Creating Connections in Teaching and Learning

Creating Connections in Teaching and Learning

edited by

Lindy Abawi
University of Southern Queensland

Joan M. Conway
University of Southern Queensland

and

Robyn Henderson
University of Southern Queensland

Information Age Publishing, Inc.
Charlotte, North Carolina • www.infoagepub.com

Library of Congress Cataloging-in-Publication Data

Creating connections in teaching and learning / edited by Lindy Abawi,
Joan M. Conway, and Robyn Henderson.
    p. cm. -- (Research on teaching and learning)
 Includes bibliographical references.
 ISBN 978-1-61735-550-9 (pbk.) -- ISBN 978-1-61735-551-6 (hardcover) --
ISBN 978-1-61735-552-3 (e-book)
 1. Learning--Social aspects. 2. Teaching--Social aspects. I. Abawi, Lindy.
II. Conway, Joan M. III. Henderson, Robyn.
 LB1060.C755 2011
 371.102--dc23   2011028162

Printed in the United States of America

DEDICATION

In memory of

Emeritus Professor Hedley Beare (1932–2010),
his inspiration, provocative predictions for the future, and
ability to reconnect educational practice and theory
in the minds and hearts of teachers

and

all of our past teachers who helped us to develop
a passion for learning, teaching, and research

A teacher affects eternity;
he [or she] *can never tell where his* [or her] *influence stops.*
Henry Brooks Adams (1938–1918)

CONTENTS

PREFACE

Lindy Abawi, Joan M. Conway, and Robyn Henderson

This book, *Creating connections in teaching and learning*, focuses on a core aspect of the work of educators, regardless of the context within which they teach. Connections are central to learning and that is one of the reasons why this book is important. If educators were asked how connections were relevant and important to their teaching and to their students' learning, we would probably be given a plethora of answers. Some might focus on the connections between new learning and prior knowledge; others might talk about the importance of social relationships between teachers and learners; others might highlight the links between theory and practice. Chances are that the list would be long and varied.

These ideas and many more have been taken up by the contributing authors. The authors represent a diverse group—beginning researchers including early career personnel and postgraduate students, novice writers, experienced researchers, and expert writers. Despite their diverse backgrounds, all the authors had some connections with a university and were working on research projects that were related to the scholarship of teaching and learning. Like most educators, the contributing authors take their work as teachers seriously, and the opportunity to create more formal connections between teaching and research was a useful way of formalizing the reflecting and thinking that "goes with the job" of being an educator.

The book explores a wide range of connections. We know that connections can encompass making links, crossing divides, forming relationships, building frameworks, and generating new knowledge. And it is this multiplicity that makes the topic of this book so interesting. In various ways, the authors explore the cognitive, cultural, social, emotional, and physical aspects of understanding, meaning-making, motivating, acting, researching, and evaluating, as they examine teaching and learning from the perspective of their own experiences. Their explorations highlight the linkages, partnerships, and networks that connect learners, educators, organizations, and communities.

Collectively, the chapters offer a wide range of educational problems, ponderings, and possibilities for transformative practices. Individually, the chapters offer insights into specific issues that relate to particular contexts, including school education, higher education, and the more recent digital or virtual worlds that are playing such an important role in education today. Many of the chapters are personal, highlighting authors' experiences, their attempts to resolve problems, or their reflections on practice. Many chapters attempt to get at the "guts" of a problem, to consider how things might be done differently, and to find a way forward in order to enhance teaching and learning.

The development of the book has been a collaborative one, with collaborations among ourselves as editors, and with and between the contributing authors. Regardless of the authors' backgrounds, however, the chapters take what is often the daily work of educators and present it in a new light. Connections are made between research and teaching, between theory and practice, and between old and new theories. Overall, the book takes a futures orientation, suggesting some possibilities for new ways of working and thinking.

The book is aimed at an academic and professional audience that is interested in the multiple ways that education can help to create connections. Because of its focus on research, on the scholarship of teaching and learning, and on connections in varied educational contexts and sectors, the book will have wide appeal. Postgraduate students will find the presentation of different research paradigms useful in formulating and clarifying their own approaches. It will also be of interest to those who want to know how connections might be forged between and among learners, educators, organizations, and communities.

The authors do not set out to provide answers for every problem in every context. What they do, however, is to open up the possibilities for transformation. They highlight their lived experiences, connect personal experiences to professional reflections, and lay out their thinking so that readers can make connections of their own. We hope that readers will engage with the ideas in this book and that they will enjoy making those connections.

Lindy Abawi, Joan M. Conway, and Robyn Henderson
University of Southern Queensland,
Toowoomba, Queensland, Australia

FOREWORD

Bryan T. Connors

The authors of the chapters that comprise this book have focused upon both change and connections. The educational orthodoxy, both the *as is* and that which is in the ascendancy, is re-examined and possibilities are suggested for the future. This is indeed a brave endeavor. The range of the educational scenes that the authors have confronted is extensive. The focus of viable connections within the elements that make up education is questioned, in terms of both the individual educator and institutional needs.

The authors look unflinchingly at what they see. In seeking to illuminate the here and now, they recognize that which obscures, and from the resulting tension they push the boundaries in other directions. The power of the familiar and the conventional is recognized rather than denigrated; it is this recognition that offers transformational change. Inherent within the authors' perspectives is the recognition that their change will, in turn, become the conventional wisdom.

The chapters represent journeys that the authors have undertaken. They have sought to provide educators with credible new perspectives; they have fought and resisted the temptation to re-gird themselves to the pull of traditional ideas. The authors' insights allow us to view activities within the education milieu from a different frame of mind. When I read a number of the chapters, I found the new perspective to be undeniable, as it is both credible and verifiable.

The concept of a journey suggests a process rather than a specific event; the current thinking of a perspective is disrupted, and possibilities for change become feasible. This journey is one of paradigm change and the creation of a collective community which supports a particular view of newly established practice. The "new thinking", in turn, needs its own assertive community.

These chapters will ask the reader to reflect, consider and hopefully change. Educators are encouraged to consider connections that are creative and of a nurturing nature. Who could ask for more?

Bryan T. Connors, PhD
Edmonton, Alberta, Canada

ACKNOWLEDGMENTS

The editors express their gratitude to the many collaborators who made this book possible. Particular thanks are extended to:

- The contributing authors, who not only wrote chapters but also engaged in writing workshops and gave feedback to other authors;
- Dr. Bryan Connors, Edmonton, Alberta, Canada, who wrote the Foreword;
- The referees, who reviewed anonymous versions of chapters:
  - Adjunct Professor Yahya Abawi, University of Southern Queensland, Australia;
  - Ms. Marion Bannister, Charles Sturt University, Australia;
  - Ms. Fariza Puteh Behak, Universiti Sains Islam Malaysia, Malaysia;
  - Ms. Alice Brown, University of Southern Queensland, Australia;
  - Dr. Bernadette Carmody, American School of Dubai, United Arab Emirates;
  - Dr. Leanne Dalley-Trim, James Cook University, Australia;
  - Dr. Beryl Exley, Queensland University of Technology, Australia;
  - Ms. Yvonne Findlay, University of Southern Queensland, Australia;
  - Dr. Todd Hartle, University of Southern Queensland, Australia;
  - Dr. Elizabeth Hirst, The University of Queensland, Australia;
  - Dr. Radha Iyer, Queensland University of Technology, Australia;
  - Associate Professor Sólveig Jakobsdóttir, University of Iceland, Iceland;

- Associate Professor Mary Keeffe, La Trobe University, Australia;
- Dr. Peter McIlveen, University of Southern Queensland, Australia;
- Dr. Allan Morgan, Educational Consultant, Queensland, Australia;
- Associate Professor Shirley O'Neill, University of Southern Queensland, Australia;
- Mr. Darren Pullen, University of Tasmania, Australia;
- Dr. Alan Roberts, Queensland University of Technology, Australia;
- Ms. Vicki Roberts, VET Consultant, Brisbane, Australia;
- Mr. Neil Stewart, The Mission Covenant Church Holm Glad Primary School, Hong Kong;
- Dr. Mark Tyler, University of Southern Queensland, Australia; and
- Ms. Lyn Wilkinson, Flinders University, Australia.

• The participants in the research symposium conducted by the Post-graduate and Early Career Researcher group, who were involved in the book's conceptualization; and

• Professor Patrick Danaher, Ms. Alison Mander, Dr. Warren Midgley, and Dr. Mark Tyler, who were involved in the early stages of the book's organization.

CHAPTER 1

EXPOSING THREADS: CREATING CONNECTIONS IN TEACHING AND LEARNING

Robyn Henderson, Lindy Abawi, and Joan M. Conway

University of Southern Queensland, Toowoomba,
Queensland, Australia

INTRODUCTION

We know that education in today's world is a complex and valued enterprise. In whatever way we look at education, we cannot but see connections to other aspects of life. Indeed, the mission of education has been described as ensuring that "all students benefit from learning in ways that allow them to participate fully in public, community, and economic life" (The New London Group, 1996, p. 60). This inextricable linking of education, society, and citizenship underpins the operations of educational institutions, the learning that students do, and the work of those who teach. Education does not, and cannot, operate in vacuum. Without connections to the other aspects of the cultural and social world, it would have no purpose and would probably cease to exist. And if we turn our focus away from the role

Creating Connections in Teaching and Learning, pp. 1–14
Copyright © 2011 by Information Age Publishing
All rights of reproduction in any form reserved.

that education plays in the cultural and social fabric of the society, and consider how education works to shape and mould individuals, we are also faced with a plethora of inter-relationships and connections. Cognitive growth, emotional development, transitions within and between educational sectors, and linkages between theoretical and practical knowledge, are just some of the associations that we might make. It is simply impossible to ignore the connected nature of education.

It is this connectedness that is the particular focus of *Creating Connections in Teaching and Learning*. The book extends conversations that began at a symposium, conducted by a group of early career and postgraduate researchers at the University of Southern Queensland in 2008. While the presentations at the symposium were about research, it became apparent that many were concerned with the scholarship of teaching and learning in a range of contexts, and that there was a wide range of connections and synergies to explore. Following the symposium, the conversations continued with a much wider group of participants. With the crystallization of interest in the topic of creating connections, it was decided to formalize the project and plan for a book publication. The call for abstracts resulted in interest from the researchers, both expert and novice, from five countries, and from several sectors, including primary/elementary, middle and secondary/high schools, vocational and technical education, and universities. Two workshops about academic writing brought the contributing authors together in real time, although a range of communication modes—electronic, telephonic, and face-to-face—were utilized, because of the authors' diverse locations. The book developed through a collegial approach that incorporated the sharing of thoughts and writing, along with the use of peer feedback to think, rethink, and refine developing ideas.

Creating connections reflects both the early career and experienced researchers' explorations of where and how connections are created and fostered in a range of educational contexts, and how the educators might continue to grow such connections as a part of their educational practice. The uses of connections in conjunction with multiple meanings of the word *create*—creativity, innovation, production, and design—enabled authors to address a wealth of diverse and dynamic topics.

This chapter explores the role of connections in learning and teaching, and exposes some of the threads that are apparent throughout the chapters by the contributing authors. We realize that the notion of creating connections might encompass making links, crossing divides, forming relationships, building frameworks, and generating new knowledge, and that it can involve cognitive, cultural, social, emotional, and physical aspects of understanding, meaning-making, motivating, acting, researching, and evaluating. However, rather than taking a broad approach, our plan is to use two examples—one theoretical and the other pedagogical—to illustrate the importance of connections to education and learning. We conclude the chapter by discussing four themes that we have distilled from the chapters: connecting within school contexts, connecting beyond school contexts, making meaning from lived experiences, and developing virtual connections. These demonstrate the connections that have been identified by the book's contributing authors as facilitating, or having the potential to enhance teaching, and learning.

EXAMPLE 1: THEORIZING CONNECTIONS

By understanding education as a social and cultural practice, we immediately locate it within social, cultural, moral, and political relationships, and as part of the network of social practices that comprise social life. If we take Chouliaraki and Fairclough's (1999) theorization as one example of how we might make sense of the social world, we begin to see that social practices are shaped, constrained, and maintained by the "relative permanencies" of social structures (p. 22), while at the same time they are practices of production, whereby "particular people in particular relationships using particular resources" can transform social structures (p. 23). This perspective recognizes that social life can be constrained by social structures, while also allowing for the effects of the agency, and the possibilities for creativity and social transformation.

Social practices, then, can be regarded as points of connection between social structures and individual actions. As an example of how we might think about education in the light of this theorization, we can focus on the work of teachers in educational institutions such as schools. Teachers are constrained by government mandated policies, by the directions of their employer—the education authority and more locally a principal—and by the ways of working and the discursive practices, that are valued and encouraged in that context.

In Henderson's (2005a, 2005b) research about the discursive practices that circulated within a school and its surrounding rural community in relation to the itinerant farm workers, their children, and their children's literacy education, it became apparent that the dominant discourses were those that identified itinerant farm workers and their children in deficit terms. Most of the teachers identified itinerancy as a significant issue, impacting on farm workers' children, and they regarded the children's low levels of achievement in school literacy learning, as predictable consequences of the families' lifestyles. They often identified the parents as culpable for the problems or difficulties that the children experienced at school. These stories were similar to the negative stories about farm workers that were circulating in the community surrounding the school—stories, that tended to regard itinerant farm workers as bad citizens and negligent or inadequate parents.

What is notable about deficit logic such as this is that "the problem" is identified as being outside the school, and beyond the control of teachers. From this perspective, it seems logical, commonsense, and "normal" to look for ways that will "fix up" itinerant students, within the school context. In taking up such views, teachers have only a limited range of options for making a difference to children's learning, and remediation seems like a sound response. In other words, contextual connections have constrained the teachers, and narrowed their options.

In contrast to the majority of teachers who drew on deficit discourses to make sense of itinerant students, there were a small number of teachers, who seemed to resist the dominant stories and explanations. They made resistant readings of the itinerant farm workers' children and as Henderson (2007, 2008) explained, identified the positive attributes as starting points for learning, and worked to find ways of engaging the students in classroom activities. These teachers were doing what Kamler and Comber (2005) described as "the kind of pedagogic, curriculum and people work" that is necessary for "connecting and re-connecting" students to learning (p. 7). In focusing on students' strengths, and using these strengths as productive resources, these particular teachers were enabled rather than constrained.

In explaining the relationship between the macro-level of social structure and the micro-level of social action as dialectical—as operating in both directions, and as constraining and enabling at the same time—this theorization often draws criticism because of its circularity (Harvey, 1996). However, it does help to make sense of the dynamic and tentative nature of connections, and to remind us that educational practice is always contextually situated and open to change. While the constraints imposed by contextual factors might sometimes seem daunting, and this might suggest that social change cannot be achieved, the potential for agency offers hope that transformative action is possible.

As a part of their theorization, Chouliaraki and Fairclough (1999) also argued, that the relationship between social structure and social action is mediated by the six elements or "moments" described by Harvey (1996)—discourse/language, power, social relations, material practices, institutions/rituals, and beliefs/values/desires. The relationship amongst these is also conceptualized as dialectical. To explain this, Chouliaraki and Fairclough argued that "discourse is a form of power, a model of formation of beliefs/values/desire, an institution, a mode of social relating, a material practice," while "conversely, power, social relations, material practices, beliefs and so forth, are in part discourse" (p. 6). Overall, this theorization of the social world fore-grounds a dynamic web of connections. It also offers a way of explaining how social life might be changed or transformed, and a way of interpreting the changes that are evident.

In this section, we have taken Chouliaraki and Fairclough's (1999) work, and used an empirical example to consider how their theorization might be used to explain the social world and educational practice. What was evident was that the teachers in the example from Henderson's (2005a, 2005b, 2007, 2008) research were connecting with the available discourses, with students, with student learning, with curriculum and pedagogy, and so on. Without these connections, learning and teaching would not have been occurring. Yet, it was also evident that different types of connections had differential effects, as in the case of connecting with deficit discourses or with less dominant discourses. Connections were shown to have an important role in the social practices of education and in society more generally.

EXAMPLE 2: CONSIDERING PEDAGOGICAL CONNECTIONS

We now move to a brief discussion of pedagogical connections. For many teachers, this is the area where connections within and between teaching and learning are recognized and enacted. Most of the teachers are cognizant of the inter-connections amongst curriculum, pedagogy, and assessment, and they work to align to them. However, recent work in the area of "new learning" (see Kalantzis & Cope, 2008) has started to bring out a detailed list of pedagogical connections that offer a much wider appreciation of connections to enhance learning.

In the mid 1990s, the work of The New London Group (1996) identified pedagogy as "a teaching and learning relationship that creates the potential for building learning conditions leading to full and equitable social participation" (p. 9). The complexity of this relationship was highlighted by Alexander (2008), who argued that pedagogy includes the performance of teaching, along with "the theories, beliefs, policies, and controversies that inform and shape it" (p. 3). In whatever way we look at it, pedagogy does not stand alone, but it relies on making connections that link teaching and learning. Pedagogy is inter-active (Murphy, 2008), and its connections with other aspects of learning and teaching are important.

Although learning might occur anywhere and at any time, considerations of pedagogy are usually in relation to the formal learning that occurs in educational institutions. It is therefore conceptualized in relation to the relevant curriculum, and the assessment of students' learning of that curriculum (Kalantzis & Cope, 2008). Although The New London Group's (1996) ideas were founded on the ways that the textual practices were changing, and the need for a re-thinking of literacy pedagogy, they offered food for thought about ways that learning, more generally, might be enhanced. More recently, many of these ideas have been expanded and elaborated (see Kalantzis & Cope, 2008; Kalantzis, Cope, and the Learning by Design Project Group, 2005), and this has fostered thinking about the need for "a broader view of learning" (Kalantzis & Cope, 2008, p. 8).

In proposing a way of thinking about "new learning," Kalantzis and Cope (2008; see also Kalantzis, Cope, and the Learning by Design Project Group, 2005) suggested a pedagogical approach that incorporates four orientations to knowledge: experiencing the known and the new; conceptualizing by naming and with theory; analyzing functionally and critically; and applying appropriately and creatively. In conceptualizing pedagogy as a way of helping students develop processes of knowing, they indicated the necessity for creating connections on many fronts.

Indeed, each of the knowledge processes is about making connections of one type or another. Kalantzis and Cope (2008) advocated that learning should involve making connections to prior knowledge and lived experiences (experiencing the known), as well as to "previously unremarked aspects of known objects, new situations, and new facts" (experiencing the new) (p. 180). They also argued for being able to connect ideas with others—to "note similarities with other things, or draw distinctions" (conceptualizing by naming) (p. 181)—and to "put concepts together into chunks of meaning" (conceptualizing by theorizing) (p. 182). Their conceptualization of learning also includes a range of social and cognitive processes, such as reasoning, using logic, inferring, predicting (analyzing functionally), and reading the world through various perspectives (analyzing critically) (p. 184), as well as using learning or new knowledge to get the job done—"doing something in a predictable or to-be-expected way in a 'real-world' situation" (applying appropriately)—or to innovate or transform (applying creatively) (p. 186).

Effective teaching, of course, involves knowing how to provide learning activities, that facilitate the types of learning connections that Kalantzis and Cope (2008) described. Yet, just as learners need repertoires of knowledge, teachers need repertoires of practices that will enable them to teach effectively, and cater to student diversity. According to Luke (1999), the work of teachers involves knowing how "to jiggle, adjust, remediate, shape, and build classroom pedagogies" so that they can achieve "quality, educationally, intellectually, and socially valuable outcomes" (p. 12). To be effective, therefore, teachers need to be able to adapt, flexibly use a range of pedagogies that are "transformative of practice" (Henderson & Danaher, in press), and to facilitate connections that will promote successful learning. Andrews and Crowther (2006) referred to this type of teacher practice as a neo-pedagogical professionalism, where teachers create new knowledge, work by sustainable values, and build future-oriented capacities.

Bransford et al. (2005), and McNaughton and Lai (2009) talked about teachers who are *adaptive experts*, those who change their practice in order to improve it. In highlighting this quality, they consider the agility of teachers to demonstrate adaptive expertise. This suggests further connections that play important roles in ensuring effective teaching and learning. McNaughton and Lai (2009) explained it as follows, "school professional-learning-communities are vehicles for changing teaching practice," and "educative research-practice-policy partnerships are needed to solve problems" (p. 55). As has been emphasized throughout this chapter, learning and teaching rely on the creation and maintenance of multiple connections.

CREATING CONNECTIONS IN EDUCATIONAL CONTEXTS

The preceding sections of this chapter have presented two examples of the role of connections in education, one theoretical and the other pedagogical. These were offered as illustrative examples of the importance of connections in education. In this section, however, we map a selection of the specific connections that the contributing authors identify in their respective chapters, and consider some of the connections that are evident between and among the chapters.

The chapters focus on explications, of how connections in educational institutions might enhance the learning and welfare of students within those institutions. In exploring specific educational contexts, one cluster of chapters investigates connections within school contexts, and another examines connections in educational contexts that have traditionally catered for adult learners, such as universities and sites of vocational education. These chapters can be found within two headings: *Connecting within school contexts* and *Connecting beyond school contexts*.

At a superficial level, some of the remaining chapters could have been placed into the clusters already described. However, these chapters were framed differently, offering insights into two other contexts for creating connections. Our analysis suggested that the topics of those chapters were not so much focused on specific educational or institutional contexts in the traditional sense. Rather, they seemed to be highlighting different types of connections that impact on those contexts. One cluster, which we have called, *Making meaning from lived experiences*, draws on a range of experiences—those of the author/s in some cases, and of the research participants in others—to explicate the importance of creating connections. The other cluster explores the virtual environment, which is changing depending on how learning and teaching are "done" by and in educational institutions in today's increasingly digital world. This final cluster—*Developing virtual connections*—thus examines some of the specific contexts of learning that have been enabled by technologies.

We now briefly discuss each of these four themes, and provide an overview of some of the connections that are highlighted within and between the chapters. In writing the first and the last chapters of this book, we have book-ended the four clusters. In this first chapter, we introduce the clusters and their foci, and in the final chapter we reflect on some of the important connections in the contributing authors' works.

Connecting Within School Contexts

The chapters that comprise the cluster we have called *Connecting within school contexts* are linked by their interest in the education of school students and the associated learning that occurs, as teachers and other educators work to enhance the learning of their students. Despite these similarities, however, the chapters demonstrate a heterogeneity of ideas, strategies, and pedagogies for teaching as well as varied approaches to research, within a range of school contexts.

In Chapter 2, Hawkins reports on the research that she conducted in conjunction with a group of pre-school educators. This participatory action research project fostered a working relationship amongst the members of the research team. It also connected early childhood educators with pedagogical strategies that proved successful in enhancing children's understandings of social justice. In Chapter 3, McLennan and Peel, who were middle-year teachers at the time of writing, provide an introspective and reflective examination of the classroom environment, in which they were teaching collaboratively. Like Hawkins, they identify effective working relationships, as essential to productive and reflective teaching. Using a motivational pedagogy that they developed, McLennan and Peel foster a range of connections to help their students become active, inspired, and engaged learners.

In Chapter 4, Casley offers insights into a school that offers holistic education for students across the full gamut of school years—from kindergarten, through primary/elementary, middle, and high school. Her investigation shows how shared values are fostered across all stakeholder groups, through character education for students, professional development for teachers, and a program for parents. In this context, connections are created through effective communication, and a shared language about values. The need for effective communication is also highlighted by Fraser in Chapter 5. Fraser offers insights into his success when working with a group of disengaged middle-year students, and turning them on to academic achievement. He advocates that teachers should listen to students' voice and let the students speak about teaching and learning. Yet, he also acknowledges the difficulties of doing this, arguing that the building of relationships and trust plays a key role in success.

Trust is also identified by Scagliarini in Chapter 6 as an important element in effective curriculum reform. Scagliarini's research at an international school in East Asia nominates relational trust, as a vital element in building school capacity for reform. As in Casley's chapter, shared values played an important role, helping to enable the staff to instigate a change in the middle school curriculum. Chapter 7 also looks at research, focusing on international schools. In this chapter, Davis investigates the change styles of teachers, working in international schools across the world. She identifies the implications of this research for a range of stakeholders, arguing that knowledge about teachers' change styles is important to international schools, where students are often reliant on the school staff for its stabilizing effects.

In our earlier discussion of Chouliaraki and Fairclough's (1999) theorization of the social world, we talked about the relationship between the social structures and individual actions, and the possibilities for constraint and enablement. Several of these chapters demonstrate the potential for agency—for individual teachers and groups of teachers, to effect change and to make a difference to student learning.

Connecting Beyond School Contexts

The chapters that comprise the cluster on *Connecting beyond school contexts* are thematically linked by their foci on educational contexts outside schools, in particular, the contexts of higher education, and vocational and educational training. However, these chapters also synergize in other ways. What is particularly noticeable is that the contributing authors tended to focus on dialectical tensions that we have discussed in an earlier section of this chapter.

In Chapter 8, Danaher and van Rensburg reflect on their experiences of supervising doctoral students as part of their work within a university, and on the doctoral student–supervisor/adviser relationship more generally. In considering three alliterative components (shibboleths, signifiers, and strategies), they identify positives and negatives—the dialectical opportunities and tensions— in the work that needs to be done to create and sustain this relationship. Chapter 9 also takes up the issue of relationships within a university context. Noble and Henderson describe a productive partnership, that developed between university support staff (in particular those working in media services) and themselves (two academics who wanted to develop a multimedia toolkit). In considering the positive relationship that developed, the chapter provides evidence that new ways of working are possible within the constraints of institutional structures.

While Chapter 9 focuses specifically on the characteristics of a successful relationship between academics and the university support staff,

Chapter 10 offers a critical examination of another university relationship. Zhou and Pedersen look at a university's arrangements with overseas partners, discussing the tensions that are evident between financial benefits and academic challenges. Their data highlight a number of disconnections which, they argue, should be addressed to ensure better connections and positive outcomes for all partners. In Chapter 11, Parry, Harreveld, and Danaher move the discussion to the context of post-compulsory vocational education and training. Here too, there are tensions and uncertainties. While the chapter offers an examination of the innovative approaches to curriculum connections, it acknowledges the challenges and highlights institutional constraints and other contextual factors that can inhibit innovative approaches.

Each of these chapters focuses on how the connections might be achieved to serve the needs of students in post-school educational environments in a better manner. The contributing authors acknowledge the challenges and tensions, but they are unanimous in their search for productive pathways that will build capacity, cultivate positive relationships, and lead to successful learning.

Making Meaning from Lived Experiences

In the chapters that focus on *Making meaning from lived experiences*, the contributing authors highlight the worth of research conducted by teachers, and for teachers, in all educational sectors. The chapters present a diverse array of strategies, which have been distilled either from their own experiences of teaching or researching, or from the experiences of participants in their research. As with some of the earlier chapters in this book, this cluster of chapters highlights the dialectical relationships that Chouliaraki and Fairclough (1999) described. However, many of the chapters focus specifically on pedagogical considerations of various types, moving the discussion towards practical considerations, rather than dwelling on theoretical concerns.

In Chapter 12, Midgley focuses exclusively on the concept of the superaddressee, and how an understanding of this concept might enhance the building of shared understandings, and forge better connections. By reflecting on his research with Saudi-Arabian students studying in an Australian university, Midgley extrapolates how an understanding of the superaddressee might help to create connections in dialogue, across multiple contexts. In Chapter 13, Conway and Abawi examine their experiences of a school revitalization project. They bring different sets of experiences to their work (one as an external, university-based facilitator, and the other as an internal, school-based facilitator), and each presents her own perspective of involvement in a collaborative school cluster. They conclude that school-university partnerships and clusters of schools working together provide a means for effecting change, and transforming schools.

Chapter 14 continues the focus on pedagogical practice. Kocher's investigation of a teacher's practice of pedagogical documentation identifies the links between the teacher's way of working and phenomenological research. As Kocher points out, the teacher was curious, speculative, thoughtful, and reflective about her everyday work with children, documenting her own lived experiences, along with those of the children she taught. Kocher's discussion foregrounds this type of teacher research as a useful strategy of professional engagement.

The challenge of balancing teaching and research in a university context is addressed by Baguley and Geiblinger in Chapter 15. Through the methodology of narrative inquiry, they delve openly into the challenges and successes that they experienced when trying to establish and work in a newly formed research team, with a membership of mostly early-career researchers. Like Conway and Abawi, they reflect on their own experiences and offer considerable food for thought for others, who are trying to do something similar. Like many of the authors in this cluster of chapters, Hatai and White take up pedagogical considerations in Chapter 16. They investigate the learning of English by Japanese high school students, who undertake a study tour in an Australian context. They found that the use of cultural knowledge in conversations between Japanese and Australian students offered a way of stimulating cognitive and social links, which would enhance trans-lingual connections and second language learning.

Several themes emerge from this cluster of chapters. One is that teachers' engagement with pedagogy is an important component of effective teaching and learning, a point made strongly by Luke (1999). Another is that teacher and researcher reflection on teaching practice provides opportunities for the type of thinking that is likely to enhance teachers' capacities to be flexible, and expert adapters of pedagogy (see Bransford et al., 2005; McNaughton & Lai, 2009). A third theme is that successful teaching and learning engages teachers in agentive action. The chapters show how teachers and researchers, either individually or collectively can work towards transformative action, and enhanced outcomes, despite contextual constraints.

Developing Virtual Connections

The final cluster of chapters under the heading *Developing virtual connections* examines the use of technologies to facilitate learning and teaching. All of the four chapters focus on the context of university teaching. The trend in recent years has been for universities to try to increase their student loads and to capture a larger share of international markets. Technologies have been used to enable the extension of study opportunities to remote areas, as well as to international locations.

In Chapter 17, Haggerty explores the design and development of an online course for postgraduate nurses in New Zealand. Like many of the other authors in this book, she considers the pedagogical implications of her work, within an educational institution. In particular, she explicates some of the challenges that were faced in offering online study, and how the course team worked to find ways around these. She concludes by suggesting a framework as an exemplar for others working in the field. Chapter 18 moves the focus to first year undergraduate studies in engineering. Brodie and Gibbings present some of the data that they have collected over several years, to examine the building of learning communities in virtual space. Their chapter offers evidence that online environments can create and sustain active participation in learning.

In Chapter 19, Redmond and McDonald compare the use of online discussion forums in the discipline areas of education and mathematics. In investigating these different contexts, they identify teaching presence, with its fostering of questioning, debate and justification, as an important component of effective online teaching, and one that is integral to active learning. In Chapter 20, the final chapter of this cluster, van Eyck reflects on her personal experiences of online learning. Through an exploration of her experiences in two contexts, she considers how online learning might make connections between theory and practice, and how it might address learning in different contexts.

In considering connections in virtual contexts, the chapters in this cluster address some of the issues that are relevant to educators, who use various forms of technology in today's increasingly technological and digital world. The four chapters address a range of pedagogical issues, and ask questions that are relevant to the rapidly changing contexts for learning that characterize today's universities.

CONCLUSION

The purpose of this chapter has been two-fold. One of the purposes has been to provide a context in which the book's themes are situated. We did this by exploring two illustrative examples, thus opening the discussion and setting the scene for the chapters that follow. Through reflecting on one theorization of the social world and considering pedagogical connections, we have framed the field in a partial and open manner. Although we wanted to highlight the way that connections are embedded in teaching and learning, we did not want to narrow or constrict how the ideas of this book are interpreted or taken up. Our intention was to leave the way open for the readers to think divergently, and to forge new meanings beyond those we have offered.

The second purpose of this chapter was to signal for readers the types of research, issues, and considerations that the contributing authors have raised. To this end, we conducted an initial thematic analysis of the chapters and we used this to cluster the chapters. However, our clustering is but one example of multiple possibilities. Only some of the possible threads have been identified by us. We see our responses as open to contestation, and we invite readers to engage in an on-going conversation about other threads and connections in teaching and learning.

ACKNOWLEDGMENT

The editors wish to thank the contributing authors for their diverse "takes" on the topic of creating connections in teaching and learning. It is that diversity that has made our task so interesting.

REFERENCES

Alexander, R. (2008). Pedagogy, curriculum and culture. In K. Hall, P. Murphy, & J. Soler (Eds.), *Pedagogy and practice: Culture and identities* (pp. 3–27). London: Sage.

Andrews, D., & Crowther, F. (2006). Teachers as leaders in a knowledge society: Encouraging signs of a new professionalism. *Journal of School Leadership, 16*(5), 534–549.

Bransford, J., Derry, S., Berliner, D., Hammerness, K., & Beckett, K. L. (2005). Theories of learning and their roles in teaching. In L. Darling-Hammond & J. Bransford (Eds.), *Preparing teachers for a changing world: What teachers should learn and be able to do* (pp. 40–87). San Francisco: Jossey-Bass.

Chouliaraki, L., & Fairclough, N. (1999). *Discourse in late modernity: Rethinking critical discourse analysis.* Edinburgh, Scotland: Edinburgh University Press.

Harvey, D. (1996). *Justice, nature and the geography of difference.* Cambridge, MA: Blackwell.

Henderson, R. (2005a). An invasion of green-stained farm workers from outer space(s)? Or a rural community struggling with issues of itinerancy? *Education in Rural Australia, 15*(1), 3–13.

Henderson, R. (2005b). *The social and discursive construction of itinerant farm workers' children as literacy learners.* Unpublished doctoral thesis, Townsville, North Queensland, Australia: James Cook University.

Henderson, R. (2007). Looking at learners: Making sense of observations. *Literacy learning: The middle years, 15*(1), 43–48.

Henderson, R. (2008). A boy behaving badly: Investigating teachers' assumptions about gender, behaviour, mobility, and literacy learning. *Australian Journal of Language and Literacy, 31*(1), 74–87.

Henderson, R., & Danaher, P. A. (in press). Moving with the times: Pedagogies for mobile students. In C. Day (Ed.), *International handbook: Teacher and school development*. London: Routledge.

Kalantzis, M., Cope, B., & the Learning by Design Project Group. (2005). *Learning by design*. Melbourne: Victorian Schools Innovation Commission, & Common Ground Publishing.

Kalantzis, M., & Cope, B. (2008). *New learning: Elements of a science of education*. Cambridge, UK: Cambridge University Press.

Kamler, B., & Comber, B. (2005). Designing turn-around pedagogies and contesting deficit assumptions. In B. Comber & B. Kamler (Eds.), *Turn-around pedagogies: Literacy interventions for at-risk students* (pp. 1–14). Newtown, Australia: Primary English Teaching Association.

Luke, A. (1999). Education 2010 and new times: Why equity and social justice still matter, but differently. Retrieved from http://education.qld.gov.au/corporate/framework/online.htm

McNaughton, S., & Lai, M. K. (2009). A model of school change for culturally and linguistically diverse students in New Zealand: A summary and evidence from systematic replication. *Teaching Education, 20*(1), 55–75.

Murphy, P. (2008). Defining pedagogy. In K. Hall, P. Murphy, & J. Soler (Eds.), *Pedagogy and practice: Culture and identities* (pp. 28–39). London: Sage.

The New London Group. (1996). A pedagogy of multiliteracies: Designing social futures. *Harvard Educational Review, 66*(1), 60–92.

SECTION I

CONNECTING WITHIN SCHOOL CONTEXTS

CHAPTER 2

CONNECTING EARLY CHILDHOOD EDUCATORS, ACTION RESEARCH, AND TEACHING FOR SOCIAL JUSTICE

Karen Hawkins

Southern Cross University, Lismore, New South Wales, Australia

INTRODUCTION

This chapter reports on a participatory action research project that con-nected early childhood educators with specific pedagogical strategies to teach for social justice in their pre-school settings. The study was conducted in a township on the east coast of Australia, and it involved two pre-school centers (providing non-compulsory, before formal school years care, with an educational purpose) to children from 3–5 years of age. Five early child-hood educators and the author were co-researchers of the research project, which spanned two school terms, and incorporated an orientation phase and an action research phase.

Creating Connections in Teaching and Learning, pp. 17–32
Copyright © 2011 by Information Age Publishing

The early childhood educators participated in the study because they had noticed bullying, gender stereotyping and exclusion occurring during play, and they wished to challenge their pre-schoolers' taken-for-granted, stereotypical assumptions, regarding difference and diversity. However, while anti-bias education and the celebration of difference were of great significance to them, the early childhood educators felt disconnected from specific pedagogical strategies to teach such a curriculum. This chapter explains how the collaborative participatory action research project empowered the early childhood educators, and connected them to strategies to teach for social justice.

Teaching for social justice is critical in the 21st century as racial, ethnic, cultural, religious, and linguistic diversity is increasing in schools throughout the world, with classrooms being shared among classmates from varying religious, political, cultural, and economic backgrounds (Banks, 2004). An optimist may claim that these classrooms are a rich source of cultural exchange. Yet, this melting pot often breeds severe discontent as racism, sexism, and prejudice are major problems in today's society (Baird & Rosenbaum, 1999; Calma, 2007; Chin, 2004; Sachs, 2002). Hence the need increases to connect students with an appreciation of diversity, difference and human dignity through inclusion, understanding, compassion, and the valuing of human rights. To achieve this, educators must be connected to specific pedagogical strategies that will assist them to implement such a curriculum. How is it possible to make these critical connections?

This chapter addresses the following sections of the participatory action research project:

- Conceptualizing the research project;
- The orientation phase;
- The action research phase;
- Presenting the findings.

It explores the connectivity of early childhood education, pre-schoolers' developing understandings of difference and diversity, and teaching for social justice.

CONCEPTUALIZING THE RESEARCH PROJECT

This research project began to germinate during my postgraduate studies in special needs education, and a master's degree majoring in children's literature. From personal observations of my own, and others' teaching practices in pre-school settings, I had noted that story time (when a picture book is read by a teacher to a pre-school group) was used at best to teach literacy skills (for example, reading directionality, comprehension, word recognition), or at worst as a transition activity to fill in 5 minutes between the end of the school day, and the collection of the children by their parents or guardians. Using children's literature for social agency in pre-school settings was, as far as I could research, untapped. The outcome of my postgraduate studies and personal observations was a desire to investigate the possibility of using children's literature in pre-school settings to heighten young children's awareness and understandings of, and sensitivities to, social justice issues related to difference, diversity, and human dignity.

This area of research has attracted considerable attention in the upper primary, secondary, and post-secondary levels of education (Siraj-Blatchford, 1995). While there is a large amount of research regarding young children's physical and intellectual development, there is much less research focusing on their development, of critical consciousness and social justice understandings (Glover, 2001; Mac Naughton, 2003). This is rather surprising, given that the pre-school years are critical in forming attitudes towards diversity and difference (Carlsson-Paige & Lantieri, 2005; Connolly, 2003; Dau, 2001; Mac Naughton, 2003; Nixon & Aldwinkle, 2005; Swiniarski & Breitborde, 2003).

Furthermore, while teaching for social justice and anti-bias curricula are of definite concern in educational circles, it was alarming to note that, at the time of this research project, many educators were struggling to promote such curricula in their classrooms, because they were not equipped with appropriate pedagogical strategies (Derman-Sparks & Ramsey, 2006; Lingard, Hayes, and Mills, 2000; Siraj-Blatchford & Clarke, 2000). Such was the case with the early childhood educators who, as co-researchers, participated in the participatory action research outlined in this chapter.

The participatory action research team was established in term 1 of the school year; the orientation phase took place during term 2; the action research phase was completed at the end of term 3, and data analysis continued during term 4. Two pre-school centers, involving 48 pre-schoolers, participated in the study, with the research team consisting of five early childhood educators: Sandra, Lisa, and Pippa (pseudonyms) from Pre-school A; Kate and Shelley (pseudonyms) from Pre-school B; and me. The pre-school group populations were mostly homogeneous in terms of socio-economic status and ethnicity, with the children coming from middle class families of Anglo backgrounds. All team members had a declared interest in exploring strategies that would promote and support teaching for social justice in their classrooms. They also wanted to investigate children's literature to discover which texts worked the best to enhance young children's interest, reflection, and understanding of social justice issues, regarding difference and diversity.

Research meetings, involving research team members, were held fort-nightly during the orientation phase to plan for the study. During the action research phase, weekly meetings were held to analyze videotaped story time sessions, regarding children's responses to children's literature read by the pre-school teachers to the pre-school groups. Data analysis was cyclical and ongoing. The action research cycle of reflection, collaborative planning, action, and observation was implemented over 10 weekly cycles, during the action research phase.

The research project's design of participatory action research was both participative and transformative, and it encouraged the educators and pre-schoolers involved to critically explore their understandings of and sensitivities to social justice issues, related to difference and diversity. They continuously shaped and re-shaped their understandings through engage-ment with, and discussion of, social justice issues that were highlighted in the children's literature read during the story time sessions.

THE ORIENTATION PHASE

It is not in the scope of this chapter to address all of the topics that were discussed during the orientation phase. Indeed, many of these topics have already been discussed elsewhere (for example, Hawkins, 2007, 2008). Nevertheless, it was clear that the orientation phase was invaluable in build-ing a strong, collaborative, caring research team. What is discussed in this section is how the research team positioned story time and the initial con-versations held with each pre-schooler prior to the action research phase.

At the first meeting, the team discussed how each pre-school used story time, and it was discovered that both the pre-schools used story time as a filler exercise. For Pre-school A story time was a transition activity between outside time and inside time. It was situated before the morning recess, after packing away the outside equipment. The children sat on a rug under an outside awning to listen to the story. A busy main road fronted the pre-school, where story time took place. In contrast, Pre-school B used story time as a "wind down" activity, after packing everything away and before home time. It was often interrupted by the parents and younger siblings moving about the pre-school, collecting paintings and sculptures created by their pre-schooler to take home. Quite often the story was not read to the end, due to the unrest of pre-schoolers eager to go home. Both Lisa and Kate admitted that they just "grabbed a book from the library shelf."

It was clear that not a great deal of thought and reflection had gone into the planning of story time at either pre-school. All of the co-researchers voiced their discomfort at this disclosure. After a bit of justification, such as "we just have not had the time" and "the books on our shelves are all pretty good," all agreed, that story time would be planned on children's interests, and it was suggested that we seek books on social justice issues that encouraged each member of the research team to join the study in the first place: appearance, gender stereotyping, exclusion, and bullying. Also, the status of story time was elevated and moved to the timeslots that were more conducive to in-depth discussion: Pre-school A re-positioned story time inside the pre-school classroom, after morning tea and before inside activities; Pre-school B re-positioned the story time to begin the pre-school day, after all the parents/caretakers had left. This re-positioning of story time not only encouraged more discussion before, during, and after the sessions but it also provided the pre-schoolers in both the settings, with opportunities to respond to the story time creatively through art, construction, and dramatic play.

During the last week of the orientation phase, a critical text was read to each pre-school group, by the pre-school teacher. Sandra, Lisa, and Pippa had noticed a slight amount of bullying from a small group of boys in the Pre-school A, who were insisting that their way was the "right and the only way to play on the fort." They chose to read *Bunyips don't* (Odgers, 2004) to the pre-school group, as the text highlights bullying and unfair behavior. Kate and Shelley had noticed gender stereotyping occurring during play, with boys ostracizing girls from their play, and a small number of girls stating that boys should not dress up in the home corner. They chose to read *The paper bag princess* (Munsch, 2006), that highlights gender issues.

Immediately, following each story time, an individual conversation with every pre-school child was held. There was no group discussion regarding the texts (*Bunyips don't* and *The paper bag princess*), as the research team wished to ensure that individual understandings and sensitivities to the social justice issues raised in the texts, were not influenced by the group. Each conversation began in the same way, with the child being greeted by name, and then asked to share his/her thoughts regarding the text; however, for the most part the conversations were child led. This meant that each child could take the conversation where he/she wished it to go. This technique lessened stress on the pre-schoolers, promoted individuality and creativity, and encouraged candid dialogue.

Initial Conversations at Pre-school A

At Pre-school A, 22 children participated in the initial conversations, and every child agreed to contribute happily. However, eight of the 22 children responded with "I do not know," "I cannot remember," or with responses unrelated to the story. Dustin (who left the pre-school, and was therefore not involved in the action research phase) made an interesting and existential comment: "In the end Old Bunyip is happy 'cos he is' doing what he wants and Young Bunyip is happy 'cos he is' got to do what he wants when Old Bunyip went away—and that is good."

Dave's response was interesting: "Kids made fun of Young Bunyip because he was big and fat so he would not sing or dance or play ever again." This is a very interesting interpretation, as both the pictorial text and the written text support the fact, that Young Bunyip was welcomed by the children. Perhaps Dave's response reflects what he expected to happen, because of Bunyip's physical appearance. Only two children, Tia and Jane, challenged the right of Old Bunyip to suppress Young Bunyip: "Young Bunyip should stand up for himself" (Tia); "Old Bunyip should not treat Young Bunyip like that" (Jane). From these responses, the research team believed that pre-schoolers from Pre-school A would benefit by exploring the texts that highlighted an individual's right to express him/herself and texts that would challenge suppression.

Initial Conversations at Pre-school B

At Pre-school B, 14 children participated in the initial conversations, with every child happily agreeing to contribute. However, three of the 14 children became very shy and almost non-verbal, during the course of the conversation. To circumvent these pre-schoolers feeling stressed or uncomfortable, the conversations were concluded amicably and quickly.

None of the children identified the bravery or resourcefulness of *The Paper Bag Princess*. All (verbal) the children concentrated on the lack of cleanliness of the Paper Bag Princess in a negative way. For example, Jedda commented that the Paper Bag Princess was "yucky and different," and when asked what she thought of Prince Ronald, she commented that he was "nice." When asked why she thought this, her response was "He is nice ... nice and clean."

Five children stated that it was "Okay for boys to save girls but not okay for girls to save boys." When asked why she thought girls should not save boys, Caddy responded: "Because boys might get angry ... and girls get happy to be saved." None of the children identified that Prince Ronald acted ungraciously. When comparing the two illustrations of Princess Elizabeth, one in her regal gown and the other in a dirty paper bag, every (verbal) child said that she would be a better, more kind, and likeable person when she was wearing her regal gown and crown to when she was dirty in a paper bag. Ally, who became almost non-verbal during the initial conversations, pointed to the illustration of the regal looking princess being the "better person."

From these responses, the research team believed that the pre-schoolers in Pre-school B would benefit by exploring the texts that challenged stereotyping through physical appearance (especially gender orientated). The research team analyzed and reflected upon the initial conversations, which supported their assumptions that children in both the pre-school groups held stereotypical ideas regarding appearance, gender, and difference. These children placed importance on maintaining a status quo that upheld the dominant discourse and culture, even though prejudice, suppression, and bullying were employed in the picture books by characters that held power in the dominant tradition. The team, however, was surprised by the pre-schoolers', rather exclusivist language; for example "All Bunyips should act the same" (Ella, Gabby); "Kids made fun of Young Bunyip because he was big and fat (different) so he would not sing or dance, or play ever again" (Dave); "She is yucky and different" (Jedda); "I do not like shabby people" (Caddy); "I would save her [pointing to the picture of the neat and clean princess in a regal gown, adopting a submissive stance to the prince] but I would not save her in that paper bag ... she is all dirty" [pointing to the illustration of a dirty, scrappy princess adopting an aggressive stance to the prince].

These examples highlight that the pre-schoolers were using the language of a hegemony that upheld the importance of physical appearance, and negated difference and diversity. The research team wished to guide the children to challenge and counter these stereotypical views, and to celebrate and uphold difference, diversity, and human dignity. Thus ended the orientation phase of our study, and set the scene for the next part of our research journey: the action research phase.

THE ACTION RESEARCH PHASE

The action research phase was situated during term 3 of the school year in 2006. It encompassed an 11 week period, in which there were 10 research cycles (weeks 1–10), followed by concluding conversations with each pre-school child (week 11). Table 2.1 displays the texts read to each pre-school group, during the action research cycles. Each week, at the research meetings, the team used critical reflection to analyze the two videotaped story time sessions from Pre-school A and the two videotaped story time sessions from Pre-school B for that week. From this analysis, strategies, and texts were planned for the following weekly cycle.

Initially, the research team wished to compare the children's responses to what it considered critical texts, against what it considered non-critical texts. We believed critical texts were children's literature that addressed social justice issues, such as race, gender, ability, class, ethnicity, sexual orientation, and/or that highlighted another's perspective. These books typically focused on social justice issues, and involved situations where the characters

Table 2.1.   Texts Examined During the Participatory Action Research Cycles in Preschool A and Preschool B

Weekly cycles	Monday: Preschool A	Tuesday: Preschool A	Thursday: Preschool B	Friday: Preschool B
1		Princess Smartypants (C[a]) (B. Cole, 1986, published by Puffin Books)		Caps for sale (NC/C[b]) (E. Slobodinka, 1987, published by Harper Trophy)
2	Snow White (NC/C) (J. Grimm, W. Grimm, & M. Deru, 2001, published by Little Pebbles)	The paper bag princess (C) (R. Munsch, 2006, published by Scholastic)	Marty and Mei Ling (C) (P. Cummings, 1995, published by Random House)	The red ripe strawberry and the big hungry bear (NC/C) (D. Wood, & A. Wood, 2003, published by Child's Play International)
3	Cinderella (NC/C) (K. Y. Craft, 2000, published by SeaStar Books)	Discussion following children's assertion of the importance of appearance.	Nickety nackety noo noo noo (NC/C) (J. Cowley, 1997, published by Scholastic)	Let's eat (C) (A. Zamorano, 1996, published by Omnibus Books)
4	The strongest girl in the world (C) (J. Nimmo, 2000, published by Koala Books)	Role play on stereotyping (C)	Bush tucker (C) (B. Hall, 2005, published by Scholastic)	Whitefellers are like traffic lights (C) (H. Reade, 1996, published by Artlook Books)
5	Nini at the carnival (C) (E. Lloyd, 1986, Puffin)	Cleversticks (C) (B. Ashley, 1993, Picture Lions)	Enora and the black crane (C) (A. R. Meeks, 1991, Ashton Scholastic)	Fish out of water (C) (H. Palmer, 1963, Collins)
6	Let's eat (C) (A. Zamorano, 1996, published by Omnibus Books)	Pumpkin Paddy meets the bunyip (C) (A. Hood, 1972, published by Paul Hamlyn)	I like myself (C) (cancelled) (K. Beaumont, 2004, published by Koala Books)	I like myself (C) (K. Beaumont, 2004, published by Koala Books)
7	A piece of string (C) (J. Morimoto, 1986, published by Collins)	Rainbow fish to the rescue (C) (M. Pfister, 1997, published by North-South Books)	Prince Cinders (C) (Cole, B. 1987, published by Hamish Hamilton)	Princess Smartypants (C) (B. Cole, 1986, published by Puffin Books)

Weekly cycles	Monday: Preschool A	Tuesday: Preschool A	Thursday: Preschool B	Friday: Preschool B
8	*The kuia and the spider* (C) (P. Grace, 1982, published by Penguin Books)	*I like myself* (C) (K. Beaumont, 2004, published by Koala Books)	*A bit of company* (C) (M. Wild, 1991, published by Ashton Scholastic)	Preschool Excursion
9	*Milly and Molly and different dads* (C) (R. R. Irons, 2002, published by Mimosa-Shortland)	*Mumma zooms* (C) (J. Cowen-Fletcher, 1992, published by Scholastic)	*The sad little monster and the jellybean queen* (C) (K. Lardner, 1983, published by Hodder-Stoughton)	*Big Al* (C) (A. Clements, 1988, published by Picture Book Studio)
10	*The race* (C) (M. Mattingly, 1994, published by Ashton Scholastic)	*Whoever you are* (C) (M. Fox, 1998, published by Hodder Headline Australia)	*Arnold the prickly teddy* (C) (K. Lardner, 1995, published by Hodder Headline Australia)	*Esmeralda and the children next door* (C) (J. Nimmo, 2000, published by Koala Books)
11	Concluding conversations: *Bunyips don't* (S. Odgers, 2004, published by Scholastic)	Concluding conversations: *Bunyips don't* (S. Odgers, 2004, published by Scholastic)	Concluding conversations: *The paper bag princess* (R. Munsch, 2006, published by Scholastic)	Concluding conversations: *The paper bag princess* (R. Munsch, 2006, published by Scholastic)

[a] Texts identified as C were regarded as critical texts.
[b] Texts identified as NC/C were thought initially to be non-critical; however, on reflection they were reconsidered as critical texts.

were marginalized in some way as a result of the existing systems of power (Leland, Harste, and Huber, 2005). We believed that non-critical texts were children's literature that addressed lighter issues than critical books. They usually attend to mundane experiences that maintain the status quo (Leland et al., 2005). However, our naïve choices of texts to fit these categories, and our assumptions regarding critical and non-critical texts were soon challenged. With the help of the pre-school children and their insights, we began to understand that all texts have the potential of critical examination, thus becoming critical texts. Hence, our misconceptions regarding critical texts and non-critical texts were quickly realized. Table 2.1 shows our initial and amended categorizations of the texts that were read.

A themed approach is a helpful tool for portraying and analyzing qualitative data (Knobel & Lankshear, 1999; Maguire, 2006; Whitmore & McKee, 2006). Therefore, a themed approach was employed to explore the pre-schoolers' developing ideas regarding issues of difference, diversity, and human dignity that occurred over the course of the action research phase of the project. The themes emerged from the data that were taken from the video transcripts of story time sessions and journal entries. These themes highlighted the issues that were important and significant to the pre-schoolers, as evidenced through their reflective and on-going discussions. They included the importance placed on outward physical appearance, skin color, indigenous issues, gender issues, issues of integrity and self worth, (dis)ability, poverty, and loneliness. Each of these themes was chosen, because the issue was raised regularly during different cycles of the action research phase, or it generated deep reflective discussion on the part of the pre-schoolers. During the last week of the action research phase, concluding conversations were held using the same books and the same techniques, as the initial conversations (discussed previously in this chapter).

Concluding Conversations at Pre-school A

At Pre-school A, 23 pre-schoolers were involved in these conversations. Nineteen children identified the bullying of Old Bunyip as inappropriate, and said that Young Bunyip should be able to dance, sing, and go to parties; therefore, it is acceptable for bunyips to be different. Twelve children said that Old Bunyip's demands on Young Bunyip were "not fair" (a phrase that was not used at all in the initial conversations).

Twenty children identified that Old Bunyip acted maliciously towards Young Bunyip. Only three children (Harley, Verity, and Darren) considered Old Bunyip's behavior to be acceptable. Twenty children said that it is reasonable and right for people to be different, with 15 children volunteering that they would play with children who looked different to them (e.g., skin color, eyes, hair, (dis)ability). Three children (Darren, Alice, and Verity) stated that all Bunyips and people should be and act, the same. Alice stated that she "would not play with people who had dark colored skin or were in a wheelchair," and her twin sister Verity said that "all people should have white skin" but "it is okay for people to have dark skin."

Mary's response was significant: "It is good for people to be different ... but I would not play with them." It appeared that Mary was developing an inclusive language; however, her intended actions communicated otherwise. Had Mary simply worked out what she thought I wanted to hear? Had she traveled a part of the journey to now tolerate people whom she perceived to be different?

Concluding Conversations at Pre-school B

At Pre-school B, 20 children were involved in these conversations; however, two children (Mark and Edward), although agreeing to be interviewed, became uncomfortable during the interview; therefore, the interview was terminated immediately. There was no stress put on these children to persist with the interview, and each conversation ended happily.

Fifteen children identified that Prince Ronald was unkind. Fourteen children identified that the Paper Bag Princess was kind and brave. Ten children stated that the Paper Bag Princess should not marry Prince Ronald, because he was "mean" to her. Even though four children—all boys (Don, Henry, Isaiah, and James)—identified that Prince Ronald was unkind to the Paper Bag Princess who saved him, they still felt that she should marry him.

Three children (Laura, Michael, and James) mentioned that it was acceptable for the girls to rescue boys. None of the children mentioned that it was not acceptable for the girls to rescue boys. Twelve children (Caddy, Ellery, Calissa, Don, Henry, Laura, Jedda, Tilly, Michael, Ron, James, and Ally) identified that Princess Elizabeth and the Paper Bag Princess were in fact, the same person inside. The words "kind," "brave," "clever," and "nice" were used to describe the Paper Bag Princess/Elizabeth. Many children mentioned that it does not matter what a person wears.

Five children (Alicia, Kirra, Ryan, Isaiah, and James) negatively commented on the Paper Bag Princess's cleanliness. Alicia, Kirra, Ryan, and Josh stated that they would not play with her because she was dirty. Isaiah said that "Prince Ronald was mad, because the Paper Bag Princess was dirty, and that is okay because he should be mad." Alicia and Ryan said that Prince Ronald should not marry the Paper Bag Princess because "she was dirty."

PRESENTING THE FINDINGS

The findings are put forward here as comparisons between the initial and concluding conversations held with each pre-schooler. Firstly, the conversations held with the pre-schoolers from Pre-school A are compared, followed by the conversations held with Pre-school B pre-schoolers. This is followed by a brief section that suggests the outcomes and subsequent strategies, which were found successful during the action research phase. These strategies emanated from the story time sessions.

Comparison of Conversations at Pre-school A

In contrast to the initial conversations at Pre-school A, where eight children were either unwilling to respond or made non-related comments, not one child fell into this category in the concluding conversations. All the children responded appropriately and willingly. In the initial conversations, only two children agreed that Old Bunyip's demands were unreasonable and inequitable, and that Young Bunyip should stand against these unfair demands. In the concluding conversations, 19 children concurred that Young Bunyip should not bend to these demands, and should stand for his rights.

As opposed to the initial conversations, where no child made the parallel between bunyips and people, 20 children made the link, and used terms such as it is "good," "right," and "okay" for the people to be different. In the initial conversations, the only children to show any concern toward injustice were Jane and Tia. In the concluding conversations, 19 children displayed concern toward injustice, with 12 children using the phrase "not fair." This phrase was not at all used during the initial conversations.

Comparison of Conversations at Pre-school B

In contrast to the initial conversations at Pre-school B, the three children who were considered non-verbal were responsive during the concluding conversations. Unlike her lack of interaction during the initial conversation, Tilly's interaction during the concluding conversation was clear and articulate, and she displayed great depth of understanding, regarding gender issues and justice. The two children, who were considered non-verbal during the concluding conversations, were not involved in the initial conversations.

During the initial conversations, no child mentioned Prince Ronald's ungraciousness or the Paper Bag Princess's bravery. During the concluding conversations, 15 children discussed Prince Ronald's unjust behavior, describing him as "mean," "nasty," "not nice," "angry," "mad," "naughty," and "a toad." Fourteen children discussed the kindness and bravery of the Paper Bag Princess. As opposed to the initial conversations, no child mentioned that it was inappropriate for the girls to rescue boys. In fact, Michael, who was adamant in the initial conversations that girls should not save boys, reconsidered his stance.

During the initial conversations, nine children discussed the impending marriage between Prince Ronald and the Paper Bag Princess. These conversations revolved around the issues of the princess's cleanliness. Alicia, Laura, Michael, Murray, Ryan, and Caddy stated that she should marry Prince Ronald "only when she gets cleaned up." Jedda, Jerry, and Ron stated that they should not get married because "she's dirty." In the concluding interview, Alicia, although still concentrating on cleanliness, felt she should not marry Prince Ronald due to her dishevelled state: "Her hair's all tangled." However, Laura, Michael, Jerry, Caddy, Ron, Jedda, Ellery, Kurt, Tilly, and Calissa now felt that the princess should not marry Ronald, due to his unkind and unjust behavior.

During the initial conversations, all children identified the better, kinder, nicer version of the princess to be the regal Elizabeth in her gown (seen in the opening illustration). Most of the children thought that Elizabeth and the Paper Bag Princess were two different characters. The concluding conversations revealed that 12 children identified Princess Elizabeth and the Paper Bag Princess as the same person, describing her as "brave," "clever," "kind," "funny," and "friendly." As opposed to the initial conversations where no child would play with the Paper Bag Princess, six children voluntarily stated, that they would play with her. However, five children said that they would not play with her "because she was dirty."

OUTCOMES AND SUBSEQUENT STRATEGIES

The comparisons between the initial and concluding conversations attest to the success of the action research project. Although compounding factors such as maturation of the pre-schoolers could also influence these results, the research team concluded that the disparity between the initial and concluding conversations was largely due to the judicious use of children's literature and the intervening pedagogical strategy of critical discussion before, during, and after the story time sessions were carried out over the preceding term. At the time of the initial conversations, the children had not engaged in critical discussion, regarding the texts that were read. If any discussion had occurred at all, it usually focussed on literal recall of the text's story. Following the action research phase, and at the time of the concluding conversations, the children were used to and enjoyed discussing social justice issues, raised during the story time sessions. They were now prepared to reflect deeply not only on the story of the text but also on the social justice issues highlighted in the texts, and to share their thoughts in a coherent and articulate manner.

Further strategies that emanated from using story time to teach for social justice are briefly:

- Elevating the status of story time sessions, from simple transition activities to important components of the pre-school day;
- Reading explicit texts that may be considered critical texts, which highlight and celebrate difference, diversity, and human dignity;
- Engaging as a group in shared sustained thinking, characterized by sustained cognitive engagements regarding picture books read during story time;
- Actively and carefully listening to children's responses (practicing a listening pedagogy), and reflectively choosing (and allowing children to choose) the texts, that consolidated the social justice issues that had been highlighted in previously read texts;
- Engaging in shared sustained thinking, characterized by sustained cognitive engagements with the individual children to gauge their understandings of, and sensitivities to, the social justice issues raised in the texts;
- Employing guided questions or comments to introduce literature, and to orientate the children to the social justice issues highlighted in the texts;
- Utilizing open-ended and higher order questioning techniques;
- Revisiting the whole texts, or parts of texts for clarification;
- Placing the social justice issues covered in the texts into real-life, and the pre-school context;
- Responding to social justice issues through action (for example, encouraging the sharing of what the children have—clothes, toys—with those who go without; supporting inclusion in play situations at the pre-school);
- Inviting, on a regular basis, people of diverse races, cultures, abilities, and backgrounds to the pre-school to share their ideas, games, food, music, art, language, wisdom, expertise, and knowledge;
- Encouraging artistic response to the texts read (for example, re-enactment, drawing, construction, dramatic play, music, singing, and dancing);
- Reinforcing and consolidating social justice issues read in the texts, by displaying the pre-schoolers' artistic responses and related posters, and making available relevant jigsaws, dolls, and games;
- Involving and informing the parents;
- Embedding teaching for social justice into the curriculum, through the above strategies.

CONCLUSION

This chapter has outlined a participatory action research project that connected early childhood educators with pedagogical strategies that helped them to teach for social justice. It also explained that the specific strategy of utilizing the story time sessions was successful in connecting very young children to an awareness of and sensitivity to social justice issues regarding difference, diversity, and human dignity. In doing this, it is hoped that other early childhood educators may adapt the study to their own contexts, and benefit in a similar way.

Although the participatory action research had a finite time-table, the educators (co-researchers) have indicated that they will continue this research in their own settings, and that it has changed the way they view story time. They now see it as a strategy to utilize picture books to teach for social justice. This desire was brought about, not only because most pre-schoolers' responses developed positively toward difference and diversity over the course of the study but because a few pre-schoolers' responses did not. Thus, research like this is ongoing, and lives in the minds, hearts, and actions of those who embrace ideals of not only the recognition of difference but also of respect and celebration.

REFERENCES

Baird, R. M., & Rosenbaum, S. E. (1999). Introduction. In R. M. Baird & S. E. Rosenbaum (Eds.), *Hatred, bigotry and prejudice: Definitions, causes and solutions* (pp. 9–20). New York: Prometheus Books.

Banks, J. A. (Ed.). (2004). *Diversity and citizenship education: Global perspectives*. San Francisco: Jossey-Bass.

Calma, T. (2007, October). *Addressing racism in Australia: Accentuating the positive and eliminating the negative (but don't forget about Mr. In-Between)*. Paper presented at the Metropolis Conference, Melbourne. Retrieved from http://www.hreoc.gov.au/about/media/speeches/race/2007/address_racism_in_australia.html

Carlsson-Paige, N., & Lantieri, L. (2005). A changing vision of education. In N. Noddings (Ed.), *Educating citizens for global awareness* (pp. 107–121). New York: Teacher's College Press.

Chin, J. L. (2004). Introduction. In J. L. Chin (Ed.), *The psychology of prejudice and discrimination (race and ethnicity in psychology): Ethnicity and multiracial identity* (Vol. 2, pp. xiii-xv). Westport, CT: Praeger Publications.

Connolly, P. (2003). The development of young children's ethnic identities: Implications for early years practice. In C. Vincent (Ed.), *Social justice, education and identity* (pp. 166–184). London: RoutledgeFalmer.

Dau, E. (Ed.). (2001). *The anti-bias approach in early childhood* (2nd ed.). Frenchs Forest, NSW: Pearson Education Australia.

Derman-Sparks, L., & Ramsey, P. G. (2006). *What if all the kids are white? Anti-bias multicultural education with young children and families*. New York: Teachers College Press.

Glover, A. (2001). Children and bias. In E. Dau (Ed.), *The anti-bias approach in early childhood* (2nd ed., pp. 1–14). Frenchs Forest, NSW: Pearson Education Australia.

Hawkins, K. (2007, November). *Participatory action research, sacred existential epistemology, the eighth moment of qualitative research and beyond*. Paper presented at the annual conference of the Australian Association for Research in Education, Fremantle, Western Australia.

Hawkins, K. (2008, December). *Addressing Lather's concerns: Practising in research endeavours what is preached in theoretical formulations*. Paper presented at the annual conference of the Australian Association for Research in Education, Brisbane, Queensland.

Knobel, M., & Lankshear, C. (1999). *Ways of knowing: Researching literacy*. Newtown, NSW: Primary English Teaching Association.

Leland, C., Harste, J., & Huber, K. (2005). Out of the box: Critical literacy in a first-grade classroom. *Language Arts, 82*(4), 257–268.

Lingard, B., Hayes, D., & Mills, M. (2000). Teachers, school reform and social justice: Challenging research and practice. *Australian Educational Researcher, 27*(3), 93–109.

Mac Naughton, G. (2003). *Shaping early childhood: Learners, curriculum and contexts*. Maidenhead, UK: Open University Press.

Maguire, P. (2006). Uneven ground: Feminisms in action research. In P. Reason & H. Bradbury (Eds.), *The handbook of action research* (pp. 60–70). London: Sage Publications.

Munsch, R. (2006). *The paper bag princess*. Sydney: Scholastic.

Nixon, D., & Aldwinkle, M. (2005). *Exploring child development from three to six* (2nd ed.) South Melbourne: Thomson/Social Science Press.

Odgers, S. (2004). *Bunyips don't*. Sydney: Scholastic.

Sachs, J. (2002). *The dignity of difference*. London: Continuum.

Siraj-Blatchford, I. (1995). *The early years: Laying the foundations for racial equality*. Staffordshire, England: Trentham Books.

Siraj-Blatchford, I., & Clarke, P. (2000). *Supporting identity, diversity and language in the early years*. Buckingham: Open University Press.

Swiniarski, L. A., & Breitborde, M. (2003). *Educating the global village: Including the young child in the world*. New Jersey: Merrill Prentice Hall.

Whitmore, E., & McKee, C. (2006). Six street youth who could …. In P. Reason & H. Bradbury (Eds.), *Handbook of action research* (pp. 297–303). London: Sage Publications.

CHAPTER 3

INSPIRE TO CONNECT
A LEARNING DESIRE

Brad McLennan and Karen Peel

University of Southern Queensland, Toowoomba,
Queensland, Australia

INTRODUCTION

A vibrant classroom environment, with an ambience of belonging, is not constructed from timber, concrete, and furnishings, or manufactured using a blueprint for success; it evolves when people who genuinely care about each other unite to form a common culture. A unique connection forms through the dynamic interrelationships within every class or group. This is not necessarily replicated from group to group, and it does not happen by chance; it is a created milieu.

This chapter utilizes snapshots to illuminate the connections that take place inside the authors' shared classroom. For example:

> As our middle school students file through the classroom door at the start of the day, we welcome them with a smile, a reassuring glance, and brief personal conversation to connect with their worlds.

The classroom environment is based on teamwork, and it provides a structure which supports both teachers and students to create a micro-community

Creating Connections in Teaching and Learning, pp. 33–45
Copyright © 2011 by Information Age Publishing
All rights of reproduction in any form reserved.

of "switched-on" learners. The walls are adorned with students' work, informative charts, photographs, and other significant memorabilia. The words *positive, proactive, prepared,* and *polite* frame the social literacy of our classroom; they are modelled by us as collaborative teachers and reinforced through self-regulation and mutual respect. Leadership is promoted, encouraged, fostered, and celebrated in support of the learners' connections that take place inside our classroom, ensuring the achievement of our vision: *students striving to become the best they can be.* This scenario is illustrated by the following snapshots:

> Assembled on the common carpeted area before us, students' body language reveals their readiness for learning. In our co-operative classroom, the parameters for optimum learning are clearly defined from the very outset of the school year.
>
> Interactive dialogue is encouraged in a courteous, non-threatening environment, where mutual respect among all stakeholders is highly valued. Free to take risks with their inquiry, students understand the advantages of having all the tools of their trade at their disposal, motivated to complete all the impending tasks to the best of their ability.
>
> Positive language rebounds back and forth around the room; justified opinions are valued, eradicating the "I cannot do it" mentality that often cripples other learning environments. Students forge individual learning pathways, utilizing their cognitive strengths within a guided inquiry philosophy that ensures effective coverage of the diverse curriculum requirements.
>
> Setting themselves up for success, by using proper initiative, highlights the instilled proactive mindset instilled. Students understand that while we are prepared to model, guide, and facilitate their learning, they are ultimately responsible for their own productivity.
>
> The social literacy introduced to the students provides the language that the culture of our micro-community is built upon. It is this literacy that is the base of communication between all the members of this community. The vocabulary is reinforced in conversations and communications related to our daily context. It is spoken, written, and heard. It enables a common infrastructure upon which everyone's learning can be constructed.

BACKGROUND

The *National declaration on educational goals for young Australians*, adopted by state Education Ministers in December 2008 (Ministerial Council on Education, Employment, Training, and Youth Affairs, 2008) commits "to supporting all young Australians to become successful learners, confident and creative individuals, and active and informed citizens" (p. 7). Curriculum and assessment provide a structure for this intention; however, we agree with Hayes, Mills, Christie, and Lingard (2006) that the quality of teaching is what makes the difference. Leading educational adviser Sir Ken Robinson, commissioned to define a British education strategy for the future of education, supports this view, and we are aligned to his philosophy which emphasizes the development of the human being and his/her ability to be productive in the world (Australian Broadcasting Corporation, 2009).

We are experienced senior teachers and, for the past decade, we have taught collaboratively in the public education system in Queensland, Australia. Through reflective practice we have developed the framework of *motivational pedagogy* (McLennan & Peel, 2008). Figure 3.1 represents the conceptual framework of motivational pedagogy, which is the foundation for maximizing student potential and establishing an inspired, engaged, and sustained classroom milieu.

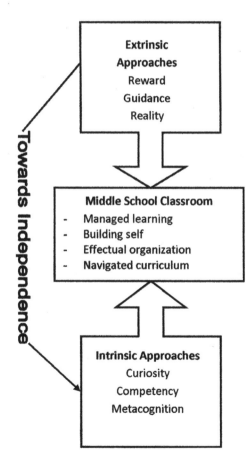

Figure 3.1. Motivational pedagogy framework

In recent years, a downward trend in middle year's student engage-ment has been acknowledged (Ryan, 2008). Gardiner (1991) suggests that, for many students education has become nothing more than drill and response, with little relevance for the expectations of classroom learning. Determined not to succumb to this drift, we recognized that motivational factors were linked to the achievements of students. The importance of motivation in learning is so much taken-for-granted, that it now seems obvious. However, knowing how to inspire the students to learn, or indeed implementing motivational pedagogy is an art form. It is a proactive approach to ensure effectual organization where student learning is man-aged, their confidence is nurtured, and the curriculum is substantial.

The curriculum is delivered through motivational pedagogy to engage and instil a love of learning in our pre-adolescent and adolescent students. A unit integrating device we have constructed generates a practical, real world context for inquiry, which can then be utilized to unveil learning throughout the term. Expectations of students are set at a high level, and the students are supported by positive, constructive, and honest feedback which builds their self-confidence and esteem. The classroom is a vibrant, evolving environment and, in this chapter, we will present evidence on how this carefully constructed learning environment contributes to the creation of individual student identity, students' sense of belonging, and a feeling of holistic connectedness. For teachers seeking reward in their profession, we think this is a proven recipe for classroom success.

It is generally accepted that there are two types of motivation. Extrinsic motivation exists when a student is compelled to do something or act in a certain way because of factors external to him or her (Petri, 1991). Intrinsic motivation occurs when people are internally motivated to do something because it either brings them pleasure, they think it is important or they feel that what they are learning is significant (Malone & Lepper, 1987). The motivational pedagogy framework identifies six approaches: the first three approaches being extrinsic—reward, guidance, reality—and the final three intrinsic—curiosity, competency, and metacognitive.

The reward motivation approach inspires the students to learn using material rewards and praise, as approval is one of the strongest social motives (Harris, 1991). An example of this approach from our classroom is:

> As Sam fulfills an expectation, we take the opportunity to "dangle the carrot"; ensuring his reward is apt, whether that is verbal praise, a photograph on the paparazzi board, or a material prize. It must be desired, instant, and well earned. The worth of any reward to Sam is measured by the level of value he attaches to it.

The guidance motivation approach provides the students with the neces-sary support, resources, knowledge, and skill base to develop a readiness to progress to the next step in their learning. As Dewey (1938) prophetically recognized, children learn more from guided experience than from authoritarian instruction. This is illustrated in our classroom as:

> Having observed the explicit modelling of a personal letter, Jennifer synthesizes her understanding via the construction of a graphic organizer. She makes use of the relevant cues we display in the classroom, including genre charts, word walls, and picture stimuli. "Building the foundation" through scaffolding and deconstructing the salient features of this genre, set Jennifer up for learning transformation and success in her own writing.

Reality motivation provides a real life purpose and short-term intent. White (1959) acknowledged that "all students need to engage intellectually, see how school activities are connected to the real world and to their own experience, and be able to use the tools to participate successfully in the knowledge economy" (p. 297). From our classroom:

> Anna understands that there is more to text, than just reading books. While acknowledging their value, she is making connections between school and her life, utilizing an array of literature. Anna is particularly interested in exploring the early Aztecs to build field knowledge, as we immerse her in this Study of Society and Environment (SOSE) topic of ancient civilizations and their relevance to the modern society. Being multi-literate allows Anna to be discerning when selecting appropriate texts and to understand the authors' intent to position her as the reader.

Teachers can employ a variety of extrinsic rewards, but a student needs to strive towards independence and intrinsic drive for self-directed competence. In fact, overuse or inappropriate use of extrinsic motivation can impede the transition to intrinsic motivation. We agree with Deci (1975), that extrinsic motivation can destroy intrinsic motivation and, at the very least, can have a negative impact upon it. Students know when they deserve rewarding, and they have a strong sense of what is fair. The aim is to nurture the transition from a short-term goal motivation to a more independent, self-regulated learning drive.

Curiosity motivation, an intrinsic approach, provides an environment for enthusiastic learning through challenges and mysteries. Beswick (2004) described curiosity as a process to create, maintain, and resolve conceptual conflicts. Teachers manage and enhance this motivation, so that children will see that guided exploration is more meaningful and satisfying than the random, spontaneous learning they encounter on their own. This motivational approach is well illustrated in our classroom:

> Over the duration of a week, Alice observes the germination of a broad bean seed, noticing the strength of the mature stem. She questions why the

cotyledons have become insignificant when compared to the flourishing twin leaves. Alice ponders the system in which the plant receives its nourishment, and identifies links with a previous experiment, where she observed how the dye revealed the transportation system of the plant. Reflecting on the perpetual dynamics of life stimulates Alice, inspiring her to explore further. Inherently curious, Alice exploits "the why factor" to increase the intellectual quality and depth of understanding.

Competency motivation occurs when students are experiencing success, gaining confidence, and developing determination to achieve goals. These feelings of competence and belief in the potential to solve new problems are derived from the first-hand experience of mastery of problems in the past, and are much more powerful than any external acknowledgment and motivation (Prawat & Floden, 1994). The excitement of this approach in our classroom is illustrated when:

Larry eyes off his self-assessment checklist that has been co-constructed among his peers and teachers, as a part of the planning phase of the inquiry process. Keen to ascertain the elements of this mathematics investigation, the checklist connects real life attributes and expectations of the task. Utilization of the checklist tool through the four phases of the inquiry (preview, plan, prove, and perfect) provides Larry with a systematic approach to enable success to breed success. As he completes each element of the task, his success concertinas, building momentum as the investigation evolves.

Meta-cognitive motivation is revealed when the students utilize an understanding of what they are learning and why they are learning it. Within this approach, students use their ability to reflect on learning, and they possess a willingness to repair breakdowns as they arise (Winn & Snyder, 1996). Higher order thinking is the outcome of this motivational approach, as illustrated from our classroom:

Acknowledging his strengths and weaknesses, Jim utilizes a vast amount of field knowledge to independently understand or seek to understand. This interdisciplinary strategy requires him to select resources judiciously, manage time effectively, and reflect on his ideas thoughtfully. This thinking about thinking is a high level cognitive device, which drives Jim's desire for self-directed competence.

IMPLICATIONS IN THE CLASSROOM

Motivational approaches can be expressed from a developmental point of view along a continuum. The teacher needs to consider the students' ages, stages, and interest levels, before employing the strategies that lead to working towards independence and intrinsic drive with self-directed competence. Students come into our classroom from lower grades with a need for short-term external rewards. It is our job as middle school teachers to wean them off these, and to create an emotional attachment with their own learning, which is crucial to becoming an intrinsic learner.

Engaging and energizing students is not an inherent skill specific to all teachers, but a fundamental element to be developed in the modern educator's armory. If we are to believe, as Geen (1995) did, that motivation is having a desire and willingness to do something, motivation within classroom pedagogy consequently becomes crucial to inspire learning. We argue that in the middle school, although it is important for teachers to understand the content and processes of learning, without effective motivational practice it is difficult to manage learning, build self, promote organization, and navigate curriculum planning and assessment for academic achievement.

Managing Learning

Through experience, we recognize that behavior management is a critical component of teaching and learning. Our observations reveal that motivated students, who are engaged and on task, have significantly reduced instances of inappropriate behavior. Although the term *boundaries* (Cloud & Townsend, 1998), referring to behavior expectations, can evoke a negative connotation when linked to the word *responsibility*, a more positive image is portrayed. Boundaries are explained as being limits applied to behaviors of people. This means that boundaries, as a principle, can apply to all people of all ages; however, the age and circumstances of the person would determine the limits that form the principle. In this way, the classroom learning management structure provides lifelong guidelines and instils resilience.

Within our classroom, the boundaries are our social literacy, promoted and modelled astutely using the alliteration of the four Ps: positive, polite, prepared, and proactive. They are collectively explored and accepted by the extrinsically and intrinsically motivated learners, thus encouraging self-discipline through responsibility. The four Ps are taught explicitly at the beginning of the year, and they are consolidated daily to become an integral part of the class culture. Astutely chosen literature stimulates conversation and creativity; consequently, our students participate in a diversity of scrapbooking activities to reinforce the literacy, incorporate elements of visual art, as well as hone their general presentation skills. Symbols are designed to represent each of the four Ps, and these are displayed prominently around the room as visual cues. Through this immersion, our students create and self-regulate their own micro-community.

Encouraging leadership within the class promotes self-regulation, and this enables the group dynamics to function efficiently, and effectively. Students monitor boundaries among themselves, removing the need for authoritarian discipline. This decreases the overall volume and anxiety of the learning environment. Boundaries are communicated to all the members of our class community, and students from our class can be identified because of the specific social literacy they demonstrate. Often, our orientation evening inspires parents to adopt the principles in their own homes, fostering consistency with rewards and consequences.

Boundaries inherently provide high expectations that align to our vision of "being the best you can be", and they supplement our desire to set the bar for all the individuals at a challenging, but achievable level. They provide a supportive classroom environment that allows all the learners an opportunity to learn and to attain productive outcomes without inappropriate distraction, as illustrated by this snapshot from our classroom:

> On entering the classroom for the first time on transfer from a nearby school, Joshua was initially anxious about the unfamiliar setting. Unsure of his social belonging, the rushed introductions to other students, where to put his bag and books, when and where is lunch, who is to be around at this time and scrambling routines, all of which to the other students seem organized. He is quickly introduced to his group and its leader, who controls the busy conversational traffic that creates this self-regulated micro-community of which he is now a member. Once seated, his senses are overwhelmed by the overt visual representation of the social literacy explicitly shaped, that forms the infrastructure of the class. At this early point of orientation, the four Ps are abstract in their intent; however, in a very short period, he soon realizes the value of these attributes in becoming a productive citizen, resilient to cope with the obstacles in his path. Joshua is soon immersed in the real life topic, surprised at the minimal inappropriate distractions, and the motivation of his new classmates. Joshua has every opportunity to be the best he can be in this supportive safe environment, and he transforms his social skills to other areas of the school and to his home life.

Building Self

Recognizing the adage that success breeds success, motivational pedagogy provides a framework for our students to grow self-confidence and esteem. We believe that those who have made the transition to be more intrinsically motivated have the ability to cope and to develop resilience and a positive self-concept. For others, the challenges appear daunting, their interest wanes, progress slows, and their self concept and sense of belonging is adversely affected. Our observations consolidate the theory that, during this middle phase of learning, young people are experiencing the greatest physical, emotional, intellectual, and social changes in their lives (Fuller, 2005).

The relationship between a teacher and a student, therefore, is especially crucial in this middle phase, as diminishing self-esteem and an erosion of confidence often occur while students begin to recognize their individualism. We acknowledge that, as children grow older, it is not uncommon for their attitude to school to deteriorate, and that as adolescents their academic motivation declines. Considering how to increase motivation and create a reciprocal connection with these students is a major issue for schools in the 21st century.

Valuing individuality, we provide a pathway structured upon the scaffolding of an array of coping skills and strategies. Our class culture nurtures and promotes the inevitable growth of self. Belonging is built through recognizing individual strengths and celebrating them amongst the entire class community. When students truly believe that teachers care about their well-being, they trust their guidance, are more prepared to explore the depths of their learning parameters, and have the self-belief to aspire to be the best they can be. We celebrate this enlightenment from our classroom:

> Emily, hiding behind her fringe, yearns to be invisible. Amongst her group, she lacks the confidence to contribute to the discussions, a resistance to cooperate with her peers is obvious and avoiding eye contact during questioning raises suspicions. Determined to uncover her values and beliefs, in an effort to illuminate how she is best motivated, and to explore her learning style and personal interests, we carefully observe and analyze the patterns of behavior. So Emily can be the best she can be, she needs to experience ongoing success and receive the subsequent extrinsic rewards attached. Measured scaffolding is designed for her individual success, building confidence and consolidating belief. As the identity grows, belonging is established and a willingness to explore challenging learning begins. Emily is willing to raise the bar and her self-belief continues on a rising plane as she realizes that her teachers care. Work is displayed in the classroom, action photographs adorn the paparazzi board, birthdays are acknowledged through song, all celebrating her value as a class member. Her ability to cope with the challenges she confronts develops resilience as a lifelong learning tool. No longer fearing failure, Emily's positive demeanor and presentation are evidence of her personal growth, reflecting increased academic and social outcomes.

Effectual Organization

Motivated students are efficient, organized, and remain focused on tasks. Setting realistic time goals and deadlines for students to demonstrate competency at their individual level, ensures a quality product or outcome.

Motivated teachers establish familiar routines, which provide their students with a supportive, non-threatening learning environment, and allow for effective inclusiveness to occur. Consistency of work patterns and of habits ensures that students understand the essential structures for learning. Within our classroom structure, timetables are balanced across the curriculum, and negotiated within the bureaucratic systems. They are flexible to ensure continuity, cohesiveness, and the fluid flow of learning. These timetables, along with other visual cues, are displayed prominently around our classroom. They are motivating, because we ensure they are topical, stimulating, and scaffold current learning. These visuals are simplified in the form of logos, symbols, acronyms, and dot points. Our goal is to establish student readiness and preparedness for learning.

Motivated learners develop teamwork, empathy for others, and co-operative skills. A sense of ownership readily develops, as the class group's identity and pride grow. Consequently, the students display the initiative to maintain their classroom environment. Recognizing that random groups are more often than not dysfunctional, we use careful blending of cognitive and social competencies to form core mixed ability groups, which enable dynamic interaction in a positive and proactive way. The promotion of leadership skills provides opportunities and responsibilities to organize efficient movement and transition of students, and the organized collection and distribution of relevant learning resources and materials. The interactive dialogue that occurs within these learning contexts is conducive for the students to teach one another.

The collaborative nature of our teaching team is underscored by numerous roles that have evolved naturally over time, but are distinctive to each individual. In our circumstance, it is significant that our individual, practical teaching knowledges complement each other, providing a balanced approach to teaching and learning. Teacher aides and significant others, who support learning in the classroom, are empowered to self-regulate, set goals, and ultimately reflect on the effectiveness of their work with the students.

Creating connections in the classroom requires a vehicle for communication between all the participants. The home-folder provides a secure, transportable storage system for such items as the communication book, which contains term overviews, relevant correspondence, and homework tasks. The assessment portfolio showcases an array of work samples for the students to self-reflect upon and for the parents to view critically. The following snapshot illustrates the effectiveness of this organizational strategy:

> As a leader, Laura understands the significance of her role in facilitating an efficient and effective group learning environment. At the beginning and throughout the year, her teachers establish routines that allow for continuity of learning. Laura is responsible for her group resource collection and distribution tasks,

which she shares among the members. She is an active listener to the teachers' initial instructions and consequently she is a capable communicator to self-regulate within her group. Members around her have been carefully selected by her teachers, according to an equitable mix of academic and social compatibility. "Dressed for success" in complete school uniform, the group is armed with the necessary materials and resources to complete the focused tasks. In Laura's classroom, this creates a mindset for a learning context, which cannot be misunderstood. She leaves the classroom and arrives each day with her communication book inside her home-folder. In this, her parents are well informed of the events in her class, through term overviews, notes, and personal messages from her teachers. Laura values classroom routines, because she is comfortable knowing what she is required to do, when she is required to do it, and where it is required to take place.

Navigating Curriculum Planning for Academic Achievement

Taking into account students' desires and curiosities, motivation is initiated through measured planning. Establishing an engaging theme, with a thought provoking question, and keeping in mind the students' prior knowledge of the learning topic, allow us to stimulate interest, and to connect learning to their real world. Being aware of gender differences, we attempt to appeal widely to individual inquisitiveness across all curriculum areas. We are careful to lead with a genre-focused, front-end assessment task that has a subject specific literacy. The unit's learning opportunities build skills and field knowledge that provide the scaffolding for the successful completion of the synthesizing task. Through careful deconstruction of the text, critical analysis of purpose and tenor, and explicit teaching of the salient features, students are provided with an infrastructure to demonstrate their competency. When students can make connections between their learning at school and their lives outside school, an opportunity for tangible cognitive development emerges. Through judicious selection and management, students manipulate resources that ultimately inspire intellectual quality in their writing and reflection. Catering for diversity in individual differences is critical, if students are to be the best they can be.

As teachers, we take on the responsibility to engage our learners, challenge them intellectually, and guide the transition from extrinsic to intrinsic motivation. While building rapport, facilitating learning, and guiding development, we are continually evaluating and diagnosing individual motivation approaches. This allows us to tailor the learning needs for all individuals within our classroom. Once we have identified an extrinsic reliance, we actively plan a transition strategy, recognizing that it is intrinsic motivation that leads to lifelong learning. Irrespective of the motivational approach, all students must be suitably catered for to achieve success; however, creating connections occurs significantly, when the transition from extrinsic to intrinsic is concrete, as illustrated in the following snapshot from our classroom:

> As Jonah scans the authentic mathematics investigation that has been introduced to the class, he previews the key components, making links to his prior knowledge and experiences in the real world. Significant elements are identified, the purpose of the problematic task is revealed, and his role is clarified. Jonah's inherent curiosity engages him in the context; consequently, assumptions are made and strategies are devised, as the planning process unfolds. Armed with a myriad of skills and field knowledge, Jonah's intent is to explore and demonstrate his competency by providing evidence of his ability to apply concepts, utilizing mathematical literacy. Peer support and group discussion opportunities, to question and challenge the direction of the inquiry process, lead to scaffolding and modelling of unfamiliar skills. Teacher intervention guides Jonah, while still allowing him to exercise his own exploration of the task. As a group, a self-assessment criterion is co-constructed, to checklist the components that need to be communicated in the proving phase of Jonah's inquiry. He has become competency driven, as the excitement of solving the problem unravels. Determined to learn more than just the answer from the inquiry, Jonah embarks on discovering the appropriateness of his strategies, and whether alternative methods would have resulted in more efficient solutions. This reflective process develops metacognition and it ensures intellectual quality and depth of understanding. Jonah's inquiry is assessment for learning, as how and what he and his peers learn, directs our future planning and teaching for each individual student.

CONCLUSION

The rewards of teaching lie within the unity of the classroom, not the physical properties of the walls, but the symbolism of the educational context, the created milieu, in which we practice. The culture of our community that evolves through social, academic, cultural, and sporting experiences always aims to provide a win-win situation; however, it is never without its perilous moments. Importantly, these problematic situations and celebrated successes are of considerable value to all, because they become teaching moments and learning opportunities that assist the creation of active, ethical, responsible, and productive citizens. It is our contention that motivational pedagogy provides the framework that establishes the robust connections existing among the primary participants, and it is crucial in enabling students to truly become the best they can be. The challenge for 21st century teachers is to embrace this pedagogy, to maximize student engagement, and to create the connections between learning at school and its relevance to real life.

REFERENCES

Australian Broadcasting Corporation. (2009). Education systems too narrow: Sir Ken Robinson. *The 7:30 report* [Television broadcast]. Retrieved from www.abc.net.au/7.30/content/2009/s2600125.htm

Beswick, D. (2004). *From curiosity to identity.* Melbourne: University of Melbourne. Retrieved from http://www.beswick.info/psychres/CuriosityIdentity.htm

Cloud, H., & Townsend, J. (1998). *Boundaries with kids: When to say yes, when to say no.* Grand Rapids, MI: Zonderban.

Deci, E. L. (1975). *Intrinsic motivation.* New York: Plenum Publishing.

Dewey, J. (1938). *Experience and education.* New York: Macmillan.

Fuller, A. (2005). *The adolescent brain.* Retrieved from http://www.andrewfuller.com.au/free/TheAdolescentBrain.pdf

Gardiner, H. (1991). *The unskilled mind: How children think and how school should teach.* New York: Basic Books.

Geen, R. G. (1995). *Human motivation: A social psychological approach.* Belmont, CA: Cole.

Harris, R. (1991). *Some ideas for motivating students* [Webpage]. Retrieved from http://www.virtualsalt.com/motivate.htm

Hayes, D., Mills, M., Christie, P., & Lingard, B. (2006). *Teachers and schooling: Making a difference.* Crows Nest, NSW: Allen & Unwin.

Malone, T. W., & Lepper, M. R. (1987). Making learning fun: A taxonomy of intrinsic motivation for learning. In R. E. Snow & M. C. Farr (Eds.), *Aptitude, learning and instruction: III. Conative and affective process analyses* (pp. 223–253). Hillsdale, NJ: Erlbaum.

McLennan, B., & Peel, K. (2008). Motivational pedagogy: Locking in the learning. *The Australian Educational Leader, 30*(1), 22–27.

Ministerial Council on Education, Employment, Training and Youth Affairs. (2008). *National declaration on educational goals for young Australians – Draft.* Canberra, ACT: Australian Government Printer.

Petri, H. (1991). *Motivation: Theory, research and application* (3rd ed.). Belmont, CA: Wadsworth.

Prawat, R. S., & Floden, R. E. (1994). Philosophical perspectives on constructivist views of learning. *Educational Psychologist, 29*(1), 37–48.

Ryan, M. (2008). Engaging middle years students: Literacy projects that matter. *Journal of Adolescent and Adult Literacy, 52*(3), 190–201.

White, R. (1959). Motivation reconsidered: The concept of competence. *Psychological Review, 66,* 297–333.

Winn, W., & Snyder D. (1996). Cognitive perspectives in pyschology. In D. H. Jonassen, (Ed.) *Handbook of research for educational communications and technology* (pp. 112–142). New York: Simon & Schuster Macmillan.

CHAPTER 4

SHARED VALUES CONNECTING PARENTS, TEACHERS, AND STUDENTS

J. Anne Casley

University of Southern Queensland, Toowoomba,
Queensland, Australia

INTRODUCTION

Internationally, there is a growing belief that teachers and schools have an important role to play in values education. In the Australian context, recent reports associated with the *National framework for values education in Australian schools* (Department of Education, Science and Training, 2005) have identified the establishment of shared values, and the consistent use of a common language as good practice in values education. As a result, the reports recommend the need for whole school communities to reach an agreement about the values that guide the schools' work. In a school which emphasizes values education, the shared values language can have profound effects on the total educational environment, and it can come to inform everything the school does and says. This chapter explores the principles

Creating Connections in Teaching and Learning, pp. 47–57
Copyright © 2011 by Information Age Publishing
All rights of reproduction in any form reserved.

that underpin the connections between parents, teachers, and students at a Queensland rural school, where values education is prioritized.

Earlier beliefs, that values were exclusively the preserve of religious bodies and families, are being affected by international research into teaching and schooling effects; schools are no longer thought to function best in a value-neutral mode (Lovat & Toomey, 2007). There now exists a growing belief that schools have an increasingly important role to play, in the understanding of personal and societal values. Also, of importance is the understanding that positive values have a significant role to play in underpinning successful school partnerships. The development of effective partnerships involves two key areas: the establishment of effective communication between the school and the family, and an understanding of underlying socio-emotional values that sustain good partnerships. Key socio-emotional values, thought to characterize successful partnerships, include respect, trust, honesty, and openness as well as valuing all the community participants (Warren, Young, and Hanifen, 2003). The notion of caring (Epstein, 1995) as well as forming partnerships that are respectful of one another's perspectives is emphasized (Risko & Walker-Dalhouse, 2009; Souto-Manning & Swick, 2006). Positive values underlying effective communication between school and family are related to a sense of trust between the participants (Swick, 2003).

Values can be defined broadly as "the principles and fundamental convictions, which act as guides to behavior, the standards by which particular actions are judged to be good or desirable" (Halstead & Taylor, 2000, p. 169). A value is a kind of belief, the object of which aims at goodness (Carr, 1991). It is a belief that integrity, honesty, compassion, wealth, or world peace, for example, "is a good to be pursued" (Carr, 1991, p. 245). Value judgements constitute bridges between people "as to the ways in which we ought to believe, to conduct ourselves, or in the things that we ought to admire" (Aspin, 1999, p. 126). In everyday language, the word *value* may be regarded as an umbrella term for things that are approved (Hawkes, 2008). People's values constitute what they believe to be important; to value truth, for example, is to believe that truth is something to strive to attain (Hawkes, 2008).

This chapter will focus on one school in the Australian context, where values education is regarded as an integral component of education. It briefly provides insights into the school's underlying educational philosophy, and its founder's worldview. The chapter then describes the approach teachers, parents, and students are encouraged to take, in order to enhance their personal growth and effective communication with each other. The underlying school support mechanisms, which were designed to facilitate these aims, are also explained. To conclude, the implications of such an approach to learning is given from my perspective as well as a consideration of the possible contribution to society more broadly.

THE AUSTRALIAN CONTEXT

Values education has played an important role in Australia's approach to education during the last 10 years. The *Values education study* (Department of Education, Science and Training, 2003), and the resulting *National framework for values education in Australian schools* (Department of Education, Science and Training, 2005) have highlighted the need for a planned and systematic approach towards values education. This approach has included key elements that inform good practice, guiding principles, and a list of core values for consideration as "discussion starters" with the school communities, interested in prioritizing values education (Department of Education, Science and Training, 2003, p. 7). Any set of values that is suggested for Australian schools needs to be the subject of discussion and debate with the school communities as values education is a "contested terrain" (Department of Education, Science and Training, 2007, p. 45).

In an address given at the Australian National Values Education Forum in 2008, Furco drew attention to the complexities of values education (see Department of Education, Employment and Workplace Relations, 2008a). In comparing the national values education efforts of one country to another, Furco highlighted many overlaps, but also striking differences. He explained these differences in terms of the fact that "values are nuanced" and consequently, are not interpreted or "operationalized" in the same way in each context (p. 30). Rowan, Gauld, Cole-Adams, and Connolly (2007), also aware of the complexities of values education, perceived common terms such as honesty, freedom, or "fair go" as being subjective, and as having different meanings in different contexts. The notion of respect, for example, could require attentiveness and eye contact towards a particular individual or group in one context, or the avoidance of eye contact in another, such as in an indigenous community (Rowan et al., 2007).

The national *Values education study* (Department of Education, Science and Training, 2003) was commissioned by the Australian Government to inform the development of a framework, and a set of principles for values education in Australian schools. The study was supported by the Ministerial Council on Education, Employment, Training, and Youth Affairs, who acknowledged, that education was as much about building character as it was about equipping students with specific skills (Department of Education, Science and Training, 2005). The council also recognized that values based education can strengthen the students' optimism and self-esteem, and help the students exercise ethical judgement and social responsibility. Developed from the outcomes of the *Values education study* (Department of Education, Science and Training, 2003) and widespread consultation on a draft framework, the *National framework for values education in Australian schools* (Department of Education, Science and Training, 2005) was introduced.

One of the key elements of the framework is the identification of nine core values, which are listed as "care and compassion, doing your best, fair go, freedom, honesty and trustworthiness, integrity, respect, responsibility, understanding, tolerance, and inclusion" (p. 4). These values are described as being consistent with Australia's democratic traditions and multicultural society.

Research associated with the *National framework* emphasizes the establishment and use of a common and shared values language across whole school communities as a means of creating an overall sense of ownership, consistency, and an inclusive school environment (Department of Education, Employment and Workplace Relations, 2008b; Department of Education, Science and Training, 2006). A case study of Modbury School in South Australia, for example, found that partnerships between teachers, parents, and other members of the wider school community were central to the school's work in values education (MacMullin & Scalfino, 2007). In this case, the school community consultation process resulted in the identification of 26 values, which were important for parents, staff, and students. These values were described as having a lasting influence in setting the direction for change in a number of key areas at the school. Other research found that community engagement was particularly significant for indigenous communities (Netherwood et al., 2007; Toomey, 2006). In these cases, exploring different language and cultural views "in a deep way," enabled the school communities to move forward with shared understandings (Department of Education, Science and Training, 2006, p. 17).

VALUES EDUCATION IN ONE SCHOOL

This chapter is based on research at a particular school, and is part of a much larger study into the school's approach. The information presented in this chapter is descriptive rather than analytical as it has been gathered in the very early stages of data collection. It incorporates an examination of particular school documents, including writings by the school's founder as well as teacher and parent handbooks, short extracts from parent and teacher interviews, and personal communication between the researcher and others.

The school, Grey Gums School (pseudonym), is located on the outskirts of a rural town, southwest of Brisbane, Queensland, Australia. Approximately 150 students attend the school across pre-school (called Kindergarten in some locations) to year 12. Established in 1981, the school is co-educational, and the teacher student ratio is generally one teacher to 12 students. In school documents, it is described as being an independent, non-denominational, and non-systemic school (Grey Gums School, 2009a).

The school's philosophy is based on the teachings/writings of the school's founder, Rajiv Mukerjee (pseudonym). His approach involves two major aspects: equipping the students with skills required for the management of a sophisticated technological society, and training in the principles of morality, defined as a practical moral approach to living, from which students can gain experience, confidence, maturity, and emotional stability (Mukerjee, 1983). Mukerjee describes western civilization as having "its roots in an objective outgoing culture," whereas eastern civilization is associated more with inwardness, and a searching of the deeper recesses of the mind in an attempt to gain real joy (p. 24). From his perspective, it is the inclusion of traditional eastern principles of education with a western approach that provides the potential for producing an individual, who is not only capable of logical thinking but is also the possessor of intuitive knowledge. According to Mukerjee (1983, 1985), both the forms of knowledge are essential for future education, in order to maintain humanity's self-development, and the progress of society at large.

Mukerjee (1983, 1985) identified refinement as the basis of proper education. In his texts, he made reference to older civilizations, where education gave a focus to character development and refinement. He explained that, in these civilizations, the disposition and state of mind of the disciples and students were given attention, and considered the important factors. In the context of holistic personality development through education, Bhatta (2009) focuses on ancient Indian cultural experiences. He states that students "were not allowed to forget that they had within them a higher self," which was thought to be beyond their personal ego, and numerous ways and disciplines were made available, by which they could realize their higher self (p. 54). Viewing life as "a process of experiencing and learning," Mukerjee (1985) seems to have a similar philosophy, as personal refinement is considered essential to understanding a spiritual reality, or "the reality of the Self" (p. 38).

The approach encouraged at Grey Gums School (2009b) is to nurture "the spirit of the child rather than the ego," and the focus is on awakening in the child "the possibility of ... on-going personal development and growth" (p. 8). The spirit of the child seems to be related to the child's personality, nature, or sunny disposition, whereas the ego is associated more with a competitive element. Signs of nurturing the ego are associated with an inability for the child to be happy in his/her own company; feeling he/she has to impress the others; needing to dominate to feel comfortable; or feeling he/she cannot make a mistake. From my understanding, teachers and parents are encouraged to nurture the spirit of the child, simply by accepting the child as he/she is right now. They are not encouraged to evaluate the child's personal worth on the basis of measurable academic achievement. From the school's perspective, each child is in need of experiencing love, and feeling lovable. In attempting to explain how the school goes about nurturing the spirit in each child, the school principal stated:

> You need to look at the idea of intrinsic motivation. What are the things that you can touch inside a person that will encourage them to grow, to learn, and to think? And that would include things like finding an interest in things; finding a sense of enjoyment in things; getting a sense of challenge out of what they are doing; aspiring to do something really well to the best of their ability. These things can only be cultivated through developing a relationship with a significant other person, such as a teacher or parent (Principal, personal communication, May 23, 2010).

The understanding of positive values such as honesty, patience, consistency, forgiveness, and responsibility appears important to this ultimate aim, and teacher modeling plays an important role in helping the students to understand these values. Positive values are linked to a student's ability to handle a western material environment, and have a role to play in assisting a child to "create in him an urge to develop his intrinsic goodness, and through goodness to develop that spiritual goodness that is deep within him" (Mukerjee, 1993, p. 48). Positive values are also linked to a person becoming someone who is capable of service, and who can see beyond personal needs and desires.

In an attempt to create a holistic approach to education, Mukerjee formed a program that provided a balance in three important areas: academic and skills training, character development, and health and physical development. Particular emphasis, however, is given to character development as this is seen as crucial to the best application of academic and skill training, and to the experiencing of good health (Grey Gums School, 2008). It would appear that the school's conception of values education is primarily "pedagogy," as it is a principle of curriculum organization and a means of shaping the whole school experience (Lovat et al., 2009, p. 3). Values education in this context appears to be influential in how the school functions, and in the relationships within its community.

The school's program is an attempt to educate the children to become future citizens with a universal outlook, awareness of the environment, their duties and responsibilities and in particular, themselves (Mukerjee, 1985). Emphasis is placed on self-development, so that the child will eventually become "a potent instrument for the growth of humanity" (p. 13). Self-development is equated with a free-thinking individual, who has self-mastery, a high vital index, and integrity. It is associated with the integration of emotional and intellectual abilities, and the development of discrimination and detachment, enabling the child to ride over problems rather than becoming their victim. Mukerjee's tradition was essentially derived from classical yoga, which gave a focus to the values and ethical norms, mental development, and physical health (Grey Gums School, 2009b).

ENCOURAGING SHARED GOALS WITH TEACHERS, PARENTS, AND STUDENTS

The school's educational philosophy is focused on enhancing the quality of relationships between all school stakeholders (Grey Gums School, 2008). The philosophy emphasizes the dimension of personal growth, and its most important task is facilitating "open communication and free-flowing inter-action" between the parents, teachers, and students (Grey Gums School, 2008, p. 3). Teachers are described as needing to take the key role of first developing themselves, understanding the problems they encounter, over-coming their own hang-ups, and putting aside their prejudices (Mukerjee, 1985). In pursuing the ideals of this approach, the teachers are encouraged to become free agents, who are capable of experiencing deeply, expressing joy in their teaching, and harnessing the positive potential of the children in their care (Mukerjee, 1985). When a teacher was asked if her understanding of the school's approach to values impacted on her approach to teaching, she stated:

> I have tried to be as loving as I can to each student. I try to understand at a deeper level; to see through to what they need at a deeper level; to under-stand their deepest needs, to try and cater to these needs, rather than the superficial needs … and to become more patient and more caring. But also, not predictable, so that learning is fun, and that the kids get an enjoyment of learning, and a sense of achievement and personal success at their own level (Teacher, personal communication, March 25, 2010).

Rather than participating in the governance of the school or in the class-room context as volunteers, parents are asked to focus on giving time and attention to becoming more mindful parents (Grey Gums School, 2008). According to Mukerjee (1983), the requirements from the parents are gen-uine love and compassion for the child, and he explains that the child is in need of love and care, before he/she can become lovable or give love. From his perspective, this means that the child will need to assimilate positive qualities that are acceptable to, if not admired by, others. In the context of the school, it appears that parents need to develop themselves, understand deeper values, and determine what they want to do and achieve for their child.

The need for the children to be relaxed in order for them to grow in a natural way is emphasized in the school's approach (Grey Gums School,

2008). According to school documents, a relaxed approach is thought to aid the students in becoming more open to learning, and to discovering their innate capacities. The students' role "is to find their unique means of expression, and to become aware of their strengths and weaknesses" (Grey Gums School, 2008, p. 3). Their role also seems to be associated with learning and developing their understanding, capacity, and skills for working with others. The students' active contributions to school life appear to be an integral part of the school's philosophy. The intention is to treat the students respectfully and in the planning of academic studies and special interest areas, their ideas and choices are sought (Grey Gums School, 2008).

SCHOOL SUPPORT SYSTEMS FACILITATING COMMUNICATION

The school has support systems to support the three stakeholder groups—teachers, parents, and students. The specialized teacher development program is designed to produce "a more innovative teacher," who has enough maturity to impact on the students' character development, academic and skills training, and the management skills to utilize resources effectively (Mukerjee, 1983, p. 107). The program focuses on the personal capacity of each teacher to implement his/her ideals in the classroom, and it is designed to assist the teacher in overcoming personal obstacles to this objective (Grey Gums School, 2008).

Mukerjee (1983) also perceives parent education to be a vital part of the school's educational philosophy. Parents who are interested in enrolling their children in the school are encouraged to focus on their own personal development as well as the children in their care. The school requires the parents to attend a weekly parents' program, where issues confronted by parents raising the children, are discussed in small groups. In this context, experiences are shared amongst parents, the teachers who may be attending the group, and parent group leaders. When asked if the parents' program had influenced her approach to values and parenting, a parent responded:

> I guess if you see parents who have older children, and you like the way their children have grown up, then you will really appreciate hearing their ideas for parenting (Parent, personal communication, March 17, 2010).

The parents' program and the teachers' development program are designed to provide support for the parents and teachers, in pursuing the ideals of the school. When examining the content of these programs, I observed an overlap on issues, such as the power of values as patience or consistency, the basis of respect, working as a team, understanding children's needs, creative discipline, school community relationships, and managing stress (Grey Gums School, 2008).

Grey Gums School recognizes the autonomous nature of young people, and its student code of conduct policy involves guidelines, based on students taking responsibility for their own behavior (Grey Gums School, 2009a). In order for these guidelines to be implemented, the key members of the school community are described as needing to accept the responsibility for their own behavior. Students are encouraged to contribute to the development of the student code of conduct to provide a positive role model for younger students, and to support each other in maintaining the code of conduct (Grey Gums School, 2009a).

CONCLUSION

Initial data collection at Grey Gums School has resulted in my becoming familiar with the school's educational ideals. From my perspective, these ideas link into research findings associated with the need for a planned and systematic approach to values education, the establishment and use of a shared value language, effective communication between school and family, and key values, thought to characterize successful partnerships. In practical terms, the school's support systems, which include the parents' program, the teachers' development program, and the character strand of the students' program, lend themselves to strengthening communication and creating connections between all stakeholders. The implications, in regard to such an approach to learning, would seem to be the need for teachers and parents to come to understand a similar philosophy of life, a focus on personal development, and a belief that values education is an integral part of the educative process. In terms of a contribution to the wider community, it would appear that the school's ideals in relation to values education link into notions of effective citizenship as students are encouraged to develop self-knowledge, an understanding of positive values, and the ability to see beyond personal needs and desires.

REFERENCES

Aspin, D. N. (1999). The nature of values and their place and promotion in schemes of values education. *Educational Philosophy and Theory, 31*(2), 123–143.

Bhatta, C. P. (2009). Holistic personality development through education: Ancient Indian cultural experiences. *Journal of Human Values, 15*(1), 49–59.

Carr, D. (1991). Education and values. *British Journal of Educational Studies, 34*(3), 244–258.

Department of Education, Employment and Workplace Relations (2008a). *National values education forum* [Report]. Retrieved from http://www.valueseducation. edu.au/values/val_national_values_education_forum_2008,24401.html

Department of Education, Employment and Workplace Relations (2008b). *Values education good practice schools project—Stage 2* [Final report]. Retrieved from http://www.valueseducation.edu.au/values/default.asp?id=8655

Department of Education, Science and Training (2003). *Values education study.* Retrieved from http://www.valueseducation.edu.au/values/values_education_ 2002-2003_archive,8778.html

Department of Education, Science and Training (2005). *National framework for values education in Australian schools.* Retrieved from http://www.valueseducation. edu.au/values/default.asp?id=8884

Department of Education, Science and Training (2006). *Values education good practice schools project—Stage 1* [Final report]. Retrieved from http://www. valueseducation.edu.au/values/default.asp?id=8884

Department of Education, Science and Training (2007). *National values education forum: Report.* Retrieved from http://www.valueseducation.edu.au/values/default. asp?id=8884

Epstein, J. L. (1995). School/family/community partnerships: Caring for the children we share. *Phi Delta Kappan, 76*(9), 701–712.

Grey Gums School. [i] (2008). *A brief explanation.* Midlands, Queensland: Grey Gums School.

Grey Gums School. (2009a). *Handbook for parents.* Midlands, Queensland: Grey Gums School.

Grey Gums School. (2009b). *Grey Gums School teachers' handbook.* Midlands, Queensland: Grey Gums School.

Grey Gums School. (n.d.) *Grey Gums School's philosophy* [Electronic version]. Midlands, Queensland: Grey Gums School.

Halstead, J. M., & Taylor, M. J. (2000). Learning and teaching about values: A review of recent research. *Cambridge Journal of Education, 30*(2), 169–202.

Hawkes, N. (2008). The purpose of values education. *Journal of Religious Education, 56*(3), 25–31.

Lovat, T., & Toomey, R. (2007). *Values education and quality teaching: The double helix effect.* Terrigal, NSW: David Barlow Publishing.

Lovat, T., Toomey, R., Clement, N., Crotty, R., & Nielsen, T. (2009). *Values education quality teaching and service learning: A troika for effective teaching and teacher education.* Terrigal, NSW: David Barlow Publishing.

MacMullin, C., & Scalfino, L. (2007). Placing values at the centre of school policy and classroom practice-case study at Modbury School, South Australia. In T. Lovat & R. Toomey (Eds.), *Values education and quality teaching: The double helix effect* (pp. 49–68). Terrigal, NSW: David Barlow Publishing.

Mukerjee, R. (1983). *The educational approach at Grey Gums School.* Midlands, Queensland: North Publications.

---

[i] To preserve the anonymity of the school, pseudonyms have been used throughout all references to school documents, for the founder, and for all school personnel.

Mukerjee, R. (1985). *The future of education*. Midlands, Queensland: North Publications.

Mukerjee, R. (1993). *A manual of education*. Unpublished manuscript.

Netherwood, K., Buchanan, J., Palmer, D., Stocker, L., & Down, B. (2007). Valuing diversity in children's voice: Case study of the Western Australian cluster. In T. Lovat & R. Toomey (Eds.), *Values education and quality teaching: The double helix effect* (pp. 91–114). Terrigal, NSW: David Barlow Publishing.

Risko, V. J., & Walker-Dalhouse, D. (2009). Parents and teachers: Talking with or past one another—or not talking at all? *The Reading Teacher, 62*(5), 442–444.

Rowan, L., Gauld, J., Cole-Adams, J., & Connolly, A. (2007). *Teaching values*. Newtown, NSW: Primary English Teaching Association.

Souto-Manning, M., & Swick, K. J. (2006). Teachers' beliefs about parent and family involvement: Rethinking our family involvement paradigm. *Early Childhood Education Journal, 34*(2), 187–193.

Swick, K. J. (2003). Communication concepts for strengthening family-school-community partnerships. *Early Childhood Education Journal, 30*(4), 275–280.

Toomey, R. (2006). *Values as the centrepiece of the school's work: A discussion paper on learnings from VEGPSP Stage 1*. Retrieved from http://www.valueseducation. edu.au/values/default.asp?id=8884

Warren, E., Young, J., & Hanifen, P. (2003). Parent partnerships within Catholic school communities: Values underpinning success. *International Journal of Education & Religion, 4*(1), 63–80.

CHAPTER 5

ENGAGING STUDENTS THROUGH STUDENT VOICE: NEGOTIATING PEDAGOGY

Ian Fraser

Nanango State High School, Nanango, Queensland, Australia

INTRODUCTION

This chapter presents a narrative case study of one high school English subject classroom, that shows how engaging with student voice can reconnect students with learning. The 2nd year of high school has been identified as a time, when students often become disconnected from learning and school and become difficult to manage (Chaplain, 1996; Cole, 2006; Knowles & Brown, 2000; Mitra, 2001; Prendergast & Bahr, 2005; Rudduck & Flutter, 2004a), something that many teachers will attest to. At the same time, the concept of student voice is gaining traction, particularly in the UK, where consultation with students has been mandated by the Education Act of 2002, which requires that schools "must provide for a pupil's views to be considered in the light of his age and understanding" (UK Government, 2002, Section 176). Student voice is seen as "ways in which youth can have the opportunity to participate in school decisions that will shape their lives"

Creating Connections in Teaching and Learning, pp. 59–69
Copyright © 2011 by Information Age Publishing
All rights of reproduction in any form reserved.

(Mitra, 2009, p. 312) and as defining "young people's 'right to be heard'" (Shaw, 2004, para. 2).

This narrative case study is an exploration of "a contemporary phenomenon in depth and within its real-life context" (Yin, 2009, p. 18) that has "spatial, temporal, and other concrete boundaries" (p. 32). By way of introduction to this chapter, the following cameo exemplifies the reason why this case study needed to be captured. Note, that the students interviewed at the time of incidence are identified by letters (A, B and so forth), while those interviewed more recently are identified by name, having given permission for this to be done. Unless otherwise noted, all quotations are from interviews or discussions on November 24, 2004.

> Early in 2003, Class 9D was seen as the worst-behaved class in the school with "no work, getting detentions, and always being very loud. We were wild dogs" (Student A). Another student wrote: "I remember, around a year and a half ago, dreading English. Every class was a disaster" (D. Pichlis, January 2005). The class was unruly, many students seemed uninterested in learning, and disputes characterized nearly every lesson; yet, within weeks, a previously totally disengaged student commented, "I love coming to English!" What happened to cause this change?

Discussions and surveys were conducted with the students at the time of incidence, and further interviews were conducted with three students 5 years later, in order to ascertain how they saw their experiences in the class from a more mature perspective and to learn from their insights. The study proposes that student voice has the potential to transform student behavior, engagement with learning, and academic achievement, although it is not without difficulties.

WHAT THE LITERATURE TELLS US?

Rudduck (2006) wrote that "schools in their deep structures and patterns of relationship have changed less over the last 20 years than young people have changed" (p. 136), and that schools have failed to recognize the degree of autonomy and responsibility that many young people have recognized outside of school, resulting in increased student disillusionment with schools. Further, the "traditional exclusion of young people from the consultative process ... is founded on an out-dated view of childhood which fails to acknowledge children's capacity to reflect on issues affecting their lives" (Rudduck, Chaplain, and Wallace, 1996, p. 172).

Student voice offers a way of addressing these issues and can be seen as having three strands: active citizenship, school improvement, and transformation of school and education (Martin, Worrall, and Dutson-Steinfeld, 2005).

The school improvement strand is based on research that argues that student voice has many advantages for students, teachers, and schools (Flutter & Rudduck, 2004; Rudduck & Flutter, 2004b; Rudduck & McIntyre, 2007), and this chapter is situated within this field. One construct of student voice categorizes levels of student involvement according to a hierarchy, with students seen as data sources, active respondents, co-researchers, and researchers (Fielding, 2001). Further, the concept of student voice was supported by the *United Nations convention on the rights of the child*, ratified by Australia in 1991, which declared that children had "the right to express [their] views freely in all matters affecting the child" (United Nations General Assembly, 1989).

The literature argues that student voice is a powerful tool for improving the schools, engaging the students in their education, improving teaching and learning, developing a sense of democracy-in-action, and even transforming schools, though it is not without its challenges. According to Rudduck and McIntyre (2007), "consulting pupils about teaching and learning proved to be difficult for pupils, teachers, and schools to manage" (p. 13). Student voice has the potential for creating powerful connections between the students and teachers and between students, their school, and their education. Further, McLaughlin's (2001) research has shown that the way students see themselves as valued by teachers is central to engagement:

> Students told us "the way teachers treated you as a student—or as a person actually," counted more than any other factor in the school setting in determining their attachment to the school, their commitment to the schools' goals and, by extension, the academic future they imagined for themselves. (p. 78)

WHAT TO DO?

How to re-engage these students was our problem. Class 9D had become very difficult to teach and many students were becoming frustrated because of "arguments between different groups ... which made it hard for others to actually learn" (A. Millikan, January 2009). One student explained: "I was a bit feral: I did not listen, I did not want to be at school, I did not want to have any part in what we were doing" (C. Yarrow, January 2009).

Research shows that "the failure to meet the particular needs of adolescent learners can manifest in disengagement from schooling, often reflected in poor achievement and behavior" (Prendergast, 2005, p. 6). The behavior of Class 9D reflected research that showed that disengaged students "were less likely to feel good about their school work.... [with] a tendency to give up more easily in school work, to do things without thinking, to make mistakes because they did not listen" (Chaplain, 1996, p. 110).

Also, the students were by now comfortable with the structures of high school and, as Rudduck and Flutter (2004a) suggests, "they may look for other sources of interest and amusement to rescue them from boredom and routine" (p. 5). This was supported by a student, who said that by year nine "people in 9D were comfortable enough with the teachers to see how far they could push them" (A. Millikan, February 2005).

At the time, we (the teaching staff) knew nothing about the theory and practice of student voice—we had not even heard the term—but by April I knew that something had to be done after all of my pedagogical repertoire had failed. In desperation, I asked the students how we should organize teaching and learning, having no idea where this would lead. We started with workshops that distilled their ideas of what makes effective learning into key concepts that Class 9D believed were essential to learning. This became the collaboratively developed *9D Statement of good teaching and learning*:

> Good teaching and learning involves a variety of new and exciting ideas for classroom activities. Where possible, activities should be hands on, creative and set in different environments. At the beginning of a unit, students and teachers should set goals to be accomplished by the end of that unit. Where possible, students should be given choices, because everyone has different interests and learning abilities. Students need to be respected and treated as equals.

This quite remarkable statement written by 13 year old students, along with a student initiated list of their own responsibilities (an early indication of their growing connection to the process), became the basis of all our future planning. Students were becoming interested in, even excited by the possibilities:

> I thought it was great, because it was so different to anything we would have ever done before. Are the students having a say? Crazy! I did not know what to expect, whether it would really work as well as we all hoped, but I was willing to give it a go! (A. Millikan, January 2009)

Over 18 months, we refined a process, whereby the students were actively engaged in devizing their course of study, learning experiences and assessment in conjunction with me, with all decisions being consensual, resulting in innovative and enjoyable learning experiences for all. We called the process "negotiating the pedagogy," since the system we developed went further than negotiating the curriculum, as the students believed that the consultative development of the processes of teaching and learning was as important as the content of classroom learning.

STUDENT VOICE: A POSSIBLE ANSWER

The changes in the class were startling. Within weeks, disruptions had become minimal as students took responsibility for their behavior and that of their peers. As one student said at the time: "Our normally ratty class was behaving and coming to class eager to get stuck in" (B) while another reflected:

> More the boys, you could see their attitude had changed toward the class. You still got some bad behavior, but you never got the real bad stuff like you had before [because they] got a say in what they wanted to do: they were more willing to learn "because it is their stuff that they wanted to learn, stuff that interested them; not the boring stuff. (C. Yarrow, January 2009)

Looking back, another student explained our success in terms of the connections being made between the students and the teacher and among the students:

> [Because] people were given a say in what they learnt, the students started getting along more, both with the teacher and with each other and we all became a lot closer. It was great to see major changes in students who did not care about their school work beforehand and enjoyed arguing—they began to have fun on the projects we did, and at the same time learn a lot as well. (A. Millikan, January 2009)

This led to a significant increase in the students' engagement with their learning. Because the students had a say in both what they learned and how they learned, they became much more involved: "It was great to have input into your learning. You have more of an interest because you choose what you learn" (C). As Rudduck and Flutter (2004a) explain, participation and engagement link "into issues of ownership and intellectual excitement, but it is also about understanding, and thereby having some control over, the nature and purpose of the task" (p. 79). One student saw it as: "More people enjoying work and getting down and doing it, instead of mucking around and playing up, because they like the work" (K, 2003).

Students also gained knowledge of pedagogy: "It gave me insight into what it is like to organize and plan how and what you learn" (C). They also recognized "that not everyone learns the same way ... that you need to take account of people's styles of learning, when planning our units" (I). The goals of their learning became important to them and, from the beginning they were able to articulate clearly, what they expected to learn from any given activity:

> We had to suddenly, instead of just blindly following the teacher ... suddenly we had to think, ok, what are we going to learn, and what are we going to

learn from that and how and what is the purpose of this for our education. (D. Pichlis, December 2008)

Reading, writing and academic attainment improved significantly: "I have learned from the process that anything is possible. I am able to write stories better, read better, punctuate" (M) wrote one student, who had begun the year with little confidence and significant literacy problems. Another student, who had severe difficulties with reading and writing said: "My grammar and my spelling picked up enormously" (C. Yarrow, January 2009). In addition, the students reported significant improvement in a range of skills—use of ICTs, problem-solving, working co-operatively, negotiating, and communicating.

Importantly, a fundamental change occurred in the class culture, with students becoming extremely supportive of each other through learning "to work with others, and the whole class works together now" (L). The class was described as "almost tribal in their loyalty to each other" (M. Ferguson, February 2005). There were also two unexpected developments: I gained a greater insight into the students' viewpoint, which was appreciated by the students—"Teachers can learn from students and school can be interesting" (J)—and the students gained a much better appreciation of the work of the teacher, furthering the connections between us:

> I have realized that there is a hell of a lot more work that the teacher has to do to prepare for lessons than I first thought. For me, after realizing just how much work a teacher has to do, you feel a lot more respect for the teacher knowing that they are actually working and not just making you work! (A. Millikan, February 2005)

CONDITIONS FOR IMPLEMENTATION

The students identified a number of conditions for a student voice project like this to be successful; the foremost was respect and trust. It was imperative that they felt they could trust me: "The teacher does not make us feel dumb when we do not understand something" (H). But respect between students was equally important: "I earned respect from other kids … because we had ideas it made me feel good about myself " (C. Yarrow, January 2009).

This was achieved only over time, but it became accepted that "the class now talks to everyone with respect—when they have a problem with someone, they talk to them" (M). Students also recognized the importance of the relationship with the teacher, inextricably linked with the twin pillars of respect and trust: "The relationship with the teacher was very important for us … the process would not work if the teacher did not respect the students, and the students did not respect the teacher or each other"

(A. Millikan, February 2005). Additionally, the relationships between the students were vital for the well-being of the class, because of the "immense importance for pupils of the social world of the classroom ... social relationships among pupils are a major positive resource for learning" (Arnott et al., p. 86). Student A described the class as "working together, and communicating better with each other and us getting along better."

The choice was also vital. As Flutter and Rudduck (2004) explain: "It is also important that we recognize and respect young people's need for autonomy in learning and imbue the pupil with a greater sense of independence" (p. 133). The students of Class 9D, and later Class 10D, embraced that independence fiercely. One student celebrated this choice, "I think, I take in more in class because it is fun and we can choose what we want to learn. I have never gone to a school that let us do that" (K, August 2004). Related to choice was the importance of control of their learning: "It was the first time I felt in control of the way I learn and I had more fun with it" (G).

Being treated like adults was very important to these growing adolescents, as "the qualities that matter to pupils tend to be as much about how they are *treated*, as how they are *taught*" (Rudduck & Flutter, 2004a, p. 78). The students described it in these terms: "We were treated as adults and allowed to decide what we wanted to do. That is why we put in so much effort—it was our choice," (E); or more memorably: "We got treated older than we were" (F). Students were also well aware of the need for structure and goals (and were critical of one unit that lacked deadlines) and of catering for different learning styles: "[We] have a choice as to the style of learning we want to use ... and also worked out what the best way of learning is" (D).

Associated with this was the importance of variety in the learning experiences and the desirability of making learning fun. This was a constant theme. One student with little academic success in other classes claimed that "we know that we are going to have fun and not just sit there and do work off the board or the textbook. We all look forward to coming to English with Frase ... in English I do as much as I can, and try hard" (A).

Important characteristics of the teacher included willingness to listen to and learn from students, with a genuine appreciation of the students' ideas and concerns; they were very quick to detect tokenism in any form. Additionally, they were firm in their desire for a teacher who was excited to teach the class, which they saw as more important than subject expertise.

CHALLENGES

Implementing such a project is difficult, particularly when it is occurring in a single classroom in a school where student voice is not integral to the school ethos. The support of administration is vital, though the support in this study was passive rather than active. Rudduck and McIntyre (2007) advocate that "there is much to be said for the senior management of schools developing both guidelines and support mechanisms so that individual teachers do not have to take risks in isolation" (p. 43). It is also desirable that student voice is part of a whole-school commitment, as "a more durable approach may be to embed student voice into the everyday habits of teaching, learning, leading and managing in schools" (Sutherland, 2006, p. 10). This was not present in this case study, and it led to some difficulties.

For instance, the teacher responsible can feel isolated from the other staff and there can be fear of what was happening. "I am not having bloody kids tell me how to teach," one teacher told me. This is supported by a comment that "I think a few teachers were rather intimidated by the concept; some did not believe that students should have a say" (A. Millikan, January 2009). Reactions of this kind are based on a fear of personal criticism and a perceived threat to teachers' positional and pedagogical power (Rudduck & McIntyre, 2007), and there was certainly a belief among some teachers that student voice was a crazy idea of mine, that was foreign to their classrooms.

Time and curriculum coverage were problems (Rudduck & McIntyre, 2007), but they were ones that we overcame by making time in class for discussions on teaching and learning and by holding voluntary planning meetings in lunch breaks. These planning meetings were very successful, with between one-third and one-half of the class attending later in year 10, because students "wanted to know more about it, wanted to get more involved in it ... we were putting across what we wanted to do at school, how we wanted to learn" (C. Yarrow, January 2009).

Curriculum coverage was ensured as I explained any mandated areas of learning, and the students readily accepted that. Rarely, the students challenged teachers in other classes when "[they] would just take advantage and yell out, you know, 'We want to do this!' ... It was like different ammunition; instead of saying, 'No, screw you, I do not want to do that!', they were using this experience as a weapon" (D. Pichlis, December 2008). Obviously, this can lead to problems with and for the other teachers.

A final caution lies in the question of whose voices are heard and how they are interpreted. Do all students have an equal opportunity to voice their opinions? Flutter and Rudduck (2004) and Arnott et al. (2004) raise this question, which Fielding (2001) puts it in these terms:

> Who is allowed to speak? ... Some voices (for example middle class girls) seem to be more willing to speak than others, partly because they may feel more at ease, with the way teachers speak about the students and with the capacity of schools to understand what matters to them in their daily lives. (p. 101)

I admit that this did not occur to us; we felt that people had the opportunity to voice their concerns in the meetings so they could not complain, and certainly two of the students, most committed to the process fit Fielding's (2001) description of "middle class girls" (p. 101). The related question of how student voices are interpreted also requires careful thought. Fielding (2004) addressed this question in an article that deals with "the problems of speaking about others," "the problems of speaking for others," and "the problems of getting heard" (p. 295). We hoped that the planning meetings would address this, but in retrospect, I mostly interpreted their ideas for lessons.

IMPLICATIONS

The most important implication is that developing student voice makes a difference to the students as individuals and as a class, and to the lives of some of the students. Students, who were totally disenchanted found they could make a difference, learning could be meaningful, and they would develop confidence: "It is weird looking back on it now ... I guess it has shaped each of us ... it kind of kept going. Yeah, it was good." (D. Pichlis, December 2008). Additionally, it takes time, energy and patience on the part of the teacher. The lunchtime meetings could be quite onerous, but they were also invigorating and exciting, as "students think deeply about educational issues, they have striking insights into them and they have a great deal to say about them" (Shultz & Cook-Sather, 2001, p. 72). The teacher must listen to the students respectfully and be open to the possibilities that working with them can bring, understanding that "students are capable of becoming active agents in the learning process" (Finney et al., 2005, p. 81).

Relationships and trust are critical, but they develop only if students see the teacher is willing to take their ideas seriously and act on them. This involves finding ways to ensure that all voices are heard, particularly those of the disengaged students whose insights may be just those needed to revitalize a class. As well, the teacher needs to be aware that relationships with the students will change—positional authority will no longer be as powerful, but a more effective relationship, built on mutual respect and trust, may develop. Communication is very important when establishing such a radical innovation, so it is vital that the teacher keeps the administration and the other teachers informed to avoid some of the problems that I faced. And finally, it can have a lasting effect on the teacher's pedagogical practices.

CONCLUSION

While it is true that giving students the right to speak about teaching and learning can be challenging for all, the rewards are clear. Students have remarkable insights into classroom interactions that are not normally accessed by their teachers, and willingness, indeed eagerness, to be involved in co-constructing their learning. As a group, we created explicit connections between the teacher and students; between individual students and the class as a collective entity; and amongst the students, their school, and their learning.

Nearly two decades ago, Fullan (1991) asked: "What would happen if we treated the student as someone whose opinion mattered?" (p. 170). Perhaps the students from 9/10D can answer him:

> I thought it was great, it gave us the chance to be really creative, to kind of branch away from what everyone else was doing, and to explore new possibilities. It was really exciting that we were doing something completely new and different. (D. Pichlis, December 2008)

REFERENCES

Arnott, M., McIntyre, D., Pedder, D., & Reay, D. (2004). *Consultation in the classroom: Developing dialogue about teaching and learning.* Cambridge: Pearson Publishing.

Chaplain, R. (1996). Making a strategic withdrawal: Disengagement and self-worth protection in male pupils. In J. Rudduck, R. Chaplain, & G. Wallace (Eds.), *School improvement: What can pupils tell us?* (pp. 101–115). London: David Fulton.

Cole, P. (2006). *Reforming year 9: Propositions for school policy and practice.* [Occasional Paper No. 96]. Jolimont, Victoria.: Centre for Strategic Education. Retrieved from http://www.edstaff.com.au/docs/Peter%20Cole%20-%20Reforming%20Year%209.pdf

Fielding, M. (2001). Students as radical agents of change [Electronic version]. *Journal of Educational Change, 2*(2), 123–141.

Fielding, M. (2004). Transformative approaches to student voice: Theoretical underpinnings, recalcitrant realities [Electronic version]. *British Educational Research Journal, 30*(2), 296–311.

Finney, J., Hickman, R., Morrison, M., Nicholl, B., & Rudduck, J. (2005). *Rebuilding engagement through the arts: Responding to disaffected students.* Cambridge: Pearson.

Flutter, J., & Rudduck, J. (2004). *Consulting pupils: What's in it for schools?* London: RoutledgeFalmer.

Fullan, M. (1991). *The new meaning of educational change.* New York: Teachers College Press.

Knowles, T., & Brown, D. (2000). *What every middle school teacher should know.* Portsmouth: Heinemann.

Martin, N., Worrall, N., & Dutson-Steinfeld, A. (2005). *Student voice: Philosopher's stone or Pandora's box?* [Electronic version]. London: National College for School Leadership. Retrieved from http://networkedlearning.ncsl.org.uk/knowledge-base/research-directory.pdf

McLaughlin, M. (2001). Somebody knows my name. In F. Crowther, D. Andrews, M. Dawson, & M. Lewis (Eds.), *Innovative designs for enhancing achievement in schools facilitation folder: Networks and resources: Readings* (pp. 1–290). Toowoomba: University of Southern Queensland, Education Queensland.

Mitra, D. (2001). Opening the floodgates: Giving students a voice in school reform. *Forum, 43*(2), 91–94.

Mitra, D. (2009). Strengthening student voice initiatives in high schools: An examination of the supports needed for school-based youth-adult partnerships [Electronic version]. *Youth and Society, 40*(3), 311–335.

Prendergast, D. (2005). The emergence of middle schooling. In D. Prendergast, & N. Bahr (Eds.), *Teaching middle years: Rethinking curriculum, pedagogy and assessment* (pp. 3–20). Crows Nest, NSW: Allen & Unwin.

Prendergast, D., & Bahr, N. (Eds.). (2005). *Teaching middle years: Rethinking curriculum, pedagogy and assessment.* Crows Nest, NSW: Allen & Unwin.

Rudduck, J. (2006). Editorial: The past, the papers and the project. *Educational Review, 58*(2), 131–143.

Rudduck, J., Chaplain, R., & Wallace, G. (1996). Reviewing the conditions of learning in school. In J. Rudduck, R. Chaplain, & G. Wallace (Eds.), *School improvement: What can pupils tell us* (pp. 172–178). London: David Fulton.

Rudduck, J., & Flutter, J. (2004a). *The challenge of year 8: Sustaining pupils' engagement with learning.* Cambridge: Pearson.

Rudduck, J., & Flutter, J. (2004b). *How to improve your school: Giving pupils a voice.* London: Continuum.

Rudduck, J., & McIntyre, D. (2007). *Improving learning through consulting pupils.* London: Routledge.

Shaw, P. (2004, September 20–26th). Are "student voices" more powerful than "student voice" in bringing about school improvement? [Discussion paper]. iNET (International Networking for Educational Transformation). Retrieved from: http://www.ssat-inet.net/resources/olc/papers/are%E2%80%98studentvoices%E2%80%80%99more.aspx

Shultz, J., & Cook-Sather, A. (2001). *In our own words: Students' perspectives on school.* Lanham: Rowman & Littlefield.

Sutherland, G. (2006). Voice of change: Embedding student voice work. *Curriculum Briefing, 4*(3), 8–11.

UK Government. (2002). Part 11, Section 176 of the *Education Act 2002.* Retrieved from http://www.legislation.gov.uk/ukpga/2002/32/section/176

United Nations General Assembly. (1989, November 20). *Convention on the rights of the child.* Retrieved from http://www.un.org/documents/ga/res/44/a44r025.htm

Yin, R. (2009). *Case study research: Design and methods.* Thousand Oaks, CA: Sage.

CHAPTER 6

RELATIONAL TRUST AS A CORE RESOURCE FOR BUILDING CAPACITY IN SCHOOLS

Richard Scagliarini

An International School, Japan

INTRODUCTION

Relational trust is conceptualized in this chapter as a core resource that connects teachers as learners, and builds a school's capacity for curriculum reform. The perspectives presented are derived from my doctoral research which was conducted at a Kindergarten to Year 12 International School in East Asia and supported the notion that an effective professional learning community is the human network necessary for building a school's capacity for reform.

It was found that embedded in the realm of a professional learning community are the fundamental reform agents of leadership, relationships, internal/external collaboration and, at the center of it all, relational trust. The interactive operation of these agents was observed as having a synergistic effect on the capacity for reform, with relational trust determined as a necessary and valuable resource that empowers and connects

Creating Connections in Teaching and Learning, pp. 71–81
Copyright © 2011 by Information Age Publishing

the teachers as learners. This impacted the reculturing experience in the school and ultimately led to a culture where enhanced student learning could take place. To illustrate these findings, a framework is presented that posits the professional learning community as a multi-dimensional and interconnected web of teachers as learners.

BUILDING CAPACITY FOR LEARNING

The central aim of education is student learning. Teachers are the main human instruments of this learning (Crowther et al., 2002) and school culture is the context in which this learning is manifested. King and Newmann (2001) provide a conceptualization of the school capacity that stresses three main dimensions: the knowledge, skills and dispositions of individual teachers; professional community among the staff as a whole; and program coherence within schools. Crowther et al. (2002) affirm that improving the teacher performance and leadership is fundamental to successful school reform, and that a new paradigm for teacher learning is needed. A focus on connecting teachers as learners provides a context for building individual and group capacity. A framework encompassing this concept is presented in this chapter as a critical process for building a school's capacity for improving student learning.

Fullan (2007) defines capacity building as "a policy, strategy, or action taken that increases the collective efficacy of a group to improve student learning through new knowledge, enhanced resources, and greater motivation on the part of people working individually and together" (p. 58). He emphasizes that, especially in the early stages of the reform process, capacity building provides the key experiences of teacher learning everyday and in context, and is thus essential. Furthermore, Fullan asserts that these experiences develop the three essential ingredients for teachers as learners—skills, clarity, and motivation. In order to engage in the change process and initiate re-culturing, teachers need to adopt new beliefs, build new knowledge, and develop closer relationships. This process of developing and connecting teachers is critical to school improvement and according to Fullan, is facilitated by the teachers engaging in new, shared, and connective experiences.

Relational trust refers to trust as a function of interpersonal interactions and it is becoming increasingly recognized as an intriguing and vital element in efficient schools (Bryk & Schneider, 2002; Powell, 1990; Scagliarini, 2010; Seashore Louis, 2007; Tschannen-Moran & Hoy, 1998). Various metaphors have been used in education literature, in attempts to capture the essence of this complex and multi-dimensional concept. These include relational trust as foundational for meaningful school improvement; as a catalyst for innovation; as a remarkably efficient lubricant (Powell, 1990); as a necessary ingredient for co-operative action; and as a bridge that reform must be carried over (Seashore Louis, 2007). Bryk and Schneider (2002) argue that relational trust is "connective tissue" (p. 144). They illustrate the omnipresence of relational trust in schools and the importance of nurturing this "connective tissue," when they explain that "good schools are intrinsically social enterprises that depend heavily on cooperative endeavor, among the varied participants who comprise the school community" (p. 144). They emphasize that it is important to organize "the work of adults and students" in such a way that "the connective tissue that binds these individuals together, around advancing the education and welfare of children" remains "healthy and strong" (p. 144).

The research I conducted at an international school in East Asia supports these propositions. Teachers played a critical role in leading the school's capacity for improving student learning. The middle school curriculum initiative identified and implemented three fundamental principles for improving learning in the middle years: addressing adolescent needs, engaging students in their learning, and aligning with the principles of the knowledge era. All three were achieved in varying degrees. This chapter focuses on findings which illuminate how the process of curriculum reform was manifested within the context of a professional learning community, where relational trust connected the teachers as learners.

THE METHODOLOGY

This study tracked the experiences of a small group of teachers and administrators (including myself) as we reformed the middle year curriculum at Bay International School (a pseudonym) in East Asia. Naturalistic inquiry was selected as the most appropriate research paradigm to realize the purpose and aim of this study. I played the role of participant-observer in this reform process, which involved participating in the reform process as an insider, while simultaneously observing and recording the experience as an outsider. Naturalistic inquiry allowed for a research design that was emergent, flexible, and responsive to contextual conditions as the process of curriculum reform unfolded over a 2 year period. The core sample consisted of the headmaster, four middle school teachers (including myself), and two other teachers who were directly involved in the reform process. The data collected included interviews, observations, documents, artefacts, and surveys (of other teachers and students).

Within the naturalistic paradigm, the process of data analysis is inductive, whereby the constructions that emerge and are gathered from the context are reconstructed into meaningful wholes. This process of inductive analysis begins with the data, from which theoretical categories or relational propositions may be arrived at by inductive reasoning processes (Lincoln & Guba, 1985). Thus, the analysis of data in this research was a progressive, on-going process that involved the continual analysis of data as they were collected. This then informed the subsequent data gathering procedures and strategies. The documentation of this research process culminated in a case report that formed the basis of a doctoral thesis (Scagliarini, 2010).

UNCOVERING THE FUNDAMENTALS

By sharing the purpose and professional dialogue and collectively learning together, the teachers at Bay International School developed into a professional learning community, whose purpose was to enhance student learning. Stoll, Bolam, McMahon, Wallace, and Thomas (2006) present five key characteristics or features of a professional learning community that intertwine and operate together to achieve this purpose: shared values and vision; collective responsibility; reflective professional inquiry; collaboration; and promoting group and individual learning. Although not school-wide as Stoll et al. imply, these features were evident in the unfolding process that occurred in the small focussed community of teacher learners at Bay International School. Furthermore, Stoll and Seashore Louis (2007) describe a professional learning community, in terms that can be aptly applied to the journey experienced by the participants at Bay International School:

> An inclusive group of people, motivated by a shared learning vision, who support and work with each other, finding ways, inside and outside their immediate community, to enquire on their practice and together learn new and better approaches that will enhance pupils' learning (pp. 5–6).

Shared Values and Vision

By drawing on their own knowledge and experience, actively uncovering new knowledge and understandings from engaging in deep conversations, interacting with internal and external sources, and sharing a vision, the teachers at Bay International School were able to connect as learners, and collaboratively construct and implement a new conceptualization of the middle years curriculum at their school. Trust played a key role in connecting the teachers at a deep level and was nurtured over time by intense and repeated interactions between the same individuals. From the early stages

Figure 6.1. The dynamics of the professional learning community at Bay International School

of introducing the curriculum initiative to the school community (initially led by the headmaster), the relational trust deepened as this group of teachers co-constructed the trust to become the "connective tissue" (Bryk & Schneider, 2002, p. 144) that bonded them and enabled them to develop and implement changes in the middle school curriculum.

Figure 6.1 illustrates how leadership, relationships, and collaboration with internal and external agents were the core reform agents that interacted with each other and powered the professional learning community. The findings from this study illuminate how these interconnected features of building capacity for change were enabled and lubricated by relational trust.

Collective Responsibility

Embedded in this concept of relational trust as the core resource for building capacity, is the manner in which leadership was manifested in the shared power relations between the school headmaster and the teachers, students, and parents. Trust is a critical resource required by the leaders to embark on effective and sustainable improvement plans. School leaders (whether they are administrators or teacher leaders) have a major responsibility for nurturing the social exchanges that are a fundamental feature of the operation of schools as a social enterprise.

The headmaster at Bay International School played a critical role in initiating, shaping, maintaining, building alliances, and energizing the learning community. He knew he could not do it alone, and he made deliberate efforts to share the leadership. He was observed playing the roles of designer, teacher, and steward (Senge, 2006), and he subsequently played a pivotal role in facilitating teacher learning, connectivity, and leadership. The joint efforts of the administrators and teachers, and the experiences that unfolded can be likened to Crowther et al.'s (2002) concept of parallel leadership, where "teacher leaders and their principals engage in collective action to build school capacity. It embodies mutual respect, shared purpose, and allowance for individual expression" (p. 38). This was observed and documented throughout the reform process.

The headmaster acknowledged that relational trust was a critical resource that he utilized as a catalyst for change (Scagliarini, 2010, p. 159). This trust had been built over his long and atypical tenure (11 years as headmaster, a rarity in the international school context), and it was evident that he had built a high trust environment, supported by (mostly) quality social relationships. He paid attention to relationships with teachers; was supported by a reservoir of trust; had enlisted teachers as co-constructors of trust, to be involved in the reform process; and he kept building trust among the stakeholders throughout the reform process. The headmaster reflected specifically on trust, and acknowledged its importance in one of the recorded interviews:

> If you are successful in certain little ways, little steps, then more and more trust comes in your direction ... Trust is fundamental, and I think in any head[master], if I was going to say what is the most important thing about a head in any schooling situation, that head has got to be trusted by all the constituencies .... When it doesn't happen that's when things start to fall apart .... And it's true in relationships all around. So trust is huge (Scagliarini, 2010, pp. 159–160).

With a focus on collective learning within the context of a community of learners, it is apparent that professional learning communities "intentionally build webs of relationships around the collective work of the participants" (Lieberman, 2007, p. 201). Sharing, interacting, participating, interdependence, mutual concern, and meaningful relationships are core features of a community (Westheimer, 1999), and these were all evident in the small Bay International School community. Trusting relationships, within the context of this social enterprise that operated as the reform group, became a core resource and helped to soothe the difficult emotions and anxieties that emerge during a school's change process (Hargreaves, 2007).

Using Lieberman's (2007) Web analogy and drawing from the data collected in this study, Figure 6.2 was constructed to provide some insights
into the existing relationships of the various groups involved in the reform
process, at around half way through the 1st year of implementation. The
lines indicate the level of relational trust based on data analysis, with a solid
line indicating the strongest relational trust and a dashed line indicating
weaker relational trust. Multiple lines indicate variations in the trust relationships. The reform group of teachers were responsible for developing
and implementing the new curriculum.

The headmaster thus enjoyed strongest relational trust with the Bay
International School Board and Teacher 1. I am Teacher 1 and a member of
the reform group, but I am presented separately here, as our trust relationship differed from that between the headmaster and the rest of the group.
The three varied lines connecting the headmaster to the school staff indicate a range of relations with this group, with some faculty members having
weak relational trust with the headmaster. Varied levels of trust are indicated
between the parents and the headmaster, and the reform group and the parents. This is unsurprising, considering the diversity and transience of the
parent group, and the affect this has on building trust. The headmaster was
certainly aware of fostering good relations with the parents throughout this
reform process in order to, as he put it, "minimize turbulence" (Scagliarini,
2010, p. 177). The external agents that had repeated interactions with the
group had strong relational trust within this learning community. These are
discussed later in this chapter.

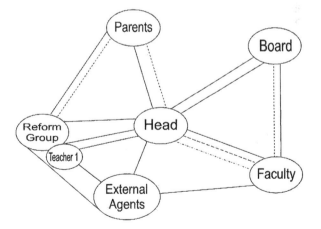

Figure 6.2. A web of relational trust in the professional learning community at Bay
International School

REFLECTIVE PROFESSIONAL INQUIRY

This study provided an opportunity to examine what goes on when teachers and administrators come together to implement change and it is revealed that the story of middle school curriculum reform at Bay International School, is a story about people and relationships. These relationships are based on trust; the trust dynamics are complex and constantly evolving and the difficulty of pinning them down is real. Figure 6.2 reveals the central position the headmaster played in building and maintaining this web of trusting relationships within the school community. Naturally, this is not a one-way venture and trusting relationships were also sought and fostered with the headmaster. Human relationships are the very essence of schooling as a social enterprise; they are the spirit of school operations and the heart of school reform. This community of learners operated as a connective network of relationships, lubricated by relational trust; it continued to learn, adapt, and evolve, providing a vehicle to build capacity and effect change in the middle school.

COLLABORATION

Collaboration is undoubtedly a critical element of the professional learning community (Kruse et al., 1994), a big idea representing a core principle of the professional learning community (DuFour, 2004), and a key component of the re-imaging of teaching (Andrews & Lewis, 2002). Unsurprisingly, collaboration emerged in this research as a significant operation in the creation of knowledge and collective learning in the reform process at Bay International School. Collaborative processes manifested in this professional learning community in two ways: as an intentional and purposeful function of interpersonal relationships; and as relationships that were differentiated as interactions within the localized group (internal) and extended to outside agents (external).

As the professional learning community became more focused and the enormity of the task became apparent, the reform group found that working collaboratively was no longer an option, but an imperative. Early on in the reform process, one of the original members of the reform group articulated the role of meaningful, collaborative relationships:

> A group of people from a diversity of viewpoints, with a diversity of interests met to negotiate a curriculum, a path, which would be satisfactory to all. It wasn't always harmonious or easy but it soon became apparent that nothing would emerge if we didn't collaborate (Scagliarini, 2010, p. 26).

As the relational trust developed, emotional and cultural barriers were relaxed, enabling the teachers to collaboratively engage in sharing and reflecting on their practice and to build individual and collective capacity for improvement. Collaboration within the group was readily observed in the story of the reform process, and trusting relationships empowered the collaboration to occur, which in turn served to deepen the trust.

PROMOTING GROUP AND INDIVIDUAL LEARNING

On the external collaboration front, the school hosted an annual community conference that provided an opportunity each year to bring in external agents, who would contribute to the knowledge building and sharing processes that were underway. Along with other visitations by experts in various disciplines throughout the year, this ongoing input of external knowledge (in the fields of human brain research, learning in the knowledge era, and curriculum design) was beneficial to the reform group, as it often served to inform and validate the curriculum initiative. This helped the reformers feel like they were creating something significant and it kept them focused and motivated. Sustained interaction with three of these external agents allowed the trust to develop and relationships to deepen—the essential elements needed to foster effective collaboration and connect the external agents as co-opted members of the professional learning community. Single visits by external agents had less impact on contributing knowledge and assimilating with the professional learning community.

This external collaboration with international experts was facilitated predominantly by the headmaster. The strategy of nurturing ongoing relationships with a few select external agents further connected the teachers as learners, by providing a broader context within which to share and expand knowledge. It added value to the collaborative process by providing new insights, resources, and validation. By pushing the existing paradigm of middle schooling, and drawing from inside and outside their community, the reformers at Bay International School enhanced the professional learning community's capacity for developing and implementing improved learning in their middle school.

CONCLUSION

The simplicity of the framework shown in Figure 6.1 is deceiving, as building capacity for curriculum reform is not simple. It is a multi-dimensional, complex, phasic, and lengthy process. Undoubtedly, the professional learning community can be the key operator of collective action for building this capacity. However, the reform agents captured in the framework must be in place: leaders need to play vital and diverse roles as facilitators of relational trust; a community of learners should be operating as a network of trusting human relationships; and collaboration must be developed as a deliberate, systematic, and systemic process.

The research that has been described suggests some advice for those who would like to enhance curriculum reform in their own contexts. The first step for educators involved in curriculum reform, is awareness. Educators need to become aware of the dynamics of Figure 6.1 as operating in their context. It is important to ask the fundamental question: What is going on here? Good advice is to observe the dynamics, examine them closely, learn about these concepts and about yourself, analyze, and reflect.

Relational trust will emerge as the "connective tissue" (Bryk & Schneider, 2002, p. 144)—the necessary and valuable resource that empowers and connects the teachers as learners. It is hard-earned, fragile, and built-up over time, through intense and repeated social interactions. It needs to be nurtured. Just like the web of a spider, which takes time and effort to form, a deliberate focus on cultivating this resource can enable a strong, flexible, and dynamic learning context to grow. Trust is vital; administrators and teachers should build it, value it, and use it, to energize the capacity for curriculum reform, and the promise of improved student learning.

REFERENCES

Andrews, D., & Lewis, M. (2002). The experience of a professional community: Teachers developing a new image of themselves and their workplace. *Educational Researcher, 44*(3), 237–254.

Bryk, A., & Schneider, B. (2002). *Trust in schools: A core resource for improvement.* New York: Russell Sage Foundation.

Crowther, F., Kaagan, S., Ferguson, M., & Hann, L. (2002). *Developing teacher leaders.* Thousand Oaks, CA: Corwin Press.

DuFour, R. (2004). What is a "professional learning community"? *Educational Leadership, 61*(8), 6–11.

Fullan, M. (2007). *The new meaning of educational change.* New York: Teachers College Press.

Hargreaves, A. (2007). Sustainable learning communities. In L. Stoll & K. Seashore Louis (Eds.), *Professional learning communities: Divergence, depth and dilemmas* (pp. 181–195). Maidenhead, UK: Open University Press.

King, M. B., & Newmann, F. (2001). Building school capacity through professional development: conceptual and empirical considerations. *The International Journal of Educational Management, 15*(2), 86–93.

Kruse, S., Seashore Louis, K., & Bryk, A. (1994). Building professional community in schools. *Issues in Restructuring Schools, 6,* 3–6.

Lieberman, A. (2007). Professional learning communities: A reflection. In L. Stoll & K. Seashore Louis (Eds.), *Professional learning communities: Divergence, depth and dilemmas* (pp. 199–203). Maidenhead, UK: Open University Press.

Lincoln, Y. S., & Guba, E. G. (1985). *Naturalistic inquiry*. Newbury Park, CA: Sage.

Powell, W. W. (1990). Neither market nor hierarchy: Network forms of organization. In B. M. Straw & L. L. Cummings (Eds.), *Research in organizational behavior* (pp. 295–336). Greenwich, CT: JAI.

Scagliarini, R. (2010). *Reforming the middle years curriculum: A new paradigm for middle schooling*. Saarbrücken, Germany: VDM Verlag Dr. Müller.

Seashore Louis, K. (2007). Trust and improvement in schools. *Journal of Educational Change, 8*(1), 1–24.

Senge, P. M. (2006). *The fifth discipline: The art and practice of the learning organization* (Rev. ed.). New York: Doubleday.

Stoll, L., Bolam, R., McMahon, A., Wallace, M., & Thomas, S. (2006). Professional learning communities: A review of the literature. *Journal of Educational Change, 7*(4), 221–258.

Stoll, L., & Seashore Louis, K. (2007). Professional learning communities: Elaborating new approaches. In L. Stoll & K. Seashore Louis (Eds.), *Professional learning communities: Divergence, depth and dilemmas* (pp. 1–13). Maidenhead, UK: Open University Press.

Straw & L. L. Cunnings (Eds.), *Research in organizational behavior* (pp. 295–336). Greenwich, CT: JAI.

Tschannen-Moran, M., & Hoy, W. (1998). Trust in schools: A conceptual and empirical analysis. *Journal of Educational Administration, 36*(4), 334–352.

Westheimer, J. (1999). Communities and consequences: An inquiry into ideology and practice in teachers' professional work. *Educational Administration Quarterly, 35*(1), 71–105.

CHAPTER 7

INTERNATIONAL TEACHERS MAKING CONNECTIONS IN TIMES OF CHANGE

Marie Davis

Educational and Counseling Psychologist, working with
international schools in Switzerland

INTRODUCTION

International schools are a rapidly growing educational reality, serving an estimated 1 million students and employing over 154,000 teachers worldwide (Brummitt, 2007). In this educational milieu, much of the research addresses such topics as international curriculum (Carber & Reis, 2004), students (Fail, Thompson, and Walker, 2004), the stress of re-location for families (Foreman, 1981), and culture shock for children (Pyvis, 2005). McLachlan (2007) discusses the impact of multiple transitions on internationally mobile families, noting the significance of the family unit in managing transition and change. Little of the literature concerning international education and the individuals involved, however, focuses on the teachers (Holderness, 2001).

Creating Connections in Teaching and Learning, pp. 83–93
Copyright © 2011 by Information Age Publishing
All rights of reproduction in any form reserved.

Hardman (2001) notes that for many students attending international schools the most important relationships and activities are centered in and around this community, with classmates and teachers. This implies that, for many children, the international school represents a secure environment. If teachers are acting as one stabilizing force for these young people, it seems essential to engage in continued knowledge and understanding of this group of educators.

A study by Hayden and Thompson (1998) shows that 40% of the 226 international school teachers, who responded to their survey, had taught in five or more schools. The Web site of the Association for the Advancement of International Education (n.d.) states that the average tenure at any one school is 3.5 years. Other studies demonstrate that there is a disturbing development among international school teachers—the non-fulfillment of a normal 2 year contract (Cambridge, 2002). Blandford and Shaw (2001, as cited in Bunnell, 2006, p. 388) see high rates of teacher turnover as a distinctive characteristic of international schools.

This chapter reports on research that focused on change, job satisfaction, and the transition process, as it affects the population of teachers working in international schools around the world. The chapter begins with an explanation of change styles, including the descriptions of *conservers*, *pragmatists* and *originators* from the work of Musselwhite (2004), who considers change style as an innate aspect of personality, which influences the preferences, attitudes, and emotions surrounding the change. Although these change style preferences are manageable and fluid within our lives, their knowledge can assist in greater self-awareness and professional satisfaction. The Musselwhite theory of change styles is then related to the aspects of personality, particularly, as described by the Myers Briggs Type Indicator (MBTI). These descriptions are then transferred to a population of international school teachers, who have chosen to work in schools outside their country of origin, and who responded to the call for data collection in this study.

Considering the concept of change and transition inherent in the lives of international teachers, the varying perceptions and approaches to the change, generally demonstrated by the individuals of different styles can then be used to consider the specific process of relocation. It is believed that increased understanding of teachers' needs when relocating, could augment orientation programs and professional development initiatives, leading to greater job satisfaction and retention among teachers in international schools. An understanding of change styles could assist in creating positive and productive connections, both professionally and personally, in the changing international school environment.

THE BACKGROUND

Before pursuing the topic, it is important to clarify the definitions and terms utilized throughout this chapter. Applying the definition determined by ISC Research (Brummitt, 2007), an *international school* is one located outside an English speaking country and in which English is wholly or partly the language of instruction. If the school is located in an English speaking country, an international curriculum must be offered, in order for it to be considered an international institution. An international curriculum is one that does not follow the national curriculum imposed by the country in which the school is situated. It may or may not include some nationally recognized subjects or objectives, but it is not limited to the host country's educational plan. With regard to the study discussed in this chapter, *international teacher* refers to the individuals of any cultural background, presently employed in an international school outside their country of origin.

The concept of change styles is born from the research of Discovery Learning (2000) and it is related to theories of personality, particularly the MBTI which is formulated in the Jungian theory. Jung hypothesized that people are wired with certain inherited preferences from birth, and that these potentials are actualized when they enter consciousness or manifest themselves in behavior or interaction with the outside world (Corey, 1996). Therefore, awareness of individual preferences and potentials can lead to greater personal development. Jungian theory has contributed many psychological approaches to human behavior and it has led to the development of an internationally recognized and applied personality assessment, the MBTI, which formed the foundation of the Change Styles Indicator (CSI), the assessment tool used in this study.

The MBTI is a self-report inventory, that helps identify natural preferences. It measures four polar dimensions of personality and is the frequent choice of educational researchers because it is particularly suited to applications in teaching and learning (Rushton, Morgan, and Richard, 2007). It is the most commonly used tool to identify individual learning preferences and teaching styles. The four scales indicate a person's psychological preference, for consistent and enduring patterns of how the world is viewed, how information is collected and interpreted, how decisions are made, and how individuals live out lifestyle choices.

Growing evidence regarding the biological basis of psychological type gives credence to Jung's assumption that type is universal (Myers et al., 2003). This premise is supported by the fact that the MBTI has been scrutinized by in-depth research and remains the most widely used personality assessment in the world (Myers et al., 2003). Many translations of the MBTI are being used successfully and many more are being developed worldwide, with analogous results being reported in different countries and cultures. Although numerous factors contribute to an individual's job performance, satisfaction, and retention, MBTI research offers a valuable conceptualization of the role of personality/type preference, as well as the implications for the use of this knowledge, in job choice and expectations.

The CSI was fashioned on the theories of the MBTI and correlates highly with the MBTI in the aspects of personality, important to the current research. Davis (2009) offers a detailed explanation of the relationship between the MBTI and the CSI. In brief, the CSI condenses the theories of the MBTI to a more specific concept of change styles, focusing on perceptions and approaches to the change process, particularly in the work environment. Individual change styles fall on the CSI continuum, ranging from conservers at one end, originators at the other, and pragmatists at the center. The CSI, while allowing for diversity among people and the strength of their predilections, attempts to categorize the change styles of individuals, into descriptions and suggestions of behavior and tendencies. Metaphorically speaking, one can regard conservers as the farmers of the world; pragmatists as hunters; and originators as the globe's explorers (Musselwhite, 2004).

Conservers are those who reap what they sow after following a systematic and defined procedure. Patient with the growing season, they cannot imagine risking a tried and true process for unknown experiments, even if the predicted harvest is greater. Conservers, believed to make up about 25% of the general population, offer predictability, structure, organization, and discipline to their environment. They value and preserve tradition, believing it is the foundation of any organization, school, or family. Conservers can be considered evolutionists, following gradual and incremental steps to reach even a minor transformation. As they are focused on details, they often overlook the big picture and future possibilities. When instituting a necessary change in an organization or team, conservers tend to involve all individuals in the decision-making process, though discreetly placing more value on the stability and experience of veteran members.

Pragmatists, the hunters, are likened to those skilled and efficient in tracking, killing, dressing, and curing their prey. While they prefer to stay within the established and known boundaries for the kill, their adaptable, broad understanding of a situation allows them to digress from a prescribed territory. Although they may overlook intricate details of a situation, they have the tools and knowledge to accomplish their goal in the time frame set before them. Their focus is the outcome, and they seek practical and functional means to get there. Pragmatists are peacemakers at heart, observing all the sides of a situation and genuinely understanding and caring about diverse positions. As a result, the change process can be prolonged at the expense of harmony. Pragmatists often frustrate conservers and originators, as they are seen as non-committal and wavering. Given their person-centered approach, they are, however, generally the most team oriented of all the change styles.

Originators, the so-called explorers of the population, seek new and uncharted territory without the least notion of what they will find. Adventure is the purpose of the voyage, and while they can adapt to most conditions, they often make adjustments that satisfy their own preferences. While the conservers are considered evolutionary, originators, also comprising approximately 25% of the population, are revolutionary, believed to create change for change sake. While they are adaptable and novel in their search for adventure and stimulation, they often overlook the possible eventualities, leaving themselves (or others) scrambling to achieve a successful outcome. Given to creative expression, originators sometimes prefer working alone, in order not to impede their imagined path. They value ideas and contributions of the individuals in the group more than they regard interpersonal processes. Seeing the future replete with possibilities, originators tend to overlook tradition, often appearing undisciplined and unconventional. While they are often regarded as change agents, they are seldom regarded for organization and efficiency.

EXPLANATION OF THE RESEARCH

Having established the definition of international schools, teachers working in them, and the concept of change styles, the process and results of the research conducted is now presented. Taking into consideration many facets of the existing literature, the design of this research was conceived with the underpinning belief that change styles are a distinct aspect of personality which can be identified and understood in different contexts. The research included both the quantitative data collected from over 200 teachers, as well as qualitative interviews from a select group of seven teachers. The quantitative data served both exploratory and explanatory functions. The quantitative element was necessary to generate a sample population of international teachers of varying change styles. From this group, individuals were identified for the qualitative component. Additionally, the quantitative data was revisited in the light of the qualitative results, to contribute to the value of the developing theory.

The population of teachers participating in the study was generated by word of mouth, within the international school community. I initially contacted international colleagues around the world, explained the research project, and asked them to disseminate information, a letter of explanation, and an informed consent form to their co-workers and international cohorts. Eventually, willing participants from around the globe responded positively, volunteering for the process. Phase 1 consisted of two online questionnaires, the CSI, as well as a personal information and rating scale, which I devised for an overview of the demographic data, information about an individual's career in international education, and rating of job satisfaction. This phase of the study identified significant diversity among the participants, contributing to the overall results, and credibility of the research.

Of the 204 participants, 67 were male and 137 female, ranging in age from 20 to over 61. All educational levels were represented, as well as teaching and non-teaching staff, including administrators, information technology specialists, student support specialists, and librarians. The duration of international school employment ranged from less than 1 year to more than 10 years. Nearly half of the respondents claimed the United States as their country of origin, with a majority of the others divided among the United Kingdom, Canada, and Australia. A small percentage was from New Zealand. Other respondents were from various countries, including Bolivia, Brazil, China, Denmark, France, India, Ireland, Jordan, Latvia, Lebanon, the Netherlands, Nigeria, Paraguay, South Africa, Sri Lanka, Syria, Turkey, Uruguay, and Venezuela. All were fluent in the English language. The geographical areas, in which the respondents reported having worked, included all the major regions of the world as categorized by the United Nations, including Africa, Eastern Africa, South-Central Asia, South-East Asia, Eastern and Southern Europe, Northern and Western Europe, the Caribbean, South and Central America, North America, Australia, and Micronesia/Polynesia/Melanesia.

From the 204 participants, seven were chosen based on their CSI scores and varied international backgrounds to participate in a more intensive interview process consisting of three rounds of dialogue. Among the seven were two conservers, two pragmatists, two originators, and one between the pragmatist and originator scores on the CSI continuum (the pragmatist-originator). The quantitative data were analyzed, using the Statistical Package for the Social Sciences (SPSS) software, while each step of the dialogical progression involved an iterative process of data reduction and coding, including consistent checking and rechecking of the topics emerging from the rich knowledge of the participants' experiences. The meaning was extracted at each level of the dialogical process to draw preliminary and final conclusions.

RESULTS

Among this specific sample of international school teachers, the frequency of conservers, pragmatists and originators corresponded with the norms of the greater population of individuals who have completed the CSI

(Musselwhite, 2004). The results reveal that among international educators change style does not indicate the regularity and predictability of an individual's choice to relocate, nor does it associate with job satisfaction. The data did exhibit, however, a consistency of preferences and approaches in managing change and transition process. Acknowledging the many personal and situational forces that influence an individual's actions in any given situation, the results indicate that teachers of different change styles presented distinct approaches and considerations, regarding adjustments to change.

For increased satisfaction and smooth transition, the conservers participating in this research, reported the need for methodical and trusted initiatives from the school administration for returning staff. Regardless of their status in the school (new or returning), teacher conservers expressed the need to feel comfortable in their classrooms and professional circumstances at the onset of the academic year before being able to address their personal lives. Conservers were most likely to disclose that they spent long hours throughout the year preparing and organizing classroom work. During relocation, they admitted to preferring to be settled in a home space and acquainted with the system around them (such as banking and shopping logistics), and they relied on the school to help manage these details, so that they could focus on job responsibilities. Relationships and connections with individuals at the professional level were reported to be more important initially than integration into the surrounding community, and they tended to spend any leisure time with and among the colleagues. Conservers tended to be most likely to choose schools based on the professional package offered (salary, benefits, safety in location, stability in the job, and living situation). They preferred schools with a well-defined hierarchy of administration, which they tended to respect. Feedback and support were reported to be crucial to job satisfaction and the change process.

Turning next to the characteristics displayed by the pragmatists, it is important to first note that the greatest number of teachers participating in this study, scored at or near center zero. This is concomitant with change style distributions in the original population of change style research, which report that the majority of the population falls in the pragmatist range. Although there are diverse preferences among the scores dispersed along the center of the continuum, pragmatists, and those with similar scores, seemed to respond in the ways summarized below.

Generally, pragmatists seemed to mix home and school life, more than conservers. This extended their choice of schools and locations, which involved both professional and personal considerations. While the package, benefits, and professional opportunity were important, they also considered the aspects of location, travel opportunity, and personal growth. They expressed the need for and the value of time in the classroom, to prepare and organize before the start of the year and throughout the academic routine; however, they were more likely than conservers to suggest that spontaneous outings and events could entice them from professional obligations. Team building and relationships were deemed important, and pragmatists, more than the other types, reported spending time and energy ensuring positive rapport among colleagues. Particularly at a time of relocation, pragmatists expressed the need to make personal connections and to form relationships with colleagues before the students arrived, in order to have both a social and professional network. Similar to the conservers, pragmatists tended to choose jobs and location based on the professional package, but they were more likely to interject personal and geographical motives into the decision process. Quality of life, as they defined it, appeared to be a strong consideration.

Looking at the other end of the continuum, the originators taking part in this research were often seen as the mavericks, the change agents, the ones who challenged both the administration and the system, and occasionally the ones who changed jobs and locations, for little apparent reason. Instinct appeared to be the impetus of an originator's choice to relocate, although salary package, benefits, and other quantifiable elements played a role. Originators reported that boredom and an exceptional intuition dictated a major change in their lives. They were known to seek adventure in new horizons. This is not to say, however, that originators moved, changed, and acted unintentionally; nor did all the originators relocate at the expiration of each contract. Many originators in the study reported the desire to remain in one place long enough to become integrated into the community, to learn the language, and to interact with the culture. Interestingly, their choices of schools were often not considered "easy" posts. Challenge and adventure seemed to be the underlying forces in the lives of originators.

At school, during relocation and throughout the year, originators were the least likely to report over-investment of time, in preparation of their professional duties; they also felt the need to become acquainted with the community around them. They required balance in their professional and personal lives, which were deemed equally significant. This is not to say that they were negligent teachers. They considered their manner of adjusting and managing a new environment necessary and logical, relying less on complete knowledge of the school system and more on their abilities to adapt and learn with each passing day.

As with all types, sociability ranged among individuals. Introversion and extraversion play a role in social dynamics, while common interests and other personal commitments of time and energy influence the comfort and perceived necessity to engage with others. In spite of these many deliberations, originators were the least likely to depend on school-arranged functions to instigate social contact and in fact many reported avoiding professional colleagues in the pursuit of contact with the local community. It appears that they valued the personal connections to the world outside their international school environment as much as the job they were hired to do.

In order to gain a clearer picture of the variances between, and among the change style type, the perspective of a teacher scoring mid-way between a pragmatist and an originator was explored. The pragmatist–originator reported many originator characteristics in the workplace (such as instigating significant change without a well-defined plan or challenging a status quo that works), as well as many pragmatist characteristics in the personal realm (for example, choosing international posts with great thought and a defined list of expectations, or maintaining harmonious relationships with friends and family at the expense of personal needs). While individuals will demonstrate different levels and unique combinations of characteristics, the pragmatist-originator suggested that elements such as team members, personal/family relationships, professional goals, and location influenced the strength of the attitudes and behaviors demonstrated. This reveals that, while change style plays a significant role in attitudes and actions, environmental and personal circumstances expand the natural preferences.

CONCLUSION

The research suggests that, although change style is believed to be an innate preference (Musselwhite, 2004), awareness, training, and situational demands allow individuals to manage those preferences in accordance with the present conditions. It is important to note that different individuals apply different change style characteristics to different elements of their lives and, while it is not possible to predict behavior, a greater understanding of the breadth of change styles and personality types could enhance individual satisfaction, professionally and personally. As administrators and teachers become more adept at responding consciously to diverse preferences, which in essence reflect relationships to structure, rules and authority, Musselwhite (2004) suggests that organizational motivation and production follow. Specific to international school communities, teachers who have a greater sense of their change styles may be in a better position to act as a stabilizing force to students and families.

For the international school administrators, knowledge about change styles may improve attentiveness to the range of styles, and their influence on leadership and motivation techniques. A basic knowledge of the input and direction and individual needs and desires could boost communication and initiatives among members of administration and staff. In addition, knowledge of the expectations contributing to a smooth transition for newly hired staff could enhance orientation programs and continued professional and personal connections. This is likely to contribute to greater satisfaction and potentially better productivity and retention.

Many could benefit from knowledge about change styles. Administrators could benefit from self-reflection, recognizing their leadership skills and preferences in relation to changes styles. Conservers would perhaps do well to challenge their internal structure and methods, and to open their eyes to new proposals and projects that challenge their innate penchant to control. Pragmatists could gain a better position among colleagues by exerting authority in making final decisions within an appropriate time frame. Originators might practice delaying important decisions by taking stock of the collective knowledge of colleagues, and easing into change with a greater acceptance of the many hesitations of others.

Individual teachers, indeed individuals of any profession, could benefit from the theory of change styles by reflecting on their natural inclinations and how this is manifested in professional and personal satisfaction. Self-understanding is the path to greater appreciation of others (Kroeger & Thuesen, 1998). Simply acknowledging differences in the approaches and perspectives of change can assist in the ongoing adjustments, intrinsic in international schools. Particularly in times of relocation, teachers could benefit from a conscious acceptance of their natural preferences, and a greater understanding of how to fulfill their unique needs.

International schools' affiliations and organizations could support these ideas through professional development opportunities at international conferences, meetings, and training programs. While these theories have been widely applied in business organizations through leadership and management training seminars, little has been done in the realm of international education. Among a community of people hailing from all the continents of the globe, often with enormous cultural differences and expectations, self-knowledge, and appreciation of others is essential. Many schools celebrate the flags and foods of their national diversity throughout the year, but greater understanding comes from searching within and looking out for a more complete acceptance of individuals, not simply cultures.

REFERENCES

Association for the Advancement of International Education. (n.d.). Association for the Advancement of International Education: The global education family of leaders and learning [Website]. Retrieved from http://www.aaie.org

Brummitt, N. (2007). International schools: Exponential growth and future implications. *International Schools Journal, 27*(1), 35–40.

Bunnell, T. (2006). Managing the role stress of public relations practitioners in international schools. *Educational Management Administration & Leadership*, *34*, 385–409.

Cambridge, J. (2002). Recruitment and deployment of staff: A dimension of international school organization. In M. C. Hayden, J. J. Thompson & G. Walker (Eds.), *International education in practice: Dimensions for national and international schools* (pp. 158–169). London: Kogan Page.

Carber, S., & Reis, S. (2004). Commonalities in IB practice and the schoolwide enrichment model. *Journal of Research in International Education*, *3*(3), 339–359.

Corey, G. (1996). *Theory and practice of counseling and psychotherapy*. Boston, MA: Brooks/Cole Publishing.

Davis, M. (2009). *The association between change styles and job satisfaction among international school teachers*. Unpublished doctoral dissertation, University of Southern Queensland, Toowoomba, Australia.

Discovery Learning. (2000). *Change style indicator: Style guide* [Brochure]. Greensboro, NC: Discovery Learning.

Fail, H., Thompson, J. J., & Walker, G. (2004). Belonging, identity and third culture kids. *Journal of Research in International Education*, *3*(3), 319–338.

Foreman, M. (1981). The effect of bilingualism on cognitive development. *International Schools Journal*, *1*, 73–81.

Hardman, J. (2001). Improving recruitment and retention of quality overseas teachers. In S. Blandford & M. Shaw (Eds.), *Managing international schools* (pp. 123–135). New York: Routledge/Falmer.

Hayden, M. C., & Thompson, J. J. (1998). International education: Perceptions of teachers in international schools. *International Review of Education*, *44*(5/6), 549–568.

Holderness, J. (2001). Teaching and managing English as an additional or second language in international schools. In S. Blandford & M. Shaw (Eds.), *Managing international schools* (pp. 63–79). London: Routledge/Falmer.

Kroeger, O., & Thuesen, J. (1998). *Type talk: The 16 personality types that determine how we live, love, and work*. New York: Dell Publishing.

McLachlan, D. A. (2007). Families in transition. *Journal of Research in International Education*, *6*(2), 233–249.

Musselwhite, C. (2004). *Dangerous opportunity: Making change work*. Greensboro, NC: Discovery Learning Press.

Myers, I. B., McCaulley, M. H., Quenk, N. L., & Hammer, A. L. (2003). *MBTI manual: A guide to the development and use of the Myers-Briggs type indicator* (3rd ed.). Mountain View, CA: CPP.

Pyvis, D. (2005). Culture shock and the international student "offshore". *Journal of Research in International Education*, *4*(1), 23–42.

Rushton, S., Morgan, J., & Richard, M. (2007). Teachers' Myers-Briggs personality profiles: Identifying effective teacher personality traits [Electronic version]. *Science Direct*, *23*, 432–441.

SECTION II

CONNECTING BEYOND SCHOOL CONTEXTS

CHAPTER 8

ENHANCING RELATIONSHIPS IN DOCTORAL STUDENT SUPERVISION: SHIBBOLETHS, SIGNIFIERS, AND STRATEGIES

P. A. Danaher and Henriette van Rensburg

University of Southern Queensland, Toowoomba,
Queensland, Australia

INTRODUCTION

Creating and sustaining viable connections in doctoral student supervision, depends on enhancing the student–supervisor relationship, as well as on navigating the complex policy and practice terrains, in which that relationship is situated. This chapter explores some of the contours of those terrains as they impinge on the supervisory experiences of the authors. It also focuses on their interpretations of the individual and institutional imperatives, framing those experiences.

Specific examples are explored of three types of phenomena held to be significant in underpinning the student-supervisor relationship and its contexts: shibboleths (here constructed as shared practices that sometimes

Creating Connections in Teaching and Learning, pp. 97–110

97

build capability and at other times develop "in groups" and "out groups"), signifiers (contextually generated meanings, often encapsulating unstated assumptions about the doctoral student journey), and strategies intended to increase the capacity of students and supervisors alike. The authors argue that these shibboleths, signifiers, and strategies function as useful reflective devices for focusing our attention on hopefully productive ways of creating and nurturing powerful connections in doctoral student supervision.

THE DOCTORAL SUPERVISION EXPERIENCE

The effective, efficient, and ethical supervision of doctoral students is increasingly the subject of serious academic scholarship (see for example, Brew & Peseta, 2004; Buttery, Richter, and Filho, 2005; Delamont, Atkinson, and Parry, 2004; Melin Emilsson & Johnsson, 2007). This is appropriate, given the high levels of cultural, economic, and social capital (understood more broadly as the number and type of resources that an individual can call on in particular contexts to achieve specific purposes) invested in completing a doctorate. Yet, the journeys traversed by doctoral students and their supervisors are not always comfortable or profitable (Grant, 2003, 2005; Holligan, 2005), sometimes being marked by high attrition, mutual misunderstanding, and potential manipulation and exploitation. Furthermore, doctoral supervision has until recently been the least professionalized form of pedagogy, it generally having been assumed that the doctoral candidates had the capacity for independent learning needed at this level of study, and that the doctoral supervisors' status as active researchers was sufficient to provide their students with the limited support that they required (Park, 2007). Increased government surveillance and concern about the relatively low completion rates have prompted universities to put in place formal induction sessions for doctoral students and training programs for their supervisors (Pearson & Brew, 2002; see also Adkins, 2009).

We argue that, worthy though these initiatives undoubtedly are, much more is needed if effective and enduring connections are to be created around doctoral student supervision. In particular, we contend that it is valuable to identify and interrogate three separate but related elements of building a sustainable student–supervisor relationship: shibboleths (understood as shared practices that need explication and examination to see whether they contribute positively or negatively to that relationship); signifiers (denoting signs and symbols that synthesize powerful yet often implicit meanings about that relationship); and strategies that might be useful in enhancing that relationship.

The chapter has been divided into six sections:

- A necessarily brief overview of the current literature and the selected elements of a conceptual framework;
- The institutional and individual contexts in which the authors work as doctoral supervisors;
- Selected shibboleths about students' and supervisors' practices drawn from those contexts;
- Specific signifiers about the doctoral student journey;
- Particular strategies intended to increase students' and supervisors' capital;
- Suggested implications for creating long-term and sustainable connections in doctoral student supervision in our institution, and more broadly.

These sections are framed by the proposition that the process of reflecting on these shibboleths, signifiers, and strategies, alert us to current practices and potentially new approaches in the journeys of doctoral students and their supervisors. Some of the connections highlighted by the analysis are healthy and beneficial; others are less so. It is vital to maximize the positive connections while replacing the negative ones and creating new ones, in order to assure the quality, and to enhance the outcomes of doctoral student supervision. Moreover, this experience of interrogating personal experience can be effective in building connections with other doctoral supervisors, and can constitute a useful starting point for further in-depth exploration to inform practice and future research.

LITERATURE REVIEW AND CONCEPTUAL FRAMEWORK

The increasing range and reach of scholarly literature about the doctoral student supervision is evident in the diversity of topics reflected in that literature. These topics include mapping students' views of their supervision (Heath, 2002), exploring the "becoming" of doctoral students (Barnacle, 2005), profiling supervisors' approaches to assessing students' work (Mullins & Kiley, 2002), noting supervisors' reflections on their supervisory practices (Boucher & Smyth, 2004; Chapman & Sork, 2001), and developing models to assist students and supervisors alike (Grevholm, Persson, and Wall, 2005).

This literature has also identified specific sites of potential tensions, attending the student-supervisor relationships that warrant further attention. These include the gendered dimension of that relationship

(Kurtz-Costes, Andrews Helmke, and Ülkü-Steiner, 2006; Leonard, 2001) and the situation when supervisors supervise their colleagues (Denicolo, 2004).

Yet, it is also clear that changes to doctoral supervision, designed to address these kinds of dilemmas have been occurring for some time (Green & Usher, 2003). For example, growing numbers of highly experienced professionals becoming part-time doctoral students have prompted changed practices to include "more collective models of supervision and collaborative knowledge sharing environments" (Malfroy, 2005, p. 165), as when several doctoral students work with the same small number of supervisors. Another development has been the efforts to make explicit, and thereby to demystify for doctoral students, previously arcane secrets of scholarly activity such as writing academic abstracts (Kamler & Thomson, 2004), by explaining the otherwise tacit knowledge required to engage in such activity.

Potentially useful concepts distilled from this literature about doctoral student supervision are also a significant indicator of the heightened breadth and depth of this field of scholarship. These concepts include performativity (Holligan, 2005) (whereby doctoral study and supervision are enacted across a range of contexts and in response to varied cues), text work and identity work (Kamler & Thomson, 2004) (where different elements of identities are called on in particular circumstances), subjectivity (Green, 2005) (the idea that, rather than identity being a fixed essence, individuals exhibit multiple and shifting dimensions of their subjectivities), disciplinary power (Bradbury-Jones, Irvine, and Sambrook, 2007) (the different ways that specific disciplines influence the identities of those who work at them), management (Gatfield, 2005), and the knowledge society (Kärner & Puura, 2008) (the economic and social valuing of particular kinds of information).

All of this suggests to us a number of important points about doctoral student supervision as portrayed and theorized in the literature. Firstly, explicitly or implicitly, many different kinds of connections have been created in the development of diverse approaches to supervising doctoral students. Secondly, these connections vary widely in terms of their perceived beneficence and effectiveness. Thirdly, several conceptual lenses have been developed and applied as a means of evaluating the utility and impact of particular doctoral supervisory practices. Fourthly, the deployment of those lenses has also prompted the elaboration of specific strategies, intended to enhance students' and supervisors' prospects of success.

Finally in this section, supervisors usually have diverse approaches and strategies; working with different students may require supervisors to change or blend the focus of different areas of their pedagogical frameworks and models (Bruce & Stoodley, 2009). Expertise in a student's research area is not the only attribute that a good quality postgraduate supervisor should have. For example, the posited ideal postgraduate

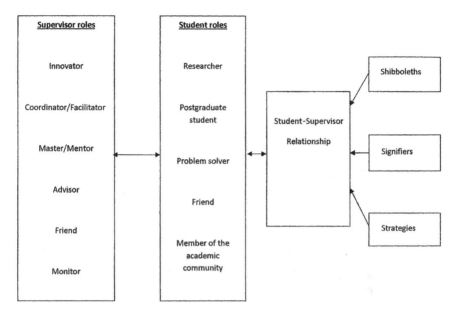

Figure 8.1. Elements of the student-supervisor relationship

student should discuss her or his needs with the supervisor, take initiative, be innovative, share responsibility, conduct research, meet deadlines, and prepare manuscripts for publication (Hay, 2008). Figure 8.1 captures some elements of the complex student–supervisor relationship as partially described by Hay (2008, p. 6) and Bruce and Stoodley (2009).

The student–supervisor relationship is flexible and may extend beyond the student's completion of the degree. It will almost certainly alter over time, as the postgraduate student's circumstances change from being a novice to becoming an experienced researcher (Hay, 2008).

Having elicited some of the salient themes in the current literature on doctoral student supervision, and having identified the elements of a provisional conceptual framework to which we return later in the chapter, we now turn to investigate how creating connections in supervision is enacted in our situation. We begin by outlining the particular institutional and individual contexts that frame that enactment.

INSTITUTIONAL AND INDIVIDUAL CONTEXTS

The University of Southern Queensland (USQ) is an Australian university that was established in 1967 and proclaimed a university in 1992 (see also De George-Walker et al., 2010). Its principal campus is located in

Toowoomba, a large regional city west of Brisbane, and its two other southern Queensland campuses are at Springfield (a western Brisbane suburb) and Fraser Coast (north of Brisbane). Currently it has nearly 25,000 enrolled students, of whom more than 7,000 are international students, studying externally or on-campus from over 85 countries (with greatest numbers originating in China, Malaysia, and India). The USQ had 43 research higher degree (doctoral and research masters) completions in 2008 (University of Southern Queensland, 2008).

This institutional history and status indicate that USQ is a so-called "new generation" university with a long tradition of teaching, having been recognized throughout Australia and internationally as one of eight nationally designated providers of university distance education. Its development as a university is more recent, and hence its experience of awarding doctorates and conducting and publishing research is much less extensive, than that of the research intensive universities in Australia. Nevertheless, USQ is benefiting from the ongoing professionalization of doctoral student retention and progression, and of research management by the office of the Deputy Vice-Chancellor (Scholarship), and the Office of Research and Higher Degrees.

The first-named author is an experienced doctoral supervisor, having co-supervised 14 doctoral students to completion to date, with another one's dissertation currently under examination, and several more in various stages of preparation. Doctoral supervision is his favourite form of teaching, partly because he learns a great deal about new topics in the process, and partly because the supervision process encourages the development of long-term intellectual and personal relationships, that often extend beyond graduation. While he strives to be open to diverse research paradigms and methods, he is most comfortable in working with students engaged in qualitative interpretivist or post-structuralist research.

The second-named author has not yet supervised a doctoral student to completion and is currently working as an associate supervisor with more experienced principal supervisors. In these situations, the principal supervisor has the main responsibility regarding supervision. The associate supervisor takes on students who match her research interests, and provides complementary expertise where needed. She has supervised several masters' students' research projects as sole supervisor, and attends workshops and conferences related to postgraduate supervision, in order to gain more experience.

These institutional and individual contexts provide the backdrop to our efforts to create sustainable connections with our doctoral students, our fellow supervisors, and the other stakeholders in doctoral student supervision at USQ. We now turn to review those efforts in relation to shibboleths, signifiers, and strategies.

SHIBBOLETHS ABOUT STUDENTS' AND SUPERVISORS' PRACTICES

Here we use the term *shibboleth* to denote shared practices that are used—consciously or otherwise—to demarcate a particular group or community and, by implication, to include some individuals as members of it, and exclude others from it. Taken to an extreme, the doctorate as a whole might be considered a shibboleth, in the sense of being positioned as the highest level of formally accredited learning and hence as the preserve of an intellectual elite (this despite the fact that the number of people enrolling in doctorates is steadily increasing). This is one way in which shibboleths can be positioned as constructing "in groups" (in this case doctoral graduates) and "out groups" (those without the opportunity to complete doctoral study). Less dramatically, shibboleths can be taken to refer to such practices, as stages in the doctoral student journey (such as application for enrolment, confirmation of candidature, pre-examination reading, and examination), as well as customs such as student–supervisor contact and supervisors providing feedback about students' draft texts.

The character of the connections created by particular shibboleths depends on the assumptions about doctoral students and their relationships with the others underpinning those shibboleths. In many ways, doctoral students embody an ambivalent status and inhabit an "in between" space, being seen as independent learners and prospective academics, and often assigned tutoring and marking roles, but nevertheless students rather than fully fledged staff members. Some supervisors respond to—and thereby replicate—this ambivalent status by constructing the doctoral student-supervisor relationship as one of "apprentice" and "master": learning the mores of this specialized community from a well-meaning but still dominant mentor (see also Manathunga, 2007). The terms used are significant as well: *supervisor* as employed in Australia and the United Kingdom implies a different set of power relations from the *adviser* as deployed in the United States. This ambivalence is also evident in Fig. 8.1, where there is considerable diversity among the listed potential roles of supervisors and students alike. There is also the possibility of considerable conflict, if the supervisors see a particular role as being appropriate but the students assume a very different kind of a role to be fitting.

More specifically, Lee's (2008) typology of research supervision is also useful to consider here (see also van Rensburg & Danaher, 2009). Her distinction among functional, enculturation, critical thinking, emancipation, and relationship development approaches evokes highly varied understandings of the shibboleths of supervision and, therefore, very diverse connections centered on doctoral students can be created. For example, from those multiple perspectives, confirmation of candidature can be variously positioned as an examination, an interrogation, an ordeal, a test of fortitude, scrutiny of the student's supervisors, constructive feedback, or contributing to the student's empowerment and development as an independent learner.

Drawing on the conceptual framework presented in Fig. 8.1, we see potentially positive shibboleths as shared practices, framing the articulation of the respective roles of supervisors and students and hence informing the student–supervisor relationship. For instance, we highlight with our students, the significant degree of overlap between their and our interests in completing their doctorates successfully and in minimum time; we communicate relevant aspects of our academic careers and intellectual development that might be useful in shaping theirs; and we seek to learn reciprocally with and from them as they progress in their doctoral journeys. The connections that we create with our doctoral students by means of these shibboleths are intended to be collegial, congenial, and mutually beneficial.

SIGNIFIERS ABOUT THE DOCTORAL STUDENT JOURNEY

We understand *signifiers* to refer to contextually generated meanings, often encapsulating unstated assumptions about the doctoral student journey. As we noted above, some of these signifiers appear confused and even contradictory, such as a doctoral student's dual roles as student and potential colleague. Another example is the multiple meanings attending on-campus doctoral students' induction or orientation. While this is an increasingly formalized process, including such issues as occupational health and safety and program rules and regulations, it is often the informal, unplanned interactions with a variety of individuals that the doctoral candidates report as being most encouraging, useful, and sustaining to them.

Returning to the confirmation of candidature mentioned above, we see that process as encapsulating a number of these competing signifiers. For instance, generally in Australia the student writes and discusses a proposal during a public presentation that in some institutions is called a *defence*. For us, this term evokes immediately its semantic opposite, *attack*, which we consider antithetical to the deep and extensive learning required in completing a doctorate. Even if *attack* is leavened to become *interrogation* or *critique*, the process can too readily turn into public criticism by the more experienced scholars that the doctoral student has to *defend*. By contrast, by calling the process *confirmation of candidature*, we imply an assumption that the proposal will indeed be confirmed (usually after specific revisions being made) and provides the basis for the presentation being conversational and dialogical.

Similarly, the examination of the completed doctoral dissertation (in Australia by two or three independent researchers, external to the doctoral student's institution) can potentially signify a process of interrogation or critique. Yet, most of the doctoral examiners assume that a dissertation that has undergone appropriate quality checks (conducted by the student, the supervisors, the faculty, and the university), is likely to be accepted for the award of the degree, albeit sometimes with required or recommended revisions, and generally they see their role as that of an external validator, rather than of a gatekeeper or interrogator (Mullins & Kiley, 2002).

Again the conceptual framework diagram (Fig. 8.1) is helpful in highlighting that diverse and sometimes competing signifiers of meaning about the doctoral student journey need to be interpreted and negotiated against the backdrop of what we see as the positive and healthy elements of the student–supervisor relationship. Specifically, supervisors who construct confirmation of candidature as a defence, and who position the assessment of the completed dissertation as an examination, are likely to communicate and explain those signifiers to their students very differently from supervisors who see those processes from a more collaborative perspective. Furthermore, we argue that the two types of supervisors posited here are liable to have very different kinds of relationships, and to create different types of connections with their students. Figure 8.1 is thus also helpful in alerting us to potentially significant contradictions between the signifiers that emerge from otherwise seemingly straightforward elements of the doctoral student–supervisor relationship.

STRATEGIES FOR INCREASING STUDENTS' AND SUPERVISORS' CAPITAL

With our fellow supervisors, we have implemented several strategies, intended to enhance our students' and our capital alike. These include the following:

- Co-authorship of publications with our doctoral students, provided that we contribute substantially (for example, by means of a literature review or conceptual framework) and ensure that the co-authorship is a collaboration, rather than an exercise in exploitation;
- Joint membership of a research team by one of us and a doctoral student, again with the focus being on shared and reciprocal opportunities to learn and contribute to the team's activities and outcomes;

- Active support of our doctoral students to participate in collaborative writing projects, whereby they can write individually about their topics while helping to sustain the wider field of scholarship (see for example, De George-Walker & Danaher, 2008; Henderson & Danaher, 2008a, 2008b);

- Attending a regularly scheduled but informal conversation with on-campus doctoral students, who are encouraged to share their achievements and any concerns or problems that they might be experiencing with one another;

- Joint membership of a Postgraduate and Early Career Researcher group that has been in operation for more than 6 years and that holds regular meetings, a series of structured and supportive writing workshops, and an annual research symposium, where members present works in progress about their research (see also Danaher, 2008; Harreveld & Danaher, 2009).

These strategies can be interpreted variously from a number of perspectives. For instance, Lee's (2008) five-fold typology of doctoral supervision noted above, evokes at least five such perspectives. Yet we contribute to and analyze those strategies most comprehensively from the perspective of relationship development, because we see the evolution of a healthy and productive synergy based on mutual rapport, respect, and trust as vital, if the strategies are to have long-term impact.

Figure 8.1 also illustrates that the kinds of strategies described here are most likely to succeed, if they are predicated on the equivalent enhancement of participants' cultural and social capital. This enhancement depends in turn on the articulation, and where possible the fulfillment of doctoral students' and supervisors' shared and separate interests. If those interests are seen as complementary and mutually reinforcing rather than competitive, the specific strategies have a heightened prospect of being effective and useful. This is a healthy process that can help to enhance and sustain the student-supervisor relationship and also create long-term and productive connections. However, in addition, Fig. 8.1 highlights how fundamental differences between supervisor and student roles can render such strategies ineffective or even counterproductive.

CONCLUSION

This chapter has examined some of the contours and terrains of a particular set of educational connections: the creation and maintenance of the doctoral student-supervisor relationship. We have considered three sites of potential tensions and opportunities associated with that relationship—what we have termed shibboleths, signifiers, and strategies—from the perspective of a provisional conceptual framework gleaned from selected literature. We see those three elements as valuable reflective devices that help to identify productive ways to enhance the experience of the doctoral student journey. They can also assist in explaining how relationships based on inequitable or contradictory behavior can lead to unhealthy situations for the participants.

We also see the exercise of reflecting critically on our personal experience as contributing to the larger field of knowledge and research about this important element of educational practice. For example, the positive connections between the doctoral students and their supervisors identified here (such as mutually respectful and trusting relationships and an identification of shared interests and benefits) are ones that we have experienced directly and that continue to sustain us as supervisors. We have also witnessed instances of the less positive connections (for example, those based on power differentials and/or irreconcilable differences), and we can attest first-hand to their deleterious impact on the student–supervisor relationship.

We conclude the discussion by suggesting a couple of possible implications of the preceding account for doctoral supervision more widely. The first implication is a vindication of placing the creation of connections at the center of approaches to teaching and learning. Policies and procedures directed at doctoral students and their supervision in contemporary universities, need to pay explicit attention to those connections, in order to maximize the individual and institutional benefits, accruing from this kind of connected and interconnected conceptualization.

The second implication is an even broader reinforcement of the relational dimension of educational relationships. Like the other chapters in this book, this account says as much about the character of current educational provision as it does about its specific object of inquiry. Creating and sustaining long-term connections is crucial, if that provision is to engage and excite, rather than alienate and marginalize—whether for doctoral students or for participants in other formal educational sectors and settings.

This suggests that identifying and analyzing the shibboleths, signifiers, and strategies associated with a particular educational enterprise are helpful in alerting us to current practices and potentially new approaches in the journeys of learners and their teachers. Some of the connections manifested in this analysis are healthy and beneficial, while others are not. Enhancing the positive connections while replacing the negative ones with new ones is crucial to assuring the quality and maximizing the outcomes of doctoral student supervision and of learning and teaching more broadly.

ACKNOWLEDGMENTS

The authors are grateful for the constructive feedback about successive drafts of the chapter provided by the participants in the writing workshops attending the production of this book, as well as for the editors' ongoing encouragement and support, particularly by Ms Lindy Abawi, the chapter editor, and also by anonymous peer reviewers. They also thankfully acknowledge that they have learned from their doctoral students and fellow supervisors.

REFERENCES

Adkins, B. (2009). PhD pedagogy and the changing knowledge landscapes of universities. *Higher Education Research & Development, 28*(2), 165–177.

Barnacle, R. (2005). Research education ontologies: Exploring doctoral becoming. *Higher Education Research & Development, 24*(2), 179–188.

Boucher, C., & Smyth, A. (2004). Up close and personal: Reflections on our experience of supervising research candidates who are using personal reflective techniques. *Reflective Practice, 5*(3), 345–356.

Bradbury-Jones, C., Irvine, F., & Sambrook, S. (2007). Unity and detachment: A discourse analysis of doctoral supervision. *International Journal of Qualitative Methods, 6*(4), 81–96.

Brew, A., & Peseta, T. (2004). Changing postgraduate supervision practice: A programme to encourage learning through reflection and feedback. *Innovation in Education and Teaching International, 41*(1), 5–22.

Bruce, C., & Stoodley, I. (2009, March). *Towards a pedagogy of RHD supervision in the technology disciplines: Project summary and conceptual framework.* Retrieved from ALTC website: http://www.altcexchange.edu.au/system/files/Pedagogy+of+Supervision+Preliminary+Paper.pdf

Buttery, E. A., Richter, E. M., & Filho, W. L. (2005). An overview of the elements that influence efficiency in postgraduate supervisory practice arrangements. *International Journal of Educational Management, 19*(1), 7–26.

Chapman, V. L., & Sork, T. (2001). Confessing regulation or telling secrets? Opening up the conversation on graduate supervision. *Adult Education Quarterly, 51*(2), 94–107.

Danaher, P. A. (2008). Teleological pressures and ateleological possibilities on and for a fragile learning community: Implications for framing lifelong learning futures for Australian university academics. In D. Orr, P. A. Danaher, G. R. Danaher & R. E. Harreveld (Eds.), *Lifelong learning: Reflecting on successes and framing futures: Keynote and refereed papers from the 5th international lifelong learning conference, Yeppoon, Central Queensland, Australia, June 16–19, 2008: Hosted by Central Queensland University* (pp. 130–135). Rockhampton, Qld: Lifelong Learning Conference Committee, Central Queensland University Press.

De George-Walker, L. R., & Danaher, P. A. (Eds.) (2008). Evaluating value(s): Issues in and implications of educational research significance and researcher identity. *Theme issue of the International Journal of Pedagogies and Learning, 4*(1), 1–93.

De George-Walker, L. R., Hafeez-Baig, A., Gururajan, R., & Danaher, P. A. (2010). Experiences and perceptions of learner engagement in blended learning environments: The case of an Australian university. In Y. Inoue (Ed.), *Cases on online and blended learning technologies in higher education: Concepts and practices* (pp. 23–43). Hershey, PA: IGI Global.

Delamont, S., Atkinson, P., & Parry, O. (2004). *Supervising the doctorate: A guide to success* (2nd ed.). Maidenhead, UK: Society for Research into Higher Education/Open Education Press.

Denicolo, P. (2004). Doctoral supervision of colleagues: Peeling off the veneer of satisfaction and competence. *Studies in Higher Education, 29*(6), 693–707.

Gatfield, T. (2005). An investigation into PhD supervisory management styles: Development of a dynamic conceptual model and its managerial implications. *Journal of Higher Education Policy and Management, 27*(3), 311–325.

Grant, B. (2003). Mapping the pleasures and risks of supervision. *Discourse: Studies in the Cultural Politics of Education, 24*(2), 175–190.

Grant, B. (2005). Fighting for space in supervision: Fantasies, fairytales, fictions and fallacies. *International Journal of Qualitative Studies in Education, 18*(3), 337–354.

Green, B. (2005). Unfinished business: Subjectivity and supervision. *Higher Education Research & Development, 24*(2), 151–163.

Green, P., & Usher, R. (2003). Fast supervision: Changing supervisory practices in changing times. *Studies in Continuing Education, 25*(1), 37–50.

Grevholm, B., Persson, L. E., & Wall, P. (2005). A dynamic model for education of doctoral students and guidance of supervisors in research groups. *Educational Studies in Mathematics, 60*(2), 173–197.

Harreveld, R. E., & Danaher, P. A. (August 27, 2009). *Fostering and restraining a community of academic learning: Possibilities and pressures in a postgraduate and early career researcher group at an Australian university.* Paper presented at the 13th biennial conference of the European Association for Research on Learning and Instruction, Vrije Universiteit, Amsterdam, The Netherlands.

Hay, D. (2008). What is postgraduate supervision all about? In L. O. K. Lategan (Ed.), *An introduction to postgraduate supervision* (pp. 5–12). Stellenbosch, South Africa: Sun Press.

Heath, T. (2002). A quantitative analysis of PhD students' views of supervision. *Higher Education Research & Development, 21*(1), 41–53.

Henderson, R., & Danaher, P. A. (Eds.) (2008a). *Doctoral designers: Challenges and opportunities in planning and conducting educational research.* Theme issue of the *International Journal of Pedagogies and Learning, 4*(2), 1–70.

Henderson, R., & Danaher, P. A. (Eds.) (2008b). *Troubling terrains: Tactics for traversing and transforming contemporary educational research.* Teneriffe, Qld: Post Pressed.

Holligan, C. (2005). Fact and fiction: A case history of doctoral supervision. *Educational Research, 47*(3), 267–278.

Kamler, B., & Thomson, P. (2004). Driven to abstraction: Doctoral supervision and writing pedagogies. *Teaching in Higher Education, 9*(2), 195–209.

Kärner, A., & Puura, V. (2008). Doctoral education in transition to knowledge-based society. *Trames: A Journal of the Humanities & Social Sciences, 12*(1), 95–109.

Kurtz-Costes, B., Andrews Helmke, L., & Ülkü-Steiner, B. (2006). Gender and doctoral studies: The perceptions of PhD students in an American university. *Gender and Education, 18*(2), 137–155.

Lee, A. (2008). *How are doctoral students supervised? Concepts of doctoral research supervision.* Guildford, UK: Information Services, University of Surrey. Retrieved from http://epubs.surrey.ac.uk/info_sci/10

Leonard, D. (2001). *A woman's guide to doctoral studies.* Buckingham, UK: Open University Press.

Malfroy, J. (2005). Doctoral supervision, workplace research and changing pedagogic practices. *Higher Education Research & Development, 24*(2), 165–178.

Manathunga, C. (2007). Supervision as mentoring: The role of power and boundary crossing. *Studies in Continuing Education, 29*(2), 207–221.

Melin Emilsson, U., & Johnsson, E. (2007). Supervision of supervisors: On developing supervision in postgraduate education. *Higher Education Research & Development, 26*(2), 163–179.

Mullins, G., & Kiley, M. (2002). "It's a PhD, not a Nobel Prize": How experienced examiners assess research theses. *Studies in Higher Education, 27*(4), 369–386.

Park, C. (2007). *Redefining the doctorate.* York, UK: Higher Education Academy.

Pearson, M., & Brew, A. (2002). Research training and supervision development. *Studies in Higher Education, 27*(2), 135–150.

University of Southern Queensland. (2008). About USQ: Facts and figures [Webpage]. Retrieved from http://www.usq.edu.au/aboutusq/facts

van Rensburg, H. M. J., & Danaher, P. A. (2009). Facilitating formative feedback: An undervalued dimension of assessing doctoral students' learning. In J. Milton, C. Hall, J. Lang, G. Allan & M. Nomikoudis (Eds.), *Assessment in different dimensions: A conference on teaching and learning in tertiary education: November 19–20, 2009 at RMIT University, Melbourne* (pp. 341–351). Melbourne, Vic: Learning and Teaching Unit, Royal Melbourne Institute of Technology University.

CHAPTER 9

PRODUCTIVE PARTNERSHIPS: CROSS-DEPARTMENTAL CONNECTIONS IN A TERTIARY CONTEXT

Karen Noble and Robyn Henderson

University of Southern Queensland, Toowoomba,
Queensland, Australia

INTRODUCTION

Teaching is recognized generally as a major part of the work of academics within universities, and academics have become used to considering the scholarship of teaching and learning as a part of their roles. However, what tends to be not as obvious is that teams of highly skilled non-teaching staff support this work, but they tend to remain in the background. Without these important connections between academics and the other staff, many exciting projects would be unlikely to achieve fruition. This chapter examines the working relationships that occurred as a group of academics and media services staff in a regional Australian university worked on a multimedia toolkit project (MMTP) for the professional development of

Creating Connections in Teaching and Learning, pp. 111–122
Copyright © 2011 by Information Age Publishing
All rights of reproduction in any form reserved.

academic staff working to support the 1st year students. It explores the use of a strengths-based approach, where the academic staff and the university staff with expertise in a range of areas, connected their knowledge and skills to ensure a successful project.

As two academics, who were fortunate to be awarded an Associate Fellowship in Learning and Teaching by our university, we quickly realized at the beginning of our project that we would not achieve our stated aims, unless we had a team with expertise in areas where we had neither knowledge nor experience. Our plans were to develop a professional development toolkit for the academics, so that they could consider and reconsider the 1st year experience that was on offer within their faculties. We were beginning the 2nd year of conducting a support program for 1st year Education students, whereby students voluntarily attended a 2 hour, weekly Learning Circle meeting to engage in social and academic problem-solving about the issues that were impacting their study. At that stage, we were comfortable with the program that we were operating, but what we did not have were the skills and knowledge to produce the multimedia artifacts for the toolkit we were planning.

We knew that staff from the university's media services division had the multimedia expertise in audio and video production and graphic design that we required. Initially, we did not know how we would be able to harness their expertise, or how we would combine their expertise with our understanding about what we hoped to achieve. However, what developed was a productive and collaborative relationship amongst all those who participated, rather than the usual client-focused or service model that exists between faculties and service divisions within the university.

In this chapter, we briefly describe the project, foreground the strengths-based approach that was used, and draw on interview data to examine the connections that developed as the project progressed. Our aim is to offer insights into one way of achieving successful project outcomes—by creating connections amongst staff with different forms of expertise that could contribute to a multi-dimensional and multi-mediated collaborative project.

THE PROJECT UNDERPINNING THE TOOLKIT DEVELOPMENT

This chapter describes the development of productive and collegial relationships in a cross-departmental capacity-building project. The MMTP built on a first year experience program—the FYI Program (using the acronym that could stand for First Year Infusion or For Your Information)—that we had designed, and had been conducting within our Faculty of Education for 1 year. Even though the program had involved a fairly small number of students, we were convinced that it had the potential to assist the 1st year students in their transition into university study. It also provided a positive faculty response to student retention and progression issues (for further details, see Noble & Henderson, 2008). We used the Associate Fellowship to extend this first year program, and to promote the approach we used through the development of a professional development toolkit.

The FYI Program is based on the view that success at university study is most likely to occur when students have the social and academic support that they need (Henderson & Noble, 2009). Thus the program fosters a supportive social environment with embedded opportunities, to develop academic skills and knowledge. It operates as a weekly meeting place, whereby students know that they can "drop in" to discuss any issues that are impacting on their study, ask questions, clarify issues, or talk with other students or staff. These weekly Learning Circle meetings (Aksim, 1998; Riel, 2006) have no set agenda. Instead, discussion develops from whatever the students choose to talk about. Several staff members attend each week, including a small group of academics, our faculty librarian, and other faculty support staff, all of whom bring a wide range of knowledge and skills.

The meetings are underpinned by a strengths-based approach, whereby no student is considered deficit of deficient (Henderson & Noble, 2011). Rather, the students are seen as learning a new Discourse (with a capital D, as per Gee, 1996) or way of "behaving, interacting, valuing, thinking, believing, speaking, and often reading and writing" (p. viii). Specifically, they are learning how to "be" university students.

FROM AN ACADEMIC PERSPECTIVE TO WIDER PARTICIPATION

While the FYI Program was part of our work in the area of learning and teaching, we wanted to use it to extend ourselves in relation to the scholarship of learning and teaching, and therefore to make explicit the links between practice and theory. As the program progressed and we began to think about its operation in terms of theoretical understandings, we found Gruenewald's (2003) human geography work to be useful. Gruenewald's five dimensions of place provided a way of conceptualizing the student learning journey as perceptual, sociological, ideological, political, and ecological. We were also interested in Biggs' (1993) notion of professional and personal presage–the environmental or situation factors, and the personal factors that influence learning—and we considered how these might work in tandem.

However, while we were comfortable with the theoretical underpinnings of our work, and we continued to think about how we could bring the work of

Gruenewald (2003) and Biggs (1993) together, we realized that we would need to find a way of translating the theory into a form that would be suitable for a multimedia toolkit. At this point, a serendipitous discussion with a member of our Faculty's support team offered a graphical solution to our problem. It was suggested that the Ishikawa Fishbone (see Skymark Corporation, 2009), a well known and widely used graphical display, might provide a way of representing the theories we wanted to use. It was at this point that we needed to seek the expertise of others to enable the translation of our ideas into something that would be suitable for a professional development toolkit. In the following sections, interview data will be used to illustrate the ways in which the project was broadened, and how the other staff came to feel a sense of belonging beyond their usual roles within the university context. We then consider the broader organizational implications of the project.

In moving the project forward, and attempting to create artifacts for communicating the FYI approach to others, we approached the management staff in our university's media services. With their assistance, the initial scope of the project was quickly realized. From then on, regular face-to-face planning meetings were held with a range of multimedia staff, with e-mail communications continuing the discussions between those meetings. It quickly became apparent that the interactions and relationships that were developing were professionally fulfilling for all those who were involved.

REFLECTING ON THE PROCESS

It was only as the project was nearing completion that we realized the potential of the collaborative approach that had developed. To capture this potential and explore its benefits, we employed a research assistant to conduct a series of focus group interviews with everyone, including ourselves, who had been involved in the team. The focus groups allowed team members to consider the project retrospectively, and to reflect on the way that the team approach developed. The data provided a set of narratives about the project and its collaborative approach.

The remainder of this chapter discusses the particular aspects of the collaborative project that the staff from media services thought were important. Excerpts from the transcripts of the focus group interviews with media services staff offer an insight into the types of connections that occurred as a part of this cross-departmental project. In drawing links to organizational development and identifying synergies to Gruenewald's (2003) work in human geography, the deconstruction of the group narratives offers an enriched perspective on what enables and enhances institutional organizational dynamics, in terms of the coexistence of stability and change (Feldman, 2000).

Shedding light on the narratives provides an opportunity to examine the ways in which they influence and construct impetus for change across organizations (Geiger & Antonacopoulou, 2009). The focused dialogues can be seen as a tool for change that enables the construction of new discourses and challenges, usual or taken-for-granted ways of working. The interviews therefore, provide an opportunity to move beyond institutional rhetoric to challenge departmental practices as well as those of the individual. As a result of reflective analysis, a diverse number of themes emerged as people made sense of the team's work. Therefore, the discourse characterizes the ways in which these "multiple, simultaneous and sequential narratives ... interweave, harmonize, and clash" (Currie & Brown, 2003, p. 566) by taking account of the effects of organizational dynamics and development on staff learning.

COLLECTIVE MEANING-MAKING

A process of collective meaning-making was privileged from the outset of the project, as we had been keen for all the members of the team to see themselves as being able to make a unique and significant contribution to the resource (toolkit) development. While it was clear to us that this was a genuine invitation to shape up the ways of working as well as the project outputs, this realization took some time for the other staff, as they had not been directly involved in the student-phase of the project. As we had done with the students, Gee's (1996) theory of capital D Discourse shaped initial interactions, in an attempt to create productive ways of assisting the media staff to see themselves as integral members of the team rather than as ancillary.

As one of the staff members commented:

> I think, perhaps one aspect would be the collaboration which I know is something they are very pleased with the way it all came together. That, as a team each of us added our own particular skills to make it happen ... That's right. And to add to value-add I suppose, in many respects to the original product. But the collaboration is the thing that ... yeah, each person did a little part of it to make the whole.

Just as had occurred in the initial student project, an enabling pedagogy promoted the social capital that each person brought to the project underpinned all the interactions with the broader multimedia team. This approach allowed us to develop a sense of collective efficacy. At the same time, each individual came to realize the important contribution that he/she made to the team. Another member of the team summed it up in the following way:

> We had to decide how each of us were actually going to work, and who could actually do the best, or the easiest way of doing it, whether we did it in

multimedia or whether it was done in video. So there were discussions between us as to who could do it most effectively, or the easiest way to get what we actually wanted.

VALUING INTERACTIONS AND BEING MINDFUL

By consciously using the Learning Circle approach to facilitate the group meetings, just as we did with the student project, it became evident that the staff came to value these interactions and they were able to draw connections between the multiple contexts of their lives within and outside the university. For example:

> My wife is an educator, and Ryan's (pseudonym) wife is an educator as well, so I guess we have a little bit of knowledge from that perspective and we can sort of throw our two cents in and say, yeah I can see where this is going. But I mean, what impact has it had on me personally or whatever? I can see where Karen and Robyn are trying to take this with the FYI Program and trying to be supportive of the students, and I think that's a good thing.

In terms of understanding the success of a planned change in culture such as the cross-departmental one outlined here, the organizational management literature builds upon understandings of the importance of reflection on-action, and the more critical aspect of reflection in-action (Macfarlane et al., 2005). Such practice is viewed in terms of the phenomenon of mindfulness (Jordan, Messner, and Becker, 2009), which is defined as "a state of mind or mode of practice that permits the questioning of expectations, knowledge and the adequacy of routines in complex and not fully predictable social, technological, and physical settings" (p. 468). Within the team, we were mindful about the possible ways to learn and to improve the motivation and engagement of all staff members (reflection before practice).

BECOMING ATTACHED TO THE PROJECT

Our experiences, collective as well as individual were significant contributors to the transformation reported here. For example, one member of the team highlighted some of the subtlety, through drawing comparisons between "normal" ways of working and the "new" way of working:

> That's right. And also with Robyn and Karen, they are very enthusiastic as well. They really get you in, don't they? You become almost attached to the job. You get involved in it. I guess one aspect of it is that it was a little bit out of the norm.

As a result, this staff member explained that there were opportunities to be involved in the project, in ways that were different from the other projects:

> There was a little bit more lateral thinking and a little bit more presentation and so forth, it was a little bit more imaginative and creative ... We added a little bit of pizzazz to it in the form of glowing and bubbles, and we just sort of added to their ideas originally because we are graphic designers and multimedia people, and they are on the education side of things. So combined, they had the good idea and we were able to expand it and make it even better.

One staff member, who was new to work at the university saw her engagement in this project as setting up a model that assisted her to see herself and her role in multimedia, in a new way:

> For me it was a sort of my first big project, because I'd only just started here. So it was really good to be able to see that lecturers do actually come across and work with you, and ... you're thrown in the media section, and you do the jobs that are brought in to you. So it's good that there is the collaboration we have got with graphics and audio and video. You felt recognized and valued for the skills and knowledge you brought ... It was a group thing; it wasn't just like this job that has to be done, who's going to do it. It was like, we need a bit of your help; we need a bit of your help, because otherwise we can't do it. So, that was really rewarding to have an experience like that straight up.

APPRECIATIVE INQUIRY AND COLLECTIVE STRENGTH

The supportive environment offered a space where all the members could confront and deconstruct the challenges or difficulties that they had. Problems became shared problems and through the value of appreciative inquiry—an organizational process of renewal, change, and focused performance (Cape Western Reserve University, 2009), there was a support for individuals to adopt change in their discourse. For example, one team member explained that:

> It's also been important that we are an integrated media group, so we're not sort of separate departments within the university, and so we have that working relationship and a personal relationship with one another. So, we get on and we know the abilities and the facilities that each of us can bring to a project. Here, Karen and Robyn have integrated us all; they haven't dealt with us individually as such; they realize that they're not necessarily just dealing with individual people but there is a collective which has a strength, which is probably more than all the individual components put together.

Another member of the team described the effect of appreciative inquiry in a different way. For him, social presence was important to his learning:

> The nice thing is having our ideas taken on board, because we have different experiences and so we can bring all that to play. They really ran with our ideas, and things expanded and snowballed and took on a life of their own almost ... the end result was more than what people expected from the outset, because everyone contributed their expertise and so forth, which ended up being a bigger, better idea in the end, than what was started with ... I think, it's a matter of then putting it all together and adjusting each part of it with all the expertise that came on board to actually work out a good solution, which met or exceeded their original expectations.

It can be seen then that appreciative inquiry needs to be well designed, both to support a change in the meaning-making processes, and to aid in understanding these processes (Bushe, 2001). It is obvious that the success of our team is as much of a socially constructed reality, as any other social system in the workplace. The critically reflective way in which the team worked, created a sense of deepened collective mindfulness, as illustrated in the following excerpt:

> I think it's the personal identification with it and then the satisfaction of being a part of it. And you can put a more personal touch on it because you can work on things together. You bounce ideas off each other and that's crucial to the success and hitting the mark with a project ... you can do what you think they want and then they may think, oh well, that's what they are getting. But to be actually able to discuss it and say, well no, they just had a slightly different approach, well okay, let's change that, you can get immediate feedback, and you can make adjustments if necessary.

The notion of presence meant that the individuals could perceive themselves, objects and other people as not only linked to the physical space of work, but importantly, they could also see themselves immersed in a socio-cultural web that connects them through interactions and relationships, that extend beyond the physical space. This meant that subjective feelings of existence within the environment (Bandura, 1997; van Manen, 1991; Zahorik & Jenison, 1998) came to the fore. Thus, causal interaction as an element of presence became important. As one team member explained, "What each of us does is fairly standard for what we do. But in this case there were more of us involved in one aspect. It was more of an integrated project." The transcript continues:

> Often we might do multimedia separately, or graphics separately, or audio separately, video separately, and each of those modules may go into a course or a presentation as an individual component of it. But this was bringing all of those together—holistically in one integrated project ... I mean, the nice thing is that

Karen and Robyn are really forward-thinking, with the interaction they've had with Jim and Ryan, and Peter in the audio section and Angela (pseudonyms), with the interaction they've had there in the past on the other projects. They were able to ask them, sort of, okay this is what we want. Can we start videoing it and filming it and can we get our librarian involved in sort of being the front man, if you like, the public face of it, for the intros and things like that?

WORKING AS AN INTEGRATED GROUP

The team became an integrated work group, a network where the members constructed themselves mutually (Cole, 1996; Mantovani, 1996). This involved information exchange and socio-emotional responses, as illustrated in the following excerpt:

> The girls had the idea of having it videoed, or having interviews with the students, of producing all this extra stuff to actually enhance that program, and show what can be done. From there it became a CD, from there it became a multimedia presentation that incorporated all the video and audio interviews etcetera. It became a website as well … They've been working together. With me, for instance, just doing the graphics and giving it to them, they've been putting the website together. So it just became bigger and bigger and bigger. All these things can expand and show the wonderful opportunities for us all … like having the foresight of gathering data and creating the stuff that then could be used, and turned into other stuff … because if you haven't had that foresight to have all those things done then the product that we've done, would never have happened.

This team member went on to explain that the MMTP project "from where I stand was pretty much a living thing. Robyn and Karen, I don't think, knew where it was going to lead; they just knew that they wanted to collect all of this material and then how to put it together was a later [decision]." She continued:

> Which makes it interesting for us because we're used to having a start, a beginning and an end and that helps us place what we're doing as well. How much we shoot, if we shoot it, if that's got to all go together in one package to get the feel of it. But we're doing so many different things sometimes that we're not even sure it was MMTP until we were into it. So yeah, it's still for that project. So, it was a little bit of that. I mean, I think projects like this help us be, put in processes to be a lot more flexible and reactive, you know with changing.

BRIDGING ORTHODOX DIVIDES

In this team member's opinion, the project "taught us to be flexible because the project was evolving." It is clear that the multimedia staff engagement in this project was empowering, and that capacity was built through their participation. This emphasizes the impact that "belonging" to such a network of staff has had in bridging the orthodox divides between academic and professional staff. As one team member explained:

> We've learnt too. We obviously observed and absorbed quite a bit of this, and we are, I guess, a little insular in some ways from what goes on out in the university life. We get on and do our job, but university life is out there in the lecture theatres ... So we don't necessarily experience what it is like out there. So we've got a better appreciation of what it's like for the students and the lecturers as well. But like the students were just saying there that every week they were just looking forward to that time, where they could meet up and could just offload, get together, share, ask questions ... we had that too because of how the group was facilitated and you don't normally have that touch ... and it gives you a deeper appreciation.

While the effects of engagement in group processes are often immediately apparent to the participants, there is also potential for application to the other domains within the institution. For example, one staff member commented that:

> This project, and the way we've put these things together, presents a model for how other people could actually use our services ... So it has benefits not just to the faculty, not just to our university, but also to other universities to sort of show, well this is the standard here; this is what you can do to improve things.

It is clear that this project has enabled participants to construct and confirm meaning in terms of "doing" and "being" a collaborative working group, traversing the binary that is often apparent in universities between academic and professional staff. The development and maintenance of authentic partnerships and relationships would appear to be key to the transformation of our work.

CONCLUSION

It is clear from this examination of the focus group narratives that this particular aspect of the MMTP fostered new ways of working in teams, and helped to disrupt orthodox departmental divides. The data suggested that the development of collective meaning-making and becoming mindful were important aspects of the process. Although the original intent of the concept of mindfulness was highly individualistic, it is a concept able to be applied equally well, to a collaborative or group endeavor such as this. In fact, Jordan et al. (2009) permit that "collective mindfulness" (p. 468) occurs at two levels: through direct interactions as well as more generally through careful examination of the existing ways of working within the context. At the latter level, it becomes evident that it is possible to evoke awareness of the impact of context on interactions and on ways of being, knowing, and doing, valuing and understanding (Gee, 1996).

For the team discussed in this chapter, the valuing of interactions among the members of the group, the feeling of "becoming attached" to the project and what it was trying to achieve and the development of ways of working as an integrated group, became important characteristics as the project developed. As a result, an artifact that exceeded everyone's expectations was produced. The toolkit that was developed, containing video and audio segments and discussion starters for academics interested in enhancing the 1st year of university experience for students, had drawn on the expertise of a range of media services staff, and had used the team's academic and professional expertise to combine and integrate video and audio clips, moving images, artwork, and academic ideas.

Through challenging existing practices to introduce the possibility of change in the working relationships of personnel, from several university departments, a certain level of uncertainty and ambiguity was evident: the whole focus of critical reflection allowed all staff to be surprised, and to adapt to the changing culture throughout each stage of the project. Therefore, while there were individual gains for each of the participants as outlined in the project, what is also evident is that the project had modeled new ways of working within the existing institutional structures.

ACKNOWLEDGMENTS

We wish to thank Sandra Adams, Jeff Black, Siân Carlyon, Greg Coombes, Eddie Flemming, Zoe Lynch, Ken Morton, and Jason Myatt from our university's media services, who were the willing collaborators who contributed to the development of the multimedia toolkit; Marilyn Dorman who suggested the Ishikawa Fishbone as a useful integrating device; our Faculty librarian, Ron Pauley, who starred in our production; and Helen Parker who conducted the interviews.

REFERENCES

Aksim, R. E. (1998). *Learning Circle basics* [Web site]. Retrieved from http://www. magma.ca/~raksim/learning_circle.htm

Bandura, A. (1997). *Self-efficacy: The exercise of control*. New York: Freeman.

Biggs, J. B. (1993). From theory to practice: A cognitive systems approach. *Higher Education Research and Development, 12*, 73–85.

Bushe, G. (2001). *Clear leadership*. Palo Alto, CA: Davies-Black.

Cape Western Reserve University. (2009). *Appreciative inquiry commons* [Web site]. Retrieved from http://appreciativeinquiry.case.edu/

Cole, M. (1996). *Cultural psychology: A once and future discipline*. Cambridge, MA: Harvard University Press.

Currie, G., & Brown, A. (2003). A narratological approach to understanding processes of organising in a UK hospital. *Human Relations, 56*(5), 563–586.

Feldman, M. (2000). Organizational routines as a source of continuous change. *Organizational Science, 11*(6), 611–629.

Gee, J. P. (1996). *Social linguistics and literacies: Ideology in discourses* (2nd ed.). London: Falmer Press.

Geiger, D., & Antonacopoulou, E. (2009). Narratives and organisational dynamics: Exploring blind spots and organisational inertia. *Journal of Applied Behavioural Science, 45*(3), 411–436.

Gruenewald, D. (2003). Foundations of place: A multidisciplinary framework for place-conscious education. *American Educational Research Journal, 40*(3), 619–654.

Henderson, R., & Noble, K. (2011). Burying the binaries: Getting discourses to converge in a program for first year university students. In W. Midgley, M. A. Tyler, P. A. Danaher, & A. Mander (Eds.), *Beyond binaries in education research* (pp. 119–130). New York: Routledge.

Henderson, R., & Noble, K. (2009). *FYI (First Year Infusion): A vaccine for the first year plague in a regional university*. In C. Boylan (Ed.), *Proceedings of the 25th National Rural Education Conference: Education in a Digital Present: Enriching Rural Communities* (pp. 85–93). Adelaide, SA: Society for the Provision of Education in Rural Australia.

Jordan, S., Messner, M., & Becker, A. (2009). Reflection and mindfulness in organisations: Rationales and possibilities for integration. *Management Learning, 40*(4), 465–473.

Macfarlane, K., Noble, K., Kilderry, A., & Nolan, A. (2005). Developing skills of thinking otherwise and critical reflection. In K. Noble, K. Macfarlane & J. Cartmel (Eds.), *Circles of change: Challenging orthodoxy in practitioner supervision* (pp. 11–20). Frenchs Forest, NSW: Pearson.

Mantovani, G. (1996). Social context in human-computer interaction: A new framework for mental models, cooperation and communication. *Cognitive Science, 20*, 237–269.

Noble, K., & Henderson, R. (2008). Engaging with images and stories: Using a Learning Circle approach to develop agency of beginning "at-risk" pre-service teachers. *Australian Journal of Teacher Education, 33*(1), 1–16.

Riel, M. (2006). *Learning circles: Teachers' guide* [Web-site]. Retrieved from http://www.iearn.org/circles/lcguide/

Skymark Corporation. (2009). *Kaoru Ishikawa: One step further* [Web-site]. Retrieved from http://www.skymark.com/resources/leaders/ishikawa.asp

van Manen, M. (1991). *The tact of teaching: The meaning of pedagogical thoughtfulness*. Albany, NY: SUNY Press.

Zahorik, P., & Jenison, R. L. (1998). Presence as being-in-the-world. *Presence, 7*(1), 78–89.

CHAPTER 10

ADDRESSING OFFSHORE DISCONNECTIONS BETWEEN CHINESE AND WESTERN BUSINESS ACADEMICS AND STUDENTS

Joe Peng Zhou and Cec Pedersen

University of Southern Queensland, Toowoomba,
Queensland, Australia

INTRODUCTION

China's growing economy has produced a huge demand for Western educated business graduates. However, Australian universities' experiences with Chinese students and vice versa, are not free of problems. This chapter reports on difficulties experienced by offshore Chinese students, while studying an Australian Business Administration program. Findings of the study indicate ways in which Western universities can improve the design of offshore joint programs with Chinese partners, to better target course content and delivery to meet the needs of Chinese students.

Creating Connections in Teaching and Learning, pp. 123–136
Copyright © 2011 by Information Age Publishing
All rights of reproduction in any form reserved.

The Dawkins reform proposals (Dawkins, 1988) regarding tertiary education in Australia, and the subsequent pursuit of international student enrolments by many universities, saw a new array of partnership arrangements in the international arena (Willis, 2005, 2006). These ranged from enrolling students in courses at host institutions in Australia, to establishing campuses in other countries, providing external study materials to students in other countries, and offering hybrid arrangements with partners, who deliver lectures and tutorials to international students in their host countries. In the 1990s in China, as part of the review of tertiary education, a number of institutions entered into the last of these options with foreign universities, including some from Australia.

One such arrangement between an Australian university and Chinese Institute provided a joint program, resulting in the awarding of a Bachelor of Business Administration to students successfully completing a four year joint program. The first 2 years of study comprised English language, writing and study skills, followed by an intensive year, in which eight business courses were taught by the international partner with the assistance of local tutors and obligatory teaching schools (required by the Chinese Ministry of Education). The final year comprised subjects from a private college in Australia, and local Chinese examinations for entry into government employment. This structure meant that the Australian partner was involved in the delivery of only one-third of the joint program.

Learning in such an eclectic international environment is always challenging, when English is a foreign language to the students. However, when the teaching is done in the students' home country, using tutors for whom both English and Western style learning and business education is foreign, and the tuition provided is only the middle third of the whole, then the situation becomes somewhat problematic.

THE CONTEXT

The increasing number of Chinese students enrolled in Western universities, both onshore and offshore, has been accompanied by a growing body of research, into the issues related to the so-called "Chinese learner". However, little research has been done with offshore Chinese students from the People's Republic of China (Xu, 2004), particularly in relation to their native language. To partly fill this gap in the literature, the authors report on four focus group interviews with offshore Chinese students, enrolled at two Chinese partner universities. The aim of the interviews was to gain insight into specific issues that the students identified with studying an Australian Bachelor of Business Administration (BBA) program. In particular, the focus group interviews were conducted in Mandarin by one author, who used to be a university lecturer in China, and therefore has a cultural understanding of the students' accounts.

Concerns have been raised over the last few years that the lure of massive international student enrolments has resulted in a significant number of universities entering into arrangements which are neither financially viable nor educationally sound (Economist Intelligence Unit, 2006). Research into the problems experienced by Western educators when teaching students of Chinese descent, or from Confucian-heritage cultures has intensified in the English literature, since the publication of Watkins and Biggs' (1996, 2001) edited books about *The Chinese learner*.

The related literature tends to center on cultural influences on Chinese students' learning styles. These include language proficiency and its impact on Chinese students' performance; ethical issues around plagiarism; cultural barriers encountered by students when studying at Western universities; and the implications of Chinese students' experiences and presence for the internationalization of the course curriculum (McGowan & Potter, 2008). The first section of this chapter discusses some of this literature. The section on research method outlines the exploratory approach of the research that is reported, and why focus group interviews were conducted in Mandarin, instead of English. Finally, an analysis of the interviews indicates that offshore Chinese students may have different expectations of the joint Australian business programs that are being delivered under transnational arrangements with Chinese partners.

WHAT DOES THE LITERATURE SAY?

Studies in this area often take an individual characteristic approach, which tends to portray Chinese learners with distinctive features. Early research typically stereotypes Chinese students as passive rote learners, who memorize from the teaching notes, take a surface approach to learning, and are unwilling to actively take part in classroom discussions (for example, Samuelowicz, 1987). More recent studies suggest that Chinese students are hard workers, who often surpass their Western counterparts, once they understand what they are expected to do, and when language is not an issue (Cooper, 2004). More specifically, Chinese learners tend to prefer concrete facts to abstract theories, and they often emphasize particulars rather than universals. Practicality is perceived by most of Chinese learners, as a central focus of their study. In addition, Nakarama (as cited in Redding, 1990) noted that Chinese learners have great concern for reconciliation, harmony, and balance. Consistent with these characteristics, learning in the Chinese context is typically passive, didactic, and teacher-centered (Liu, 2008).

Biggs (1996) indicates that Chinese students have learning approaches deeply rooted in their national culture, and heavily influenced by Confucianism. The traditional Chinese way of teaching views students as empty vessels, that need to be filled with unarguable knowledge from their teachers (Liu, 2008). Teachers in the Chinese context are supposed to engage students in learning, by providing detailed and well-structured teaching notes to make the transition of knowledge happen. As a result of this traditional didactic teaching approach, there is a tendency among Chinese students to seek definitive answers from their expert teachers (Newell, 1999), and not to try to construct their own understanding or discover knowledge by questioning authorities' opinions.

Critical thinking, which underpins Western business education philosophy, is incompatible with the traditional Chinese culture, and this often causes frustration among Chinese students in the early stage of studying the Western business course (Choo, 2007; Liu, 2008). The tradition in Chinese culture of discouraging questioning, argumentation, and criticizing, coupled with an unfamiliarity with Western academic ethics and writing conventions, often leads to unintentional copying in written assignments, and accusations of plagiarism within many Western universities (Robinson & Kuin, 1999).

Ironically, crucial critical thinking skills and academic writing conventions, such as correct referencing, are not always explained explicitly to Chinese students because these are assumed to be obvious in the Western culture (Lillis, 2001). In addition, limited English capability prevents many offshore Chinese students from actively interacting with, and purposefully seeking support from their Western teachers. However, as Volet and Kee (as cited in Watkins & Biggs, 1996) highlight, once Chinese students jump those initial hurdles, they perform as well as or even better than their Western counterparts.

CONDUCTING EXPLORATORY FOCUS GROUPS IN MANDARIN

An exploratory approach was taken for this research to identify as many issues as possible, and to understand difficulties or problems that offshore Chinese students have experienced, when studying an Australian Bachelor of Business Administration (BBA) program under transnational arrangements with Chinese educational partner institutes. The exploratory approach was appropriate in this situation, as there was little previous research available on the topic (Steward & Shamdasani, 1990). Most previous research has used either on-campus students from mainland China as convenient samples (for example, Thompson & Ku, 2005), or students of Chinese descent from Hong Kong, Taiwan, Singapore, and other countries in South East Asia as representative of Chinese learners. However, the Chinese learner is not a homogeneous group. Findings based on teaching Hong Kong or Singapore Chinese students may have little relevance to students from mainland China, because significant variations may exist between Chinese students in different countries (Jones, 2005).

Accordingly, focus groups interviews were used to discover the "social reality" (Minichiello et al., 1995, pp. 69, 75), through verbal accounts by multiple respondents, and thus to build a "grounded theory" (Taylor & Bogdan, 1998, p. 91) about the difficulties and problems offshore Chinese students experienced while studying an Australian BBA program. More specifically, four focus group interviews (two sessions with students from each of the two Chinese partners) were conducted with 26 offshore Chinese students during April and May 2008. Both Chinese partners have a joint BBA program, under transnational arrangements with an Australian university.

Participants of the focus groups had either just finished their joint Chinese-Australian BBA program, or were in their final year of study. They were invited to participate in the research on a voluntary basis. With participants' informed consent, all four focus groups were videotaped for convenience of later analysis. There was an imposed time limit of 1 hour for each session. No pre-prepared questions were developed, and the researcher/moderator began each focus group session with a brief introduction to help the participants understand the purposes of the research, and the rules for the focus group interview. After the introduction, all the participants were invited to deliberate on particular difficulties or problems they had with studying the joint Chinese-Australian BBA program. The researcher/moderator intervened occasionally with probe questions, such as: So, what other difficulties have you experienced with the teaching schools conducted by the Australian lecturers?; Is there anything else that you can think of in this regard?

The focus group interviews were purposefully conducted in Mandarin, to allow the participants to express their opinions freely. The exploratory approach and interpretive nature of this research indicates that the purpose of the focus group interviews was to seek culturally derived and historically situated interpretations of the students' social life-world (Crotty, 1998). Given, that many of the Chinese participants in the focus groups had problems with clearly expressing themselves in English and the researcher/ moderator shared the same cultural background as the participants, it was logical for the focus group sessions to be conducted in Mandarin. In this way, the accounts were understood in a meaningful "ethnographic context" (Minichiello et al., 1995, p. 72), and with little "cultural bias" (Craig & Douglas, 2000, p. 164).

Nevertheless, the researcher attempted to distance himself from the participants by positioning himself as an outsider, so as not to impose his own insights into the problems identified by the participants. Conducting the focus group interviews in Mandarin worked well, with the participants in all sessions actively taking part by talking and interacting with others, and adding comments on related issues or opinions. The participants felt comfortable expressing themselves in their mother tongue, and each session was successfully completed in about 50–55 minutes, with approximately 25 issues emerging during each session.

A limitation to the study was the lack of graduate records and statistics because the researchers did not have access to the limited information of partners or information that the Chinese government collects. It is important to note that Chinese students have little choice about where they study because of parental and government allocations, and in this particular joint program they had no choice about which courses they would undertake or when they would study them.

WHAT DID WE FIND?

Initial analysis of the focus group interviews identified two streams in the participants' verbal accounts. One stream raised by the participants related to cultural differences. Issues included mismatches between Australian course materials and the reality of Chinese society. In particular, the participants identified:

- a lack of familiarity with the Western style academic writing conventions;
- unrealistic expectations of the Chinese students' English capability and the impact of that capability on assessments;
- differing instructions from local Chinese tutors and Australian lecturers, causing confusion amongst the Chinese students.

The second stream was more contextual in nature and included:

- how assessment design may significantly affect Chinese students' performances;
- the need to sequence the courses, so that students build on prior knowledge;
- a lack of direct communication between the Chinese students and Australian lecturers;
- teaching schools conducted by visiting course leaders were too short, and contained too much material for the Chinese students to digest;
- raising awareness of how slow internet access speed makes it difficult for the Chinese students to utilize online resources effectively.

The findings from this research suggest eight key areas for further improvement of the joint programs. These are:

1. Content mismatches;
2. Unfamiliar conventions;
3. Lack of consistency;
4. Unrealistic expectations;
5. Assessment design;
6. Sequencing issues;
7. Lecturer visit ineffectiveness;
8. Online issues.

Finding 1: Content Mismatches

Participants from three of the four focus groups explicitly identified mismatches between the Australian course materials and Chinese social reality as a major issue. For example, one participant identified that because there are significant differences between Australian and Chinese financial management and reporting systems, it is almost useless for the Chinese students to study Australian financial courses, which are specific to the Australian context. This is because most of the students enrolled in the Chinese-Australian joint program, will end up with a career in the domestic China labour market. A similar issue was raised by a participant, who indicated that it was difficult for the Chinese students to relate many Australian business theories to Chinese business practices.

However, many students wanted to learn useful and practical business ideas and concepts from their Australian lecturers. Almost all Chinese university students at the bachelor degree level had not had any kind of work experience with any organization. It was suggested that ideally, the Chinese-Australian program should have an internship component that would enable them to relate what they learned to what is happening in the real world. The students thought that this might help to encourage a comprehensive understanding of abstract business theories, accompanied by relevant examples from Chinese reality.

Finding 2: Unfamiliar Conventions

Lack of familiarity with the Western style academic writing conventions was another issue that emerged from the focus group interviews. One participant pointed out that Australian assignments, such as essays, reports, and case analysis are foreign concepts to Chinese students. Yet, no bridging course was provided to help the Chinese students prepare for such unfamiliar assignment types. Another participant described the situation as "only after obtaining many Cs in my study of the Australian courses did I begin to roughly understand what my Australian course leaders expected from me in the essay type assignments." Her insight was supplemented by another participant, who added that "if it is so important for our study of the Australian courses, why not have a Western academic writing skills course for us, before we begin studying these Australian courses?" All participants noted that what they learned in the fundamental English preparation courses had little to do with what they were expected to do in their later study.

Finding 3: Lack of Consistency

The issue of confusing instructions on how to prepare assignments from Australian lecturers and local Chinese tutors was identified by all four focus groups. Under transnational partnership arrangements, students at the two Chinese partner universities were provided by the Australian university with all English teaching materials. A local Chinese tutor was appointed to provide weekly face-to-face lectures to the students in English, and in accordance with the corresponding Australian course leaders' requirements.

However, often the local Chinese tutors did not have necessary insights into Australian culture and context, and their interpretations of the course materials and assignment requirements were different from those of the Australian lecturers. On some occasions, the students obtained poor marks in their assignments by following the local tutors' misinterpreted instructions. Many deemed this unfair by saying, "Why should we be punished for our local Chinese tutor's fault?" It was suggested that all local Chinese tutors should be systematically trained to fully understand the Australian course requirements and teaching practices, before being employed to teach in a Chinese-Australian joint program.

Finding 4: Unrealistic Expectations

Another issue that emerged across the board from all focus groups was unrealistic expectations of the Chinese students' English capabilities. It was identified by several participants that bulky Australian textbooks are difficult for Chinese students to understand. This was exacerbated by many students, not understanding the differences between the textbooks and other study materials provided by the Australian university. One participant said that "many of my classmates did not even bother to read the English textbooks; instead they simply borrowed a translated version of an English textbook, to help them understand what they were supposed to learn for a particular course." Also, because of a lack of confidence in their English capabilities, many Chinese students were unwilling to participate in online discussions. One participant explained this issue in the following manner:

> If I have the English capabilities expected by my Australian lecturers, why should I spend so much money to get enrolled into a Chinese-Australian joint program like this, when with just a little bit more money, I can go abroad to study either in the United States or in the United Kingdom?

Finding 5: Assessment Design

Related to English proficiency, the issue of how assessment items are designed was raised in all focus groups as an important factor that may significantly affect Chinese students' performances. Participants of two focus groups complained that online quizzes were not a good way to test students' understanding, because many students have problems understanding the questions. Additionally, the time limit set for online quizzes is unrealistic, because internet access speed in the mainland China can be very slow. There were perceptions from some students that a few poor performers cheated in the online quizzes without being detected, and this was considered unfair.

Similarly, participants of the other two focus groups raised issues of "unfairness" in the Australian assessment system. It was said that the assessment formats used in the Australian courses, forced most of the Chinese students to learn by rote, in order to pass the assessments. Many students felt their results were not in proportion to the effort they put into studying. As a result, many students who initially enrolled into the Chinese-Australian program decided to transfer to other Chinese programs, because poor final results would make it difficult for them to obtain a good job in the domestic Chinese market.

Finding 6: Sequencing Issues

Participants from two focus groups found that the sequencing of Australian courses made no sense. Under transnational arrangements with their Chinese partners, the Australian university offers only a limited selection of courses, from those on offer in the same Australian semester. Typically, Chinese partner students had no choice about which courses they would study, and the limited availability of courses often meant, that they did more advanced level courses out of sequence. Many students viewed themselves as victims of the inadequate establishment of the joint programs between the Chinese and the Australian partners. One participant commented: "How could I be expected to understand a year three Australian course, before I had touched the more fundamental year one courses?"

Finding 7: Lecturer Visit Effectiveness

Conflicting opinions were expressed over the issue of whether teaching visits made by the Australian lecturers were useful and effective. Participants from the four focus groups stated that they valued the teaching visits, because these visits were the only opportunities for them to interact with their Australian lecturers in face-to-face situations. However, common complaints across the four focus groups were that teaching visits were poorly scheduled, that they were too short (usually 3 days), and that there were too many ideas to digest. One participant described this by saying that "the duration of the teaching school is so short, that we do not even have time to get used to our Australian lecturers' accent before they fly back."

Another participant from the same focus group commented that:

> We actually wish that our Australian lecturers did not just focus on talking us through PowerPoint slides, because this makes us think that the whole purpose of teaching visits is just to help us to pass the assessments. What we really want to learn during the teaching school is something totally new from our Australian lecturers such as some contemporary management ideas and skills, or even just some interesting group activities in the classroom.

Finding 8: Online Issues

Finally, slow internet access speed was identified as an important factor that prevents Chinese students from making better use of the online resources provided by the Australian university. One participant complained that:

> Because of the slow and unstable internet access, most of our classmates had to stay up after 12 am to take the online quizzes, but what our Australian lecturers did not know is that in China, most of the university students actually live in university dormitories which had a strict regulation to switch off the power supply and internet access after 11 pm.

Another participant commented on the internet access speed issue, by saying that:

> Slow internet access speed did affect us when downloading large files from the Australian university. I think, it will be helpful if you can take advantage of the technology, by video-shooting some of your on-campus class sessions, and then make them available to our Chinese students, by burning them on to CDs.

One participant found the Australian university's online teaching platform a positive experience, as she had not only found the format interesting, but also useful, in terms of helping her improve her English while studying the Australian courses. However, she also suggested that, to help the Chinese students make full use of the Australian university's online resources, the university should provide orientation courses to help Chinese students familiarize themselves with the online environment.

IMPLICATIONS FOR TEACHING AND LEARNING

The findings of this exploratory research have three significant implications for creating connections between teaching and learning. The first implication is that cultural conflicts and mismatches between the West and the East—which may affect learning outcomes of students from a different culture—must be addressed proactively. Unless the educators and their institutions are willing to change their mindsets, and to really embrace the idea of internationalizing the curriculum and developing culturally appropriate pedagogy, offshore Chinese students will struggle to succeed in a Western educational environment.

More specifically, to help the offshore Chinese students prepare for their study of Australian business courses in a better manner, both Australian lecturers and local Chinese tutors need to be aware of, and make stronger connections between, the cultural differences in the two education systems. Arguably, the most effective way to do this is to involve academics from both countries in undertaking systematic training before they are assigned to their jobs. Also, the Chinese students enrolled in joint programs should be introduced explicitly to fundamental Western academic skills, such as library searches, critical thinking, essay and report writing, and referencing during an induction or orientation process, before they embark on studying Australian business courses. Ideally, the bicultural and bilingual teaching staff of both the educational partners should be utilized to connect the Chinese students and the Australian academics at this early stage (Edwards & Ran, 2006).

The second implication relates to the reality that most of the offshore Chinese students are still struggling with their English, and this needs to be taken into account when designing and developing course assessments. While it can be argued that all international students enrolled in an Australian education program should have an expected level of English proficiency, many Chinese students who choose to study a Chinese-Australian joint program in their own home country make their decision based on a realization that their English is not good enough to go and study abroad in an English-speaking country. If this is not taken into account when designing course assessments, Chinese students may feel frustrated and intimidated by the high language hurdle.

However, some Australian academics would argue, that by accommodating the Chinese students with insufficient language capabilities and rote memorizing learning styles, we may end up with having to lower our academic standards, or even our educational ethics (McGowan & Potter, 2008). This is a serious challenge to long-held educational philosophies, and academic integrity principles. A solution for this challenge is pro-active flexibility. There should be more flexibility in our educational system to develop tailor-made approaches, which will assist the offshore Chinese students to obtain the positive outcomes they desire, when enrolling in the course. Transnational educational services need to provide value for money, and they should not expect that existing materials and a one-size-fits-all approach will meet the needs in a different context. A pro-active approach based on the appreciation and acceptance of difference must be taken, rather than the deficit model which is currently in place.

One final implication that can be drawn from this research is that to make joint transnational educational programs work for Chinese students, consideration must be given to fundamental course structural issues, such as the sequencing of courses, internet access, and the scheduling of teaching visits. While many Chinese students think that it should be easy to ask for the adjustments to course sequencing, and for extensions to the duration of teaching visits, the reality is that teaching staff simply cannot make these changes, unless universities and faculties are willing to commit more resources to servicing and supporting offshore partners.

Furthermore, many Chinese students have no knowledge of how to use online course websites as useful platforms to help them study Australian business courses, so scaffolding of learning in such an environment is necessary. Because Chinese students are used to learning directly from teachers who give detailed instructions, if these are not developed and provided explicitly in the early transition process, students feel that they are being left alone to figure out "the rules of the game." Therefore, consideration must also be given to improving the impact of teaching visits, and to developing more supportive teaching resources, such as live lecture videos with English subtitles, to help the offshore Chinese students overcome the language hurdles, while simultaneously catering for visual learning preferences (Nguyen, Terlouw, and Pilot, 2006).

CONCLUSION

The growing numbers of offshore Chinese students enrolled in Chinese-Australian joint business programs under transnational arrangements have presented both financial benefits and academic challenges for Australian universities. By conducting focus group interviews with 26 offshore Chinese students from two Chinese partners, this exploratory research identified several significant disconnections between the Australian and Chinese tertiary education systems. These appear to adversely affect the Chinese students' experiences, and their performances in studying Australian business courses. A number of concerns that were raised could be examined in more detail, in a subsequent and much larger study.

There are major implications for Australian educators in terms of internationalizing course curriculum, and developing culturally appropriate pedagogy. Unless these disconnections are systematically addressed by all parties engaged in transnational joint education programs, offshore Chinese students will remain frustrated with trying to understand unfamiliar Western business education concepts, such as critical thinking, evidence-based logical argumentation, and the use of referencing styles to avoid plagiarism. However, with clear understandings of these issues, the way is opened up for creating better connections between both parties, enabling the Chinese students to achieve their goals, and Australian universities to further benefit from their increased capability to meet the growing demands of lucrative offshore markets.

REFERENCES

Biggs, J. (1996). Western misperceptions of the Confucian-heritage learning culture. In D. Watkins & J. Biggs (Eds.), *The Chinese learner: Cultural, psychological and contextual influences* (pp. 45–67). Hong Kong: Comparative Education Research Center & Australian Council for Educational Research.

Choo, K. L. (2007). The implications of introducing critical management education to Chinese students studying in UK business schools: Some empirical evidence. *Journal of Further and Higher Education, 31*(2), 145–158.

Cooper, B. J. (2004). The enigma of the Chinese learner. *Accounting Education, 13*(3), 289–310.

Craig, C. S., & Douglas, S. P. (2000). *International marketing research.* New York: John Wiley & Sons.

Crotty, M. (1998). *The foundations of social research: Meaning and perspective in the research process.* London: Sage.

Dawkins, J. S. (1988). *Higher education: A policy statement ("The white paper").* Canberra, ACT: Australian Government Publishing Service.

Economist Intelligence Unit. (2006). *The international education market in China: A report commissioned by Australian Education International in the Australian Government Department of Education, Science and Training.* Canberra, ACT: Commonwealth of Australia.

Edwards, V., & Ran, A. (2006). *Meeting the needs of Chinese students in British higher education.* UK: The University of Reading.

Jones, A. (2005). Culture and context: Critical thinking and student learning in introductory macroeconomics. *Studies in Higher Education, 30*(3), 339–354.

Lillis, T. M. (2001). *Student writing: Access, regulation and desire*. New York: Routledge.

Liu, J. (2008). From learner passive to learner active? The case of Chinese postgraduate students studying marketing in the UK. *International Journal of Management Education*, 7(2), 33–40

McGowan, S., & Potter, L. (2008). The implications of the Chinese learner for the internationalization of the curriculum: An Australian perspective. *Critical Perspectives on Accounting*, 19, 181–198.

Minichiello, V., Aroni, R., Timewell, E., & Alexander, L. (1995). *In-depth interviewing: Principles, techniques, analysis*. Melbourne: Longman.

Newell, S. (1999). The transfer of management knowledge to China: Building learning communities rather than translating Western textbooks. *Education and Training*, 41, 286–293.

Nguyen, P. M., Terlouw, C., & Pilot, A. (2006). Culturally appropriate pedagogy: The case of group learning in a Confucian Heritage Culture context. *Intercultural Education*, 17(1), 1–19.

Redding, G. (1990). *The spirit of Chinese capitalism*. New York: Walter de Guyter.

Robinson, V. M. J., & Kuin, L. M. (1999). The explanation of practice: Why Chinese students copy assignments. *Qualitative Studies in Education*, 12(2), 193–210.

Samuelowicz, K. (1987). Learning problems of overseas students: Two sides of a story. *Higher Education Research & Development*, 16(2), 121–132.

Stewart, D. W., & Shamdasani, P. N. (1990). *Focus groups: Theory and practice*. Newbury Park: Sage Publications.

Taylor, S. J., & Bogdan, R. (1998). *Introduction to qualitative research methods: A guidebook and resource*. New York: Wiley.

Thompson, L., & Ku, H. Y. (2005). Chinese graduate students' experiences and attitudes toward online learning. *Educational Media International*, 42(1), 33–47.

Watkins, D. A., & Biggs, J. B. (Eds.). (1996). *The Chinese learner: Cultural, psychological and contextual influences*. Hong Kong: Comparative Education Research Center & Australian Council for Educational Research.

Watkins, D. A., & Biggs, J. B. (Eds.). (2001). *Teaching the Chinese learner: Psychological and pedagogical perspectives*. Hong Kong: Comparative Education Research Center & Australian Council for Educational Research.

Willis, M. (2005). An identification and analysis of students' expectations and views regarding foreign-sourced tertiary education programs delivered in China: Investigating the next stage of internationalisation and market entry for foreign universities. *Journal of Marketing for Higher Education*, 15(2), 1–30.

Willis, M. (2006). Why do Chinese universities seek foreign university partners?: An investigation of the motivating factors behind a significant area of alliance activity. *Journal of Marketing for Higher Education*, 16(1), 115–141.

Xu, R. (2004, September. 15–18). *Chinese mainland students' experience of teaching and learning at a Chinese university: Some emerging findings*. Paper presented at the BERA 2004 Conference, UMIST, Manchester.

CHAPTER 11

CURRICULUM CONNECTIONS: LESSONS FROM POST-COMPULSORY VOCATIONAL EDUCATION AND TRAINING

Lindsay Parry, *James Cook University, Townsville, Queensland, Australia;*
R. E. (Bobby) Harreveld, *CQUniversity Australia; Rockhampton,
Queensland, Australia;* **P. A. Danaher,** *University of Southern
Queensland, Toowoomba, Queensland, Australia*

INTRODUCTION

Curriculum, as one of the three educational message systems (with pedagogy and assessment), can be understood as potentially complicit with disconnections and missed opportunities for creating connections in teaching and learning. This is particularly the case if the curriculum is removed from the lived experiences and situated aspirations of groups of learners. At the same time, curriculum can function as the vehicle for creating and sustaining meaningful connections in teaching and learning, if it engages respectfully with those experiences and helps to fulfill those aspirations.

Creating Connections in Teaching and Learning, pp. 137–150
Copyright © 2011 by Information Age Publishing
All rights of reproduction in any form reserved.

This chapter explores curriculum's capacity to create educational connections by interrogating a previously marginalized field of educational provision and research: post-compulsory vocational education and training, incorporating senior secondary schooling, Technical and Further Education Colleges and their non-Australian equivalents, and private providers. Framed by selected concepts from contemporary curriculum theorizing, the chapter draws on evidence presented in the recent issues of *VOCAL: The Australian Journal of Vocational Education and Training in Schools*. Specifically, the authors argue that post-compulsory vocational education and training provides several examples of curriculum, creating powerful connections for young adult learners that must be understood against the backdrop of broader socio-economic trends, enacted locally, nationally, and globally. More broadly, this field makes a distinctive and important contribution to wider research endeavors, related to teaching and learning.

Separately, curriculum and post-compulsory vocational education and training are both contested and politicized fields of scholarship, policy, and practice. This chapter examines these two fields in combination, in order to identify the opportunities for creating productive and sustainable connections in teaching and learning that they exhibit, as well as some of the obstacles to such a creation. In doing so, we also consider what those opportunities and obstacles might prognosticate for enabling and empowering curriculum connections more widely.

THE CHAPTER FOCUS

As elaborated below, curriculum is the key element of teaching and learning research, policy-making, and provision (see for example, Kelly, 2009; Miller, 2007; Pinar et al., 2004; Slattery, 2006). Some see curriculum's vital function as being to facilitate socio-cultural resistance and transformation (Apple & Buras, 2006). If it is to discharge this function effectively, it must create connections among learners, educators, administrators, government officials, community members, and other stakeholders, who contribute directly to lifelong and life-wide learning that is fulfilling for individuals and productive for communities. Creating curriculum connections is therefore crucial to the broader agenda of researching and enhancing teaching and learning outcomes and it forms the central focus of this chapter.

Post-compulsory vocational education and training constitute a particular field in which effective curriculum connections must, and can be created. In many ways, this field encapsulates the vicissitudes of contemporary life in the early 21st century. This can be seen as the forces of late capitalism to confront such challenges as the recent global financial crisis, with direct and ongoing implications for assumptions about workforce development and individual capacity building. This field also engages foursquare with debates about what learning is, how it is facilitated, measured, and assessed, when and where it takes place, and who benefits from its outcomes. If this field is to prosper and thereby maximize those benefits, it needs to create long-term connections that cross traditional divides such as school and work, and education and training, as well as professional and vocational knowledge.

The chapter is arranged in five sections:

- A background overview of selected current developments in post-compulsory vocational education and training;
- A conceptual framework, outlining selected concepts derived from contemporary curriculum theorizing;
- An initial mapping of the terrain of post-compulsory vocational education and training (VET), gleaned from the recent issues of *VOCAL: The Australian Journal of Vocational Education and Training in Schools*;
- A focused analysis of those maps, informed by the selected concepts of curriculum theorizing;
- A concluding synthesis of suggested implications of that analysis for creating enduring curriculum connections, both within the post-compulsory vocational education and training, and in teaching and learning contexts more broadly.

Overall, we adopt a cautiously optimistic view of the capacity of curriculum to create and carry through teaching and learning connections that benefit learners in vocational education and training, their communities, and the wider society. Broader socio-economic trends constitute an influential backdrop against which individual learners and educators interact. Yet the connections between those learners and educators can fuse with the curriculum, generating new and powerful understandings in their own right. They can also contribute distinctive perspectives on the wider project of researching teaching and learning.

BACKGROUND

All sectors of formal education have experienced substantial change, in concert with an equally fundamental transformation of the socio-economic system, with which these sectors are inextricably connected. One manifestation of this change has been the dynamic character of post-compulsory vocational education and training in many Western countries. This has been centered on the raising of the de facto school leaving age from 15–17 or 18, and the introduction of several vocational subjects and school-based apprenticeships and traineeships to senior secondary schooling. It has also been evident in the lessening of the emphasis on senior secondary schooling's function in ranking the entrants to universities, and the dilution of the division between academic and vocational subjects, during and after senior secondary schooling. There has been an elaboration of formal pathways linking senior secondary schooling, vocational education and training colleges, and universities as well. This set of changes has entailed the breaking of some existing connections—curriculum and otherwise—and the creation of new ones.

More specifically, the vocational education and training literature has simultaneously explored several themes related to these changes. One such theme has been the degree of effectiveness of school vocational education and training programs (Anlezark, Karmel, and Ong, 2006). Another theme has been the impact of those changes on the work and identities of educators and trainers (Harris, Simons, and Clayton, 2005; Tyler, 2009), with important consequences for teacher training for this sector (Holloway, 2009). Yet another theme has been the link between vocational education and training programs, and the development of sustainable learning communities, such as in the regional areas (Allison, Gorringe, and Lacey, 2006), and through rural extension systems (Coutts & Roberts, 2007). There has also been scholarly interest in the association between such programs and increased entry to formal employment (Stanwick, 2006), and between such programs and heightened access to higher education (Harris, Rainey, and Sumner, 2006; Harris, Sumner, and Rainey, 2005). All these themes involve different kinds of connections being envisaged and implemented, if the associated changes are to be positive and productive.

Closely associated with these themes has been the application of specific concepts, designed to separate the realities of change and stasis in post-compulsory vocational education and training from rhetorical statements about such provision. These concepts have included capability (Harreveld & Singh, 2008), competence (Mulder, Weigel, and Collins, 2007), entrepreneurship (Henry, Hill, and Leitch, 2005; Isaacs et al., 2007), leadership and hope (Singh, Chen, and Harreveld, 2009), and learning pathways (Young, 2006). They have also involved learning support (Robson, Bailey, and Mendick, 2008) and professionalism (Gleeson, Davies, and Wheeler, 2005). Once again, all these concepts have in common, a focus on varied types of connections linking individual learners, particular education and training institutions and systems, and the broader communities in which they are situated.

This necessarily selective overview of current developments in post-compulsory vocational education and training, as distilled from some of the contemporary literature, demonstrates the recurring relevance and significance of creating connections conceptually, via policy-making and in practice. It also highlights the crucial intersection among such connections, vocational education and training, and curriculum that is at once fluid, innovative, and responsive. We now turn to outlining specific concepts of the curriculum that theorize those characteristics and in doing so, provide a framework for applying them to the key elements of vocational education and training.

CONCEPTUAL FRAMEWORK

Contemporary curriculum theorizing is extensive, diverse, and complex. Consequently, we do no more than elicit a small number of concepts that we consider central to creating connections, to constitute the framework that we use to analyze the examples of post-compulsory vocational education and training provision, examined below. Concept selection has been facilitated by our proposition, that such provision invites particular attention to the wider individual and societal contexts in which various forms of schooling are enacted.

The first group of concepts selected on that basis is drawn from Billett (2008). In particular, we highlight the notions clustered around Billett's (2008) tripartite distinction among the potential elements of a workplace curriculum. He identified these elements as: "the *intended curriculum*—what is intended to occur; the *enacted curriculum*—what actually happens when the curriculum is enacted; and the *experienced curriculum*—what learners experience, construe, and learn as a result of its enactment" (p. 61). We consider this a useful framework for analyzing the curriculum, as it has also been proven particularly applicable to post-compulsory vocational education and training, because of Billett's (2006, 2007; Billetts & Somerville, 2004) renowned researching in that field.

This tripartite distinction resonates with Kelly's (2009) evocation of two related differentiations: between the planned and the received curriculum; and between the formal and the informal curriculum. Our second selected concept is therefore, a logical extension of these pairs of curriculum constructions: the hidden curriculum, which recognizes the pervasive and ongoing impact of forces, broader than the education system. Kelly conceived of the hidden curriculum somewhat narrowly, but reasonably clearly. He contended that "our definition must embrace all the learning that goes on in schools, whether it is expressly planned and intended or is a by-product of our planning and/or practice" (p. 11; see also Anyon, 2006).

This focus on the wider relationships, influencing formal curriculum enactments, resonates with the third concept selected for our framework: curriculum as ecosystem. Barab and Roth (2006) elaborated this concept as underpinning an ecological theory of knowledge and as being underpinned by "affordance networks, effectivity, sets, and life-worlds" (p. 3). This approach highlights the dynamism, fluidity, and responsiveness of curriculum, and its interdependence on a host of other factors affecting formal educational provision, many of them outside the control of the participants.

In combination, then, the distinction among the intended curriculum, the enacted curriculum, and the experienced curriculum; the hidden curriculum; and curriculum as ecosystem, constitute our provisional conceptual framework. We consider that this framework is likely to assist our exploration of the evidence for viable curriculum connections being created by post-compulsory vocational education and training. Below, we apply that framework to an analysis of the terrain of that field, after we have mapped that terrain.

POST-COMPULSORY VET: MAPPING THE TERRAIN

As *The Australian Journal of Vocational Education and Training in Schools*, *VOCAL* is published biennially by the VETnetwork Australia, "a national network of teachers, trainers, career advisors, program coordinators, administrative, and support personnel committed to vocational learning and youth transition" (VETnetwork Australia, n.d.). The VETnetwork Australia was established in 1995 by a group of senior secondary teachers in the Australian Capital Territory, and it has since spread to all Australian states and territories. It also has links with government departments, universities, industry groups, and education and training bodies (VETnetwork Australia, n.d.). As well as publishing *VOCAL*, the organization hosts an annual conference, publishes the *VETnetworker Magazine*, and provides several professional learning opportunities for its members.

The *VOCAL* was first published in 1998, with its editorial proclaiming its intention of being a "reader-friendly, stimulating, reasonably erudite, perhaps challenging journal aimed at teachers and coordinators of vocational education and training" (Frost, 1998, p. 3). The goal was to "draw its material from the growing range of inspirational thinkers, writers, researchers and 'doers' both within Australia and overseas" (p. 3).

The changing topography of the terrain traversed by the journal since its inception was encapsulated in the editorial of the publication's 10th anniversary volume (Harreveld & Frost, 2008–2009). For example, the inaugural issue covered topics such as assessment, national policy, industry and international perspectives, different notions of workplace learning, and the concept of multiple pathways linking the specific components of formal post-compulsory education. Ten years later, while a great deal had changed in the interim (such as the rapid expansion in the number of learners and subjects involved in vocational education and training in senior secondary schools), the journal was still addressing similar themes. These included promoting community partnerships and industry work experience programs, enhancing work and education pathways, aligning workplace and school-based learning experiences, and examining the school-work mix. It is noteworthy, in view of this chapter's focus, to reflect on the theme of the 10th anniversary issue of the journal. This was "What works for vocational education and training in schools, in terms of developing connections, building capacity, and enhancing collaboration"—enduringly significant concerns of the journal, and the educational sector that it represents.

These concerns were also evident in two recent editions of the journal. Volume 5, published in 2004–2005, had as its theme "Young people and VET, transitions, transformations, research, and implications: The politics and passions of VET in schools." The editorial observed the potential opposition between the two strands in the subtitle:

> "politics" evokes brokerage and deal-making in a "real world" context, where resources are finite and compromises are sometimes necessary among different stakeholders' conflicting aspirations and expectations, while "passions" suggest the idealistic commitment to making the world a better place for young people, held by individuals and communities (Harreveld & Danaher, 2004–2005, p. 4).

This opposition was taken up in several of the articles in the issue, which covered topics as diverse as quality, experiential learning and teaching, training and learning paradigms, and the links between vocational education and training, and life-long learning. Perspectives were provided from China, Ireland, the Netherlands, and South Africa as well as from Australia.

Volume 6 of the journal, published in 2006–2007, had as its theme "Transitions in senior phase learning." The potential challenges and triumphs of those transitions were synthesized at the end of the editorial:

> Helping young people manage these complex transitions is the work of teachers, parents/guardians, employers, youth workers, and so on. All participate with the goodwill and intent of engaging young people in worthwhile learning—and eventual earning—as knowledge workers of the 21st century (Harreveld & Danaher, 2006–2007, p. 9).

The volume explored the reality, as well as the rhetoric of these transitions in several Australian states and also in Botswana, Canada, China, Greece, Hungary, Nigeria, Taiwan, the United Kingdom, and the United States. This coverage highlighted the wide diversity of government and industry approaches to senior secondary schooling. It also revealed the continuing commonalities involved in the efforts to upskill young people and help them to enter the paid workforce, while also trying to facilitate their self-actualization as individuals and citizens.

Thus the terrain of post-compulsory vocational education and training is undulating, variegated, and sometimes difficult to navigate. Mapping that terrain requires attentiveness to confusing and sometimes contradictory features (for example, related to government priorities and industry imperatives), if pathways that lead to productive destinations and meaningful outcomes are to be constructed and pursued. Yet, that mapping is crucial if relevant curriculum connections are to be created in ways that help to empower learners, fulfill educators, and also benefit society as a whole. The next section of the chapter interrogates the possibilities of that creation by applying the conceptual framework outlined above, to selected accounts in the recent issues of *VOCAL*.

POST-COMPULSORY VET: ANALYZING THE MAPS

None of the concepts distilled from the curriculum theory literature outlined above was referred to explicitly, in the selected issues of *VOCAL* that we examined. Nevertheless, there were specific references to curriculum that drew on one or more of those concepts. In doing so, they demonstrated some of the contemporary patterns of curriculum in facilitating and/or hindering the creation of lasting and meaningful connections for learners and other stakeholders in that process.

For example, in their examination of vocational education in China, Han and Singh (2004–2005) enumerated several "problems" with that education (as well as a number of strategies designed to address those problems) (p. 17). In noting that "the quality or outcome of the VET graduates is less than satisfactory," for instance, they contended that "the curriculum standards upon which their skills are built, are frequently outdated and irrelevant to the needs of industry" (p. 17).

This constituted a striking illustration of the disparity among the intended, enacted, and experienced curriculum, as it applied to those learners. Similarly, Han and Singh (2004–2005) asserted that "VET in China has been and still is considered to be the poor relation of higher education" (p. 17). They also observed that the implementation of "curriculum linkages between the VET and higher education sectors—is not widespread" (p. 17). From the conceptual perspective of curriculum as the ecosystem, this would suggest a lack of alignment among key features of the system that needs to be in sync, if such pathways were to be effective. Simultaneously, "developing common curriculum frameworks" (p. 18) was identified as a principal instrument deployed by the Chinese government to "open the channel between VET graduates and higher levels of study"

(p. 18). This indicated an awareness of the required policy shifts, even if those shifts were not easy to achieve in practice.

There were some striking similarities between the vocational education and training sectors in China and the Netherlands. Onstenk (2004–2005) located "curriculum content and didactic methods in vocational education" as being at the center of demands and pressures for change from students and from the occupations to which they aspire (p. 22). This was intended to maximize the degree of fit between what the students learn and the character of their work roles. Again the notion of curriculum as ecosystem comes to the fore, suggesting a complex interplay of micro, meso, and macro forces, exercising multiple and sometimes conflicting influences on the way curriculum is designed and implemented. For instance, Onstenk described "the choice between broad (and much) content versus deep (and selective) content" as a "dilemma" centered on the "the temptation to put as many aspects as possible in a curriculum" (p. 23). This depiction highlighted that the impact of that choice extended far beyond the immediate classroom into the work readiness of current and future workers, and the industries that rely on them to develop and sustain themselves.

This position of curriculum as the object of broader influences and the potential vehicle for productive change simultaneously was encapsulated in two issues, pertaining to vocational education in South Africa (Frauendorf, 2004–2005). The first issue was the optimistic claim that technical and vocational colleges are effective at helping learners to prepare for self-employment in small, medium, and micro-enterprises. They do this, for example, by developing their "orientations and skills to prepare learners for entrepreneurship—across the curriculum" (p. 30). The second issue related to democratic citizenship, with the argument that:

> The formal curriculum must expand its focus beyond vocational knowledge and skills, and include a component that will provide the learners with knowledge and skill base that will enable them to function as described by South African Qualifications Authority (SAQA): "informed consumers, and responsible parents, community members, and citizens" (Frauendorf, 2004–2005, p. 31).

This argument recalled Kelly's (2009) distinction between the formal and informal curriculum. It also evoked some of the key elements of the hidden curriculum hindering learning, if there is a significant divide between the cultural, economic, and social capital, and habitus operating in the educational setting and those obtaining in the home setting.

In Australia, curriculum has likewise been at the forefront of both criticism and change in relation to creating productive connections. In a system where, constitutionally, education is the responsibility of state and territory jurisdictions, developments that are sometimes in tandem with one another and at other times reflect the distinctive history and context of a particular state, have occurred. For example, Tasmania recently enacted policies that included "extensive pathways planning, intensive support for young people at-risk of disengaging from education, a completely overhauled senior secondary curriculum, and a new senior secondary graduation certificate" (Evans, 2006–2007, p. 35). Similarly, in Western Australia "there have been changes taking place in relation to curriculum, with a move to an outcomes based approach for courses of study in Years 11 and 12" (Morrison, 2006–2007, p. 43). Students have been able "to undertake VET within the new courses, as well as separately" (p. 43). Finally, in a cluster of schools in regional Queensland, "the issues pertaining to curriculum provision" (Harreveld, Danaher, and Kenny, 2004–2005, p. 65) reflected considerable complexity. The schools also demonstrated "the need to maximize scarce resources (including meeting the human resource requirements placed upon teachers of particular subjects)" (p. 65).

Despite these pressures, the schools were generally effective at sustaining business and industry partnerships, and developing productive networks and pathways for their students. These specific examples highlighted anew the intersection of various types of curriculum, some formally mandated and some reflective of broader forces, and all of them reinforcing the proposition, that creating curriculum connections is a highly complex and contentious undertaking.

CONCLUSION

So, what do the preceding mapping and analysis of the post-compulsory vocational education and training terrains, as outlined in *VOCAL*, mean for the creation of enduring curriculum connections both within those terrains and in teaching and learning more broadly? As noted above, overall we are cautiously optimistic about the capacity of this sector to generate and sustain connections between formal education and individual students' and communities' lifeworlds. This has been evidenced by some of the innovative approaches to curriculum (and also pedagogy/andragogy and assessment) outlined earlier. Those approaches work well when they can be aligned with wider socio-economic and political trends with common assumptions and interests related to the education of young people. From that perspective, it is possible for the connections among learners, educators, and curriculum to engender new understandings and lasting change to learning opportunities and outcomes.

On the other hand, we do not downplay the significance of the complexity of this task or the influence of sometimes countervailing forces hindering the creation of those connections. Educational institutions like schools,

Technical and Further Education colleges, and universities are often less adaptable than they might see themselves as being, and the cultural practices that characterize them are remarkably resilient. Moreover, in a context of competition for scarce resources (including student numbers), it is not always in institutions' interests to engage in the collaboration needed to create these kinds of curriculum connections (such as through the recognition of current and prior learning). Furthermore, educational partnerships can be difficult to envisage and enact, particularly when government departments are involved in them (Cardini, 2006).

All of this suggests that the creation and implementation of enabling and empowering curriculum connections are a fraught exercise, needing to satisfy multiple stakeholders and traverse extensive and varied terrains. At the same time, the specific examples of effective curriculum connections portrayed in successive issues of *VOCAL* demonstrate that it is both feasible and desirable to strive for such connections. Indeed, these associations can benefit significantly and sustainably learners, educators, communities, industries, governments, and other stakeholders alike. These are key lessons to be learned from post-compulsory vocational education and training in Australia and elsewhere. They also have much of value to say about agendas and issues, involved in researching, teaching, and learning.

ACKNOWLEDGMENTS

The authors have benefited considerably from the editors' assistance and facilitation, particularly our chapter editor Ms Lindy Abawi. They are grateful also for the helpful feedback on earlier drafts of the chapter by participants in the writing workshops, associated with producing this book and by anonymous peer reviewers.

REFERENCES

Allison, J., Gorringe, S., & Lacey, J. (2006). *Building learning communities: Partnerships, social capital and VET performance*. Adelaide, SA: National Centre for Vocational Education Research.

Anlezark, A., Karmel, T., & Ong, K. (2006). *Have school vocational education and training programs been successful?* Adelaide, SA: National Centre for Vocational Education Research. Retrieved from http://www.ncver.edu.au/research/core/cp0302.rtf

Anyon, J. (2006). Social class and the hidden curriculum of work. In G. Handel (Ed.), *Childhood socialization* (2nd ed., pp. 369–394). Pistcatway, NJ: Aldine Transaction.

Apple, M. W., & Buras, K. L. (Eds.) (2006). *The subal tern speak: Curriculum, power, and educational struggles*. New York: Routledge.

Barab, S. A., & Roth, W. M. (2006). Curriculum-based ecosystems: Supporting knowing from an ecological perspective. *Educational Researcher, 35*(5), 3–13.

Billett, S. (2006). Relational interdependence between social and individual agency in work and working life. *Mind, Culture, and Activity, 13*(1), 53–69.

Billett, S. (2007). Exercising self through working life: Learning, work and identity. In A. Brown, S. Kirpal, & F. Rauner (Eds.), *Technical and Vocational Education and Training Series: Identities at work* (Vol. 5, pp. 183–210). Dordrecht, The Netherlands: Springer Netherlands.

Billett, S. (2008). Constituting the workplace curriculum. In P. Murphy & R. McCormick (Eds.), *Knowledge and practice: Representations and identities* (pp. 61–73). London: Sage Publications.

Billett, S., & Somerville, M. (2004). Transformations at work: Identity and learning. *Studies in Continuing Education, 26*(2), 309–326.

Cardini, A. (2006). An analysis of the rhetoric and practice of educational partnerships in the UK: An arena of complexities, tensions and power. *Journal of Education Policy, 21*(4), 393–415.

Coutts, J., & Roberts, J. (2007). *Adding value to extension programs: A user's guide to aligning extension programs with vocational education and training (VET): A report for the Cooperative Venture for Human Capacity Building for Innovation in Rural Industries.* Barton, ACT: Rural Industries Research and Development Corporation.

Evans, N. (2006–2007). Tasmania is guaranteeing futures for young people. *VOCAL: The Australian Journal of Vocational Education and Training in Schools, 6*, 30–35.

Frauendorf, M. (2004–2005). Technical and vocational education and training: A progressive approach to human resource development in the post-apartheid South Africa. *VOCAL: The Australian Journal of Vocational Education and Training in Schools, 5*, 29–31.

Frost, M. (1998). Editorial. *VOCAL: The Australian Journal of Vocational Education and Training in Schools, 1*(1), 3.

Gleeson, D., Davies, J., & Wheeler, E. (2005). On the making and taking of professionalism in the further education workplace. *British Journal of Sociology of Education, 26*(4), 445–460.

Han, J., & Singh, M. (2004–2005). Vocational education in China. *VOCAL: The Australian Journal of Vocational Education and Training in Schools, 5*, 16–19.

Harreveld, R. E., & Danaher, P. A. (2004–2005). Editorial: The politics and passions of VET in schools. *VOCAL: The Australian Journal of Vocational Education and Training in Schools, 5*, 4.

Harreveld, R. E., & Danaher, P. A. (2006–2007). Editorial: Transitions in senior phase learning. *VOCAL: The Australian Journal of Vocational Education and Training in Schools, 6*, 6–9.

Harreveld, R. E., Danaher, P. A., & Kenny, M. D. (2004–2005). VET delivery in a Queensland regional community: Issues and implications. *VOCAL: The Australian Journal of Vocational Education and Training in Schools, 5*, 64–67.

Harreveld, R. E., & Frost, M. (2008–2009). Editorial. *VOCAL: The Australian Journal of Vocational Education and Training in Schools, 7*, 1–2.

Harreveld, R. E., & Singh, M. (2008). Amartya Sen's capability approach and the brokering of learning provision for young adults. *Vocations and Learning, 1*, 211–226.

Harris, R., Rainey, L., & Sumner, R. (2006). *Crazy paving or stepping stones? Learning pathways within and between vocational education and training and higher education.* Adelaide, SA: National Centre for Vocational Education Research. Retrieved from http://www.ncver.edu.au/research/proj/nr4005.pdf

Harris, R., Simons, M., & Clayton, B. (2005). *Shifting mindsets: The changing work roles of vocational education and training practitioners.* Adelaide, SA: National Centre for Vocational Education Research.

Harris, R., Sumner, R., & Rainey, L. (2005). *Student traffic: Two-way movement between vocational education and training and higher education* [Support document]. Canberra, ACT and Adelaide, SA: Australian National Training Authority and National Centre for Vocational Education Research. Retrieved from http://www.ncver.edu.au/research/proj/nr3003s.pdf

Henry, C., Hill, F., & Leitch, C. (2005). Entrepreneurship education and training: Can entrepreneurship be taught? (Part I). *Education + Training, 47*(2), 98–111.

Holloway, D. (2009). Reforming further education teacher training: A policy communities and policy network analysis. *Journal of Education for Teaching, 35*(2), 183–196.

Isaacs, E., Visser, K., Friedrich, C., & Brijlal, P. (2007). Entrepreneurship education and training at the further education and training (FET) level in South Africa. *South African Journal of Education, 27*(4), 613–630. Retrieved from http://ajol.info/index.php/saje/article/viewFile/25136/4335

Kelly, A. V. (2009). *The curriculum: Theory and practice* (6th ed.). London: Sage Publications.

Miller, J. P. (2007). *The holistic curriculum* (2nd ed.). Toronto: University of Toronto Press.

Morrison, L. (2006–2007). Where VET in schools has come from in Western Australia. *VOCAL: The Australian Journal of Vocational Education and Training in Schools, 6*, 42–45.

Mulder, M., Weigel, T., & Collins, K. (2007). The concept of competence in the development of vocational education and training in selected EU member states: A critical analysis. *Journal of Vocational Education & Training, 59*(1), 67–88.

Onstenk, J. (2004–2005). Innovation in vocational education in The Netherlands. *VOCAL: The Australian Journal of Vocational Education and Training in Schools, 5*, 20–24.

Pinar, W. F., Reynolds, W. M., Slattery, P., & Taubman, P. M. (2004). *Understanding curriculum: An introduction to the study of historical and contemporary curriculum discourses (Counterpoints Vol. 17).* New York: Peter Lang.

Robson, J., Bailey, B., & Mendick, H. (2008). Learners' emotional and psychic responses to encounters with learning support in further education and training. *British Journal of Educational Studies, 56*(3), 304–322.

Singh, M., Chen, X., & Harreveld, R. E. (2009). *Leading secondary schools through vocational education and training: Reforming to senior learning in Queensland.* Paper presented at the 12th annual conference of the Australian Vocational Education, Training and Research Association, TAFE New South Wales Sydney Institute, Randwick, NSW. Retrieved from http://www.avetra.org.au/papers-2009/papers/48.00.pdf

Slattery, P. (2006). *Curriculum development in the postmodern era* (2nd ed.). New York: Routledge.

Stanwick, J. (2006). *Outcomes from higher-level vocational education and training qualifications*. Adelaide, SA: National Centre for Vocational Education Research. Retrieved from http://www.ncver.edu.au/research/core/cp0405.doc

Tyler, M. A. (2009). *Torquing up TAFE teacher traction through a critical spirit discourse*. Paper presented at the 12th annual conference of the Australian Vocational Education, Training and Research Association, TAFE New South Wales Sydney Institute, Randwick, NSW. Retrieved from http://www.avetra.org.au/papers-2009/papers/32.00.pdf

VETnetwork Australia. (n.d.). About us [Webpage]. Retrieved from http://www.vetnetwork.org.au/01_cms/details.asp?ID=1

Young, M. (2006). Reforming the further education and training curriculum: An international perspective. In M. Young & J. Gamble (Eds.), *Knowledge, curriculum and qualifications for South African further education* (pp. 46–63). Cape Town, South Africa: Human Sciences Research Council.

SECTION III

MAKING MEANING FROM LIVED EXPERIENCES

CHAPTER 12

LOOK WHO'S LISTENING: USING THE SUPERADDRESSEE FOR UNDERSTANDING CONNECTIONS IN DIALOGUE

Warren Midgley

University of Southern Queensland, Toowoomba,
Queensland, Australia

INTRODUCTION

Regardless of what theories of learning and pedagogy are espoused or adopted, people engaged in any of the activities that might be described broadly as education are required to communicate effectively in order to facilitate the process of learning. This book, *Creating connections in teaching and learning*, seeks to explore ways in which this communication might be improved by creating connections. In this chapter, I explore one way of conceptualizing the process of creating connections, using the bakhtinian concept of the superaddressee.

The *superaddressee* is a theoretical concept drawn from the work of Bakhtin (1981) which posits the necessary existence of a higher level

Creating Connections in Teaching and Learning, pp. 153–163
Copyright © 2011 by Information Age Publishing

153

addressee in every dialogic exchange. This other listener is conceptualized as one who is valorized more highly than the speaker and the listener, and who listens sympathetically and understands justly. I use the unconventional lower case *b* for *bakhtinian* to emphasize the theoretical stance that I have adopted towards the theories drawn from the writings of M. M. Bakhtin (especially Bakhtin 1981, 1986); namely that I have appropriated them as useful concepts for a new context. I do not claim to represent the historical Bakhtin (see Midgley, 2010).

In this chapter, I outline how this concept can help to explain the success of efforts to create connections in dialogue. When both parties in a dialogue are addressing a similar superaddressee, connections are more likely to be created than if the superaddressees are quite different. To begin, I briefly explain the concept of the superaddressee, in the context of the broader bakhtinian concept of dialogue. I then demonstrate the influence of superaddressees by analyzing transcripts from a larger research project which explored the experiences of male Saudi Arabian nursing students at an Australian university. By applying this concept to an analysis of transcripts from conversations with the students about diversity in education, I demonstrate the operation of superaddressees in dialogue. I conclude by drawing out implications and suggestions for how a theoretical framework, developed around the concept of the superaddressee, might enhance educators' attempts at creating connections with various and diverse stakeholders.

DIALOGUE

Dialogue, as a theoretical concept in the bakhtinian sense does not simply mean conversation; rather, it refers to a complex relationship that operates on several different levels (Bakhtin, 1981). In its most basically conceived form, it is an engagement between two people who are communicating. This engagement may be localized in time and space (two friends who have met for a chat), or it might be distanced in either time (asynchronous chatrooms) or space (a telephone conversation), or both. However, dialogic engagement does not always involve the presence of a specific, embodied interlocutor. A novelist may write with a general readership in mind, and likewise a student may write an essay for an unidentified marker. In these instances, the interlocutor is an imagined or idealized person.

The presence of this "indefinite, unconcretized other" (Bakhtin, 1986, p. 95) is significant, because this interlocutor influences the outcome of the dialogue. For example, I now write for an idealized reader. In my conceptualization of the way in which my idealized reader responds to the previous point, I sense the need for further explanation. Hence, I have included this illustration in an attempt to clarify the point. Whether the person I am speaking or writing to is real or imagined, present or distant in time and space, my dialogue is influenced by the other to whom it is addressed. This concept is referred to as addressivity (Bakhtin, 1986).

SUPERADDRESSEE

One important aspect of addressivity in bakhtinian theory is the theorized existence of a third party, or superaddressee, in dialogue. While my writing or speaking is directed to and influenced by an addressee, it is also at the same time directed to and influenced by a superaddressee. Bakhtin (1986) described this superaddressee as an ideal listener in the mind of the speaker—one who hears from a position above self and other, and who listens sympathetically and understands justly.

Morson and Emerson (1990) suggested that the superaddressee was the embodiment of hope, without which all attempts at dialogue would degenerate into some kind of "special terror" (p. 136). The reason for this lies in the contingent nature of all dialogic encounters: I do not know whether or not you truly understand what I am saying, nor whether you really agree with what I am saying. You may agree with what you think I am saying, but if you have not understood my meaning, then you have not agreed with me. Morson and Emerson noted that, in this discussion, Bakhtin related the need to be heard with the need for God—possibly in the Russian Orthodox tradition, although the exact nature of the religious activities for which Bakhtin was exiled is not known (Clark & Holquist, 1984). Adopting a postmodern perspective, Morson and Emerson argued that the superaddressee should be considered as a meta-linguistic fact, rather than as the expression of an ideological or theological belief.

Bryzzheva (2006, 2008) has discussed important implications of the role that the superaddressee—or third listener as she renamed it—plays in providing support for those in threatening situations. In the case she discussed, teachers in classrooms, she argued that teachers may find strength to carry on in difficult situations, despite opposition from various quarters, because they carry with them in their minds an idealized mentor who agrees that what they are doing is right. An example of this might be when the teacher says, "You have to do your homework." Even if all the students in the classroom disagree, the superaddressee hears and (from his or her superior position of knowledge and understanding) affirms that the teacher is correct. This affirmation would give support to the teacher.

The presence of the superaddressee may be clearly observed in the use of sarcasm. For instance, were an embittered acquaintance to say, "It is about trust, not that you would know what that means," the speaker is appealing to the superaddressee to acknowledge the veracity and validity of the claim to having been betrayed (an acknowledgment that the listener may be unwilling to make). The fact that the speaker articulates a view that he/she knows the listener will not necessarily agree with can be seen to be evidence of the operation of a superaddressee in dialogue. The form of the utterance suggests that the speaker is addressing the listener, whereas the content of the utterance suggests that the speaker is addressing a super-addressee who is somehow above or beyond the listener.

The superaddressee can be conceptualized as an actual transcendent being, or as a meta-linguistic property of the dialogue. In either case, exploring the role of the superaddressee in dialogue can provide useful insights into the way in which connections between interlocutors are created. In the following section, I demonstrate this potential in a brief analysis of interview data. Following that, I outline suggestions for how the theoretical construct of the superaddressee might be further employed as a strategy for creating connections.

THE SUPERADDRESSEE AT WORK

In a larger study investigating the experiences of male Saudi Arabian students at an Australian university, I recorded discussions with several small groups of Saudi participants. These discussions were open-ended conversations, which arose from a general prompt question— "Tell me about your experiences here." I transcribed the recordings for analysis.

The data below are excerpts from the transcript of one episode in one discussion in which two Saudi Arabian students—Wadi and Halim (both pseudonyms)—and I discussed cultural differences. To make the transcript easier to follow, I have removed back-channeling comments and repeated or grammatically unnecessary words (replacing the latter two with ellipsis marks) from the data. I have not used capital letters at the beginning of turns or full-stops at the end of turns because, in a free flowing conversation, sentences are often incomplete. However, I have used capital letters and full stops within longer turns in an attempt to represent the sentential intonation used by the speaker.

The data is analyzed through the theoretical lens I have called *bakhtinian discourse analysis* (see Midgley, 2010). This approach focuses on the utterance as the unit of analysis. An utterance is a turn in a dialogic encounter, which is contingent upon the immediate content of the dialogue, the context of previous encounters with the utterances employed in the dialogue, and the utterances which are anticipated in some possible future response. Another distinctive of this bakhtinian approach is that specific bakhtinian concepts (such as the superaddressee) are used as lenses (Chase, 2005) to interpret the dialogic construction of meaning (Dop, 2000). Thus, in the analysis that follows, I read the transcript from my epic position (Whittemore, Chase, and Mandle, 2001) as one of those engaged in the dialogue and looking for the influence of superaddressees.

The data is broken into three excerpts, all from the same part of one conversation. In the first excerpt, Wadi begins by talking about something that he had recently been taught in a class on communication skills—that cultural differences are not bad just different.

Excerpt 1

Wadi: I'm involved in one course … now and that's about … communications skills, and I find that's very good for students. They teach … about … other cultures. So they told them that if you … see somebody doing anything [emphatic tone] don't think that's bad. No, it's their culture. You cannot say that's better than … our culture. It's different. Totally different

Wadi's assertion, that cultural differences are neither good nor bad is supported by what he had been taught in class, which I have discussed elsewhere as explicit authoritative discourse (see Midgley, 2010). This kind of discourse involves a version of truth that demands to be accepted as truth on the basis of the authority behind the truth claim. The authority behind this truth claim is the teacher as expert. This is evident in expressions such as "they teach" and "they told them."

Following on from this conversation about cultural differences, Wadi talks about his impression that Australian people do not like to talk to strangers. He gives as an example the fact that his home-stay family and neighbors do not communicate. This is evident in Excerpt 2, which begins 34 turns after the end of Excerpt 1, counting back-channeling. The turns in Excerpts 2 and 3 are numbered to facilitate discussion.

Excerpt 2

1 Wadi: the home-stay I live with … have neighbors and they said, "We don't know anything about them." They are their neighbors since 10 years or more than 10 years

2 Me: more than 10 years? [incredulous tone]

3 Wadi: yes [emphatic] and they don't know anything about their neighbors

4 Me: hmm, and that's very strange?

5 Wadi: yeah. Totally <u>different</u>. You know, I am living in my house and I have to know all the neighbors. I have to communicate with them. I have to invite them. If somebody sick, I have to visit them. If somebody want anything, I have to help. That's the difference. But here no it is different, totally different

Wadi's emphatic "yes" and the repetition of the assertion that the members of his home-stay family do not know anything about their neighbors (turn 3) expresses a degree of negative evaluation of the situation. The "different" (underlined in turn 5) is used by Wadi as a synonym for my "strange" of the previous turn (turn 4). This "different," repeated twice by Wadi in turn 5, has another meaning from the word "different" used by Wadi in Excerpt 1. To simplify, I have called the "different" in Excerpt 1 *different (neutral)* and I have called the "different" in Excerpt 2 *different (negative)*.

The degree of negativity in the evaluation expressed by the *different (negative)* remark is difficult for me to determine. It may simply have been "I do not understand" or "I find it hard to believe," or it may have been more judgmental (different = bad). Whichever it was, this use of the word "different" was not the same as its earlier usage in Excerpt 1, and this is further evidenced by the fact that, at the end of Excerpt 2, Wadi seems to become aware of the disjuncture himself. Before anybody else takes a turn, he attempts to negotiate a self-repair (numbering continues from Excerpt 2):

Excerpt 3

5   **Wadi:**   that is their culture I cannot say anything
6   **Me:**   (laugh) it's [emphatic tone] different you can say that
7   **Wadi:**   it is different
8 Halim: different, yeah
9   **Wadi:**   I cannot say it's bad or good or no. It's different

Half way through turn 5 (between Excerpt 2 and Excerpt 3), Wadi attempts to revert to the previous discourse with the words "I cannot say anything." Picking up on this cue for a switch, I laughed. I interpret this laugh as my acknowledgment that we—Wadi and I—had both strayed from the parameters of the *different (neutral)* explicit authoritative discourse of the earlier discussion. We had done what the teacher had taught Wadi we must not do. Although it was Wadi's story, as a participant in the dialogue I co-operated in the operation of the other *different (negative)* discourse, both with affirming back-channeling and through tone. My laugh was a non-linguistic way of saying, "We have been caught out." I then affirmed Wadi's switch by re-introducing the word "different" from Wadi's earlier recount of the *different (neutral)* discourse. Both Wadi and Halim joined in this dialogic move, with the almost mantra-like repetition of the word "different."

This episode highlights an intriguing question: How is it that the same people in the same place in the middle of the same conversation can accept something as true, then act (in speaking) as though it were not true, and then come back to affirm it as true again? In this episode, it is clear that Wadi, Halim, and I affirm our acceptance of the explicit authoritative discourse that cultural differences are not good or bad, just different. However, shortly thereafter, we begin a discussion which seems to indicate that we do not believe it to be true. In the middle of that discussion, we all correct ourselves and re-affirm the teaching as true.

This dialogic behavior can be explained using the concept of the superaddressee. I would suggest that, for some reason in the middle of turn 5, Wadi suddenly remembered that our conversation was being recorded for my research or (in a similar vein) that I was not just a friend having a chat, but a researcher collecting data. Throughout Excerpt 2, Wadi and I were speaking in the presence of a superaddressee, who agreed that never speaking with your neighbors was strange, incomprehensible, or wrong; that is to say *different (negative)*. In the middle of turn 5, another superaddressee became powerfully present in our conversation, and hence, like schoolchildren caught whispering in the corner, we quickly reverted back to what we were supposed to be talking about.

It is interesting to reflect upon the character of the superaddressee that was present throughout Excerpt 2. Clearly, the superaddressee agrees with Wadi and me, that it is strange for neighbors to not talk to each other. However, it is unlikely that we had exactly the same superaddressee in mind. In the course of this very episode, Wadi explained the importance of maintaining close relationships with neighbors in Saudi Arabia, so it is reasonable to presume that Wadi had in mind a Saudi superaddressee or at least a superaddressee who was familiar with and sympathetic to Saudi customs.

At the time of this discussion, I was completely unfamiliar with the Saudi customs regarding neighborly relationships. Therefore, we were not addressing exactly the same superaddressee. However, I had spent 12 of the 13 years prior to this discussion, living in Japan where maintaining strong relationships with neighbors is also highly valued. My superaddressee (who agreed with us both, that it was strange for the neighbors to know nothing about each other) was more likely to have been Japanese or someone familiar with, and sympathetic to Japanese customs.

Japanese and Saudi customs are, of course, quite different in many respects. However, in this respect (neighborly relations), they appear to be similar, and therefore Wadi and I were able to speak to different superaddressees and still come to agreement. While Wadi and I may not agree on many issues, as we continue to seek mutually agreeable superaddressees (which are not exactly the same, but do have some points of agreement), we may be better able to achieve the goal of getting to know one another.

IMPORTANCE FOR CREATING CONNECTIONS

The influence of powerfully present superaddressees in dialogue suggests important implications for educators seeking to create connections with various and diverse stakeholders. The examples given in this section are illustrations that represent possible applications of the theoretical concept of the superaddressee. They have not been empirically tested; rather, they have been extrapolated from the theory and data analysis outlined in the previous section.

The possible usefulness of understanding the concept of superaddressees for creating connections may be seen in the following hypothetical case. A teacher may explain the objectives of a learning activity to another teacher in terms of raising awareness. It may be that both teachers are addressing a superaddressee who advocates critical pedagogy, and therefore, for both of these teachers, the term *raising awareness* calls up theories, beliefs and values about which they share a common understanding. They may have different beliefs about the relative value of the theories or their applications to a specific context, but they are at least talking about more or less the same thing. A connection has been created through a common superaddressee.

However, if the same teacher attempts the same conversation with a parent who is unaware of theories relating to critical pedagogy, then it is less likely that the same type of connection will be made. The term *raising awareness* may carry for the teacher, deep and significant social justice implications; whereas, for the parent, it may imply learning the things their children need to know. The teacher and parent may continue to talk at cross-purposes because, while they appear to be talking to each other about the same thing, they are actually talking to quite different people (superaddressees) about quite different things. Indeed, it is possible that both the parties in this conversation could come away thinking that they are in agreement, when in fact there has been very little cognitive or conceptual connection at all.

Speaking in the presence of similar superaddressees, therefore, can be conceptualized as a mechanism for creating connections in dialogue (see also Midgley, Henderson, and Danaher, 2010). This does not necessarily mean that the two parties in the dialogue agree on everything; however, with similar superaddressees, the two parties stand a better chance of connecting on the basis of having a mutual understanding of the parameters of the dialogue and a common understanding of the concepts and terms being used. Likewise, speaking in the presence of superaddressees who are very dissimilar would tend to work against creating connections at a deeper level of understanding.

In order to use the concept of the superaddressee for effectively creating connections in dialogue, at least three possible applications suggest themselves. One is *listening for superaddressees*. This means that, as the listener/reader, we be attentive to cues in our interlocutor's utterances which indicate the kind of superaddressee who may be present. For example, the use of the word *conscientization* may indicate a superaddressee who advocates critical pedagogy as conceptualized by Freire (1970, 1970/1998). The use of other terms that are commonly used in discussions on critical pedagogy, such as *cultural action*, would further suggest the presence of such a superaddressee. Other cues to be attentive to might include making reference to the names of specific theories, experts, belief systems, and so on. Noticing these cues may provide an insight into the superaddressee to whom our interlocutor is speaking.

If we are able to identify the kind of superaddressee that is present in our interlocutor's mind, and we have some knowledge of a similar superaddressee, we would have a better chance to connect on the basis of common understandings, theoretically. One way of reinforcing this connection is by *acknowledging the superaddressees*. This may simply be through affirming back-channeling ("yes," "I know," "uh-huh," and so forth), or it may be more proactively enacted through the use of aligned cues. In the above example, my interlocutor may talk about conscientization and I may respond with the words: "yes, some kind of cultural action." If indeed my interlocutor is speaking in the presence of a superaddressee who endorses cultural pedagogy, then this kind of statement will affirm the presence of similar superaddressees.

The third process that might be employed in helping to create connections is *calling upon superaddressees*. This is perhaps the most difficult, because it requires some degree of guesswork as to which superaddressees might be potentially present in the thought worlds of our interlocutor. In this process, I as speaker would proactively employ cues such as key terms in such a way as to invite a common (or similar) superaddressee to join the dialogue. If my interlocutor is able to read the cues and is also willing to call upon a similar superaddressee, we can then engage in dialogue with some degree of shared understanding. Theoretically, this would also increase the chances of effectively creating connections in dialogue.

These three suggestions have arisen out of my reflections upon the role of the superaddressee as a theoretical concept, and also in the data analysis I have outlined in this chapter. I am not aware of any study that has sought to test the viability or usefulness of these approaches to effectively create connections, although the analysis and discussion summarized in this chapter suggest to me that this would be a useful area for further research.

CONCLUSION

In order to engage effectively with the various stakeholders involved in education and education research, creating connections in dialogue is essential. One mechanism for supporting and enhancing these connections is through being mindful of the presence and influence of superaddressees. The analysis of the data presented in this chapter points to the significant influence that superaddressees can play in dialogue. Understanding the significance of mutually recognizable and acceptable superaddressees may help overcome communication breakdowns and enhance the degree of shared understanding that can be achieved in dialogue. Three processes have been suggested as ways to attempt to employ that understanding to improve dialogue. These are listening for superaddressees, acknowledging superaddressees, and calling upon superaddressees. Proactively employing these processes in dialogues may help in the process of creating connections more effectively.

REFERENCES

Bakhtin, M. M. (1981). *The dialogic imagination: Four essays.* In C. Emerson & M. Holquist (Trans.). Austin, TX: University of Texas Press.

Bakhtin, M. M. (1986). *Speech genres and other late essays.* In M. Holquist & C. Emerson (Trans.). Austin, TX: University of Texas Press.

Bryzzheva, L. (2006). Superaddressee or who will succeed a mentor? *Studies in Philosophy and Education, 25*(3), 227–243.

Bryzzheva, L. (2008). Who watches over a teacher? On knowing and honoring a teacher and her third listener. *Educational Studies, 43*(3), 175–187.

Chase, S. E. (2005). Narrative inquiry: Multiple lenses, approaches, voices. In N. K. Denzin, & Y. S. Lincoln (Eds.), *The SAGE handbook of qualitative research* (3rd ed., pp. 651–680). Thousand Oaks, CA: Sage.

Clark, K., & Holquist, M. (1984). *Mikhail Bakhtin.* Cambridge, MA: Harvard University Press.

Dop, E. (2000). A dialogic epistemology: Bakhtin on truth and meaning. *Dialogism: An International Journal of Bakhtin Studies, 4,* 7–34.

Freire, P. (1970). *Pedagogy of the oppressed.* New York: The Seabury Press.

Freire, P. (1970/1998). Cultural action for freedom. *Harvard Educational Review, 68*(4), 471–521.

Midgley, W. (2010). *Seeking to understand the experiences of male Saudi Arabian nursing students at an Australian university.* Unpublished Doctor of Philosophy thesis, Toowoomba, Australia, University of Southern Queensland.

Midgley, W., Henderson, R., & Danaher, P. A. (2010). Seeking superaddressees: Research collaboration in a doctoral supervisory relationship. In C. Arden, P. A. Danaher, L. De George-Walker, R. Henderson, W. Midgley, K. Noble,

M. A. Tyler (Eds.), *Sustaining synergies: Collaborative research and researching collaboration* (pp. 87–102). Upper Mt Gravatt, Qld: Post Pressed.

Morson, G. S., & Emerson, C. (1990). *Mikhail Bakhtin: Creation of a prosaics.* Stanford, CA: Stanford University Press.

Whittemore, R., Chase, S. K., & Mandle, C. L. (2001). Validity in qualitative research. *Qualitative Health Research, 11*(4), 522–537.

CHAPTER 13

EFFECTIVE CLUSTER COLLABORATIONS: TRANSFORMATION THROUGH SCHOOL AND UNIVERSITY CONNECTIONS

Joan M. Conway and Lindy Abawi

University of Southern Queensland, Toowoomba,
Queensland, Australia

INTRODUCTION

Clusters of schools which allow conversations between participants from different contexts are a useful mechanism for creating connections for professional networking and learning among teacher professionals. In recent years, the creation of clusters—designed to deliver significant school revitalization—has strengthened connections across schools and education sectors Australia wide. The prospect of schools coming together, exchanging ideas, assisting each other and making connections for deeper learning and understandings is for many innovatory. Furthermore, the idea of teachers

Creating Connections in Teaching and Learning, pp. 165–176
Copyright © 2011 by Information Age Publishing
All rights of reproduction in any form reserved.

interacting with colleagues from across sectors, and leading professional conversations about pedagogical practice is refreshing and visionary of the leading teacher professional.

Teachers as leaders is a growing phenomenon of the 21st century teaching profession (Crowther, Ferguson, and Hann, 2009) and as teachers increasingly realize the benefits of collaboration in their quest for collective responsibility, the formation of clusters seems to be a logical movement. A *cluster* in this instance is the gathering of teachers from a number of schools that are engaged in school renewal. Clusters offer opportunities for teachers to meet with fellow professionals from other schools to make professional contacts, exchange pedagogical ideas, and interact with professionals connected by a shared purpose. This sets the scene for a rich networking formation, herein referred to as the cluster. Such clusters are integral to the school revitalization process called IDEAS (Innovative Designs for Enhancement of Achievement in Schools; see Crowther et al., 2002), as supported by the University of Southern Queensland's Leadership Research International team.

The IDEAS process engages schools in a developmental journey of self-discovery for the enhancement of pedagogy while simultaneously aligning action to the key elements of whole school organization (Andrews et al., 2004; Crowther et al., 2002). Clusters of schools engaged in the IDEAS process across Australia continue to benefit from the professional networking of teachers who are committed to enhancing pedagogy. This reinforces the need to focus "on teachers' beliefs and on how these beliefs shape school reform/restructuring attitudes, intentions, and actions" (Block & Hazelip, 1995, p. 25).

This chapter shares the co-authors' lived experiences and insights—from the perspectives of an external university-based facilitator and an internal school-based facilitator working within one of the cluster schools—into the benefits of cluster-based learning. Understandings gained by the co-authors' working with the school revitalization process of IDEAS (see Crowther et al., 2002) highlight the benefits of cluster collaboration as a vehicle for celebrating school successes, stimulating thinking, and refocusing action in positive and empowering ways. At times, the narratives shared are more than the views of the authors and include those of other cluster participants. This reflects the authors' deliberate intent to share the collaborative nature of the learning and professional transformation that took place.

LEADERSHIP WITHIN PROFESSIONAL LEARNING COMMUNITIES

It is apparent that educational research has contributed very positively over a substantial period of time to an understanding of the work of the individual teacher in creating and sustaining classroom effectiveness (Connolly & Clandinin, 1999; Seashore Louis & Marks, 1998). Indeed, some argue that a new age in education is now being led by teachers who have acquired deep understandings of how learning occurs and can be supported (Hattie, 2003; Moran, 2007). At the same time, it can be argued that appreciation for the characteristics and benefits of co-operative learning (Johnson & Johnson, 1999, 2004), coupled with growing understanding of the notion of professional learning communities (Seashore Louis & Marks, 1998; Wenger, 1999), has led to recognition of the importance of the teacher's role as a learner in his/her social context.

Recent findings from England (Swann et al., 2009) illustrate that the issues of professionalism and professional development among teachers are complex, but they are probably most dependent on a sense of commitment as key to teachers' professional identity (Day et al.,2007). However, Conway (2009) claimed that collective intelligence in schools "pushes the boundaries of teachers' work beyond the notion of teachers, engaging as individual players" (p. 243). It manifests as "a capacity to deal with discontinuous change within the unknown complexity of a 21st century institution," and "the capacity to generate significant new knowledge in response to temporal demands of the knowledge society" (p. 246).

In *The fifth discipline: The art and practice of the learning organization*, Senge (1990) identified the attributes of a learning organization and challenged the way organizations approach leadership and cultural and productivity issues. Educational leadership researchers (Hargreaves & Fink, 2003; Mulford, 2007) have continued to highlight the importance of nurturing staff through vision development, relationship building, and effective conflict resolution strategies. Andrews and Lewis (2007) found that "teachers work together in new ways, responding to challenges by collectively seeking solutions and developing new approaches that better meet the needs of their students" (pp. 145–146). Collaboration and a sense of the importance of the collective are promoted as outstanding features that prepare teams for change implementation. The Leadership Research International at the University of Southern Queensland has spotlighted that teacher leadership of change processes produces a sense of collective responsibility which results in effective pedagogical reform and is the key to school improvement (Andrews & Crowther, 2002; Crowther et al., 2009).

Holden (2008) reported that researchers at the University of Cambridge Faculty of Education have explored the notion of networking as "the relationships, norms, and values that characterize the work of the members of the network" (p. 308). This resulted in the recognition of an ongoing iterative process, where "the network is both a vehicle for and an outcome of the building and sharing of new knowledge" (p. 308). This finding provides a substantial backdrop to cluster experience as explored in this chapter.

Furthermore, Edge and Mylopolous (2008) purport from a recent study in Canada that "cross-school teacher leader networking presents significant opportunities for the teacher leaders to connect with colleagues, share personal and professional experiences, and develop their leadership and instructional expertise" (p. 147). It is this notion of networking that has similarly consolidated our view of the benefits of the cluster.

METHODOLOGY: PRESENTING DIFFERENT PERSPECTIVES

Our perspectives—as an external university-based facilitator and as an internal school-based facilitator—have been documented within this chapter as a means of capturing the richness of the lived experiences of those within such a cluster. Our dual perspectives are presented as separate lived experiences within a hermeneutic phenomenological research approach (van Manen, 1997), and the combined essence of these has been captured in the conclusion to highlight the multi-faceted benefits of networking in a cluster.

The object of human science research is essentially a meaning-making exercise, which aims "to make some aspect of our lived world, of our experience, reflectively understandable, and intelligible" (van Manen, 1997, pp. 125–126). As the authors of this chapter, we believe that a reflective professional discourse delivers a heightened level of consciousness that enriches understandings about the worth of a school revitalization process via a cluster format. Schrag (1988, as cited in Lanigan, 1992) elaborates heightened consciousness as "a rhetorical consciousness, stitched into the very warp and woof of the multiple forms of discourse and action, which in concert occasion a hermeneutical reference to the world, a hermeneutical self-implicature of the subject and a disclosure of the other" (p. 180).

A further dimension to this reflective understanding might be gleaned from the work of Agee (2002), in her support of a multilayered picture of the participants' lived experiences. In light of Agee's metaphor of unraveling to show "the potential to enrich findings and theorizing about the complex connections that inform the lives of those we study" (p. 583), we have endeavored to illustrate the richness of cluster collaboration. Within clusters of schools engaged with the IDEAS process, teachers with other teachers from different schools, and teachers with university researchers, engage in a significant meaning-making process (Conway, 2009). We argue that this meaning-making process is directly linked to the quality of the professional conversations that occur.

Developing the art of professional conversation is vital to the success of the IDEAS process and as demonstrated by Isaacs (1999), dialogue is more than just the exchange of words. It is the art of thinking together when different points of view are embraced. This becomes the heart of quality learning communities, providing a space "where people continually expand their capacity to create the results they truly desire, where new and expansive patterns of thinking are nurtured, where collective aspirations are set free, and where people are continually learning how to learn together" (Senge, 1990, p. 3).

Our stance of taking an emic posture and choosing to interpret the lived experience of teaching practitioners in their life world, celebrates the worth of quality interpretations and the reflective practices of teacher professionals. The anecdotes and interpretations of our lived experiences are presented as two separate vignettes in the first person. This presentation then forms the data base from which significant benefits of cluster collaboration can be concluded.

THE UNIVERSITY-BASED FACILITATOR'S PERSPECTIVE

As a university member of the IDEAS team, I (the university-based facilitator and chapter co-author) provide external facilitation in support of the process as adopted by the schools in search of school revitalization. I adopt the multifaceted role of being the initial expert of the knowledge underpinning the process, as well as the workshop facilitator for the guidance of each school's development of the process (Crowther et al., 2002). Furthermore, as the school's visitor, I become a mentor and a critical friend of the IDEAS School Management Team and in so doing, the opportunity for co-research (Erwee & Conway, 2006) in the ongoing conceptual and practical development of the IDEAS process becomes a reality.

Erwee and Conway (2006) use the concept of co-research in recognition of the multidimensional roles of external university researchers and internal school-based researchers, where "each person's value is acknowledged, regardless of their experience or expertise ... mind-sets and conceptual maps changed. They became willing to learn from one another" (p. 181). As the external facilitator and a university researcher, I continually take the vantage point of learning from the school participants as they ask questions, seek answers, reflect on their school's needs, and increasingly demonstrate, a commitment to knowing their context and consequently meeting their challenges.

In recalling the experience of facilitating within a number of schools in a large regional city, it became evident that there were major benefits to be gained, when school facilitators, principals and other staff members gathered several times a year to share their ongoing development of the process within their schools. Their increasing confidence and ability to network, and gain from these meetings grew exponentially, as illustrated by the following comments of various school-based personnel:

> We find it boring to talk about housekeeping stuff at meetings now—to talk about our profession is more common and more meaningful.

> Relationships with other zealots are at a wonderfully productive and professional level—we say things that others are thinking.

> I enjoy the dimensions that critical evaluation adds to our job; I became a teacher because I wanted a job that occupied my mind—this process has renewed that belief.

Although each school was visited individually for the benefit of monitoring and supporting the ongoing development of the process, it soon became evident that the cluster meetings were a major forum for the schools as they gathered informally to share their experiences, learn from one another, and bolster flagging confidences. This occurred as they simultaneously celebrated and further grappled with how best to develop the process, pertinent to their school's needs. It also became a major source of fulfillment from both external and internal perspectives when school-based personnel gradually took on the responsibility of organizing and leading these cluster meetings. In the midst of one such gathering, one member was heard to say in response to my input, alongside all others present, "Oh! We forgot you were there—that is good." There was definitely an increasing awareness amongst the school-based personnel, that they were able to share their significant meaning in ownership of the developing process within each of their schools.

> I am not sure what this means for "shared meanings" except that perhaps we need to frequently revisit and re-share, the understandings that we reach as a group at different junctions—in fact, a meaning may emerge at one point and be forgotten by the group, until it is really crucial at a different time.

Furthermore, I observed and interpreted that the teachers were increasingly empowered by the opportunities to share their insights and to gain from those of others:

> I think one cannot underestimate the power of a group of people having fun with the work of IDEAS and the energy that comes from working together with good humor and patience with each other.

> We have all come back from the cluster meetings and got inspired about something and got excited. That is something that has been really impressive to me. The cluster meetings have been really good value. Just when it is flagging at school, you go there and you come away excited.

The significance of the professional conversation skills being practiced and honed during these cluster meetings was also an enlightenment that reinforced for me the power of dialogue in a professional learning community. Together there were many instances of realizing the importance of professional conversation, both for themselves within the cluster meetings, and as a powerful tool for their school community.

> Sometimes it's been X that's put this thing out there, and another time Y has put up something, and then we've all played with it. There've been some amazing processes and discussions.

It became increasingly obvious that the story of the other, shared in person by the other, was more powerful as a benchmark for progress, than the retelling of the story by me or any other external support personnel. The authenticity of the story could not be disputed, and there was an economy of scale when the stories of each school were heard and discussed together.

An increasing sense of collegiality built through collaboration and a sense of importance of the collective emerged as outstanding features of the effective cluster, where teachers across schools developed a high level of relationship trust (Bryk & Schneider, 2002) and respect for each others' work.

THE SCHOOL-BASED FACILITATOR'S PERSPECTIVE

As the school-based facilitator and chapter co-author, I provide the following reflections. These offer a melding of my own experiences, recorded in a learning journal, with the insights from cluster colleagues, taken from a collegial brainstorming activity undertaken by the group during the preparation of a conference presentation. I became involved in cluster meetings at the beginning of the 2nd year of my school's IDEAS journey, when one of the school's key facilitators was transferred to another school. My first meeting with the whole cluster group proved fairly overwhelming, as I realized the extent to which I had committed myself to be one step ahead of my staff. I lacked confidence in my ability to help lead the process within my school, and I felt constrained by my lack of knowledge. Even the ice breakers of food and drink at these early meetings failed to render me comfortable.

However, this uncertainty did not last. As my familiarity with the members of the cluster group grew, I heard many echoes of this experience in the words of other school facilitators:

> I must admit I did not feel I belonged in this group—I often wondered "what was I thinking?" I would have never thought of myself as a teacher leader.

> It was so refreshing to be a part of the cluster group, because the educators were enthusiastic and excited by what was happening in their schools. Uncertainties were shared, difficulties raised, and small victories or insights celebrated, the sense of belonging to our cluster became very strong.

Meetings were held in different schools, allowing for greater understanding of the context, and the easy sharing of materials and ideas. Although the university team resource materials served as models, it was the way in which each school adapted and developed these, that provided the school facilitators with the confidence to innovate. What evolved was a competitive slant to these show-and-tell meetings, with no facilitator wanting to appear uncreative or ineffective in front of his/her peers. This was an exciting experience, and confidence grew as each new challenge was undertaken. As an entry in my learning journal stated:

> My co-facilitator spoke to me this afternoon to explain that he is finding it more and more difficult to spend the time on the IDEAS stuff because his role as our IT [information technology] guru is becoming overwhelming. He is willing to help me ... but is no longer able to contribute to cluster meetings or host meetings at our school ... I am surprised by my reaction! I relied on him being there when I took on the facilitator role and yet, as much as I will miss him, I actually no longer need him. The cluster people are there if I need them!

Each school team, while striving to make improvements within their own community, learned together and inspired each other to maintain focus and direction within the process and to adhere to key timelines. The strong sense of empowerment, that came into being as teachers shared professional conversations in a no-blame environment (Andrews et al., 2004), had developed a rich professional learning community (Hord, 1997). In my learning journal, I noted:

> Looking at our school's data was pretty disappointing at first, but adhering to the no-blame policy—that was pretty well accepted now—meant that we could see which year-level teachers needed support, and in which areas. There was a real sense of what "we" can do to improve. The great thing is by sharing our areas of concern with others in the cluster our principals have decided to pool their resources and we are going to do some combined professional development around micro-skilling, as so many of our problems were issues for others as well.

The resonances between our collective understandings gave a sense of energy and substance to our cluster experience. There had developed a real appreciation of what was evolving within our cluster. My learning journal states:

> When I have something exciting to share or a problem that needs heads other than mine ... there are people who give this support.

No matter how much we wanted "the answers" to be given, we had to find "our" answers. It has been fascinating to see how our answers aren't the same as the answers of others.

The complexities of questions and variety of answers emerging within the group are taking our learning as a collective into heights, breadths, and depths I have never before experienced.

By the time the formal 3 year involvement with the university support was complete, the relationships for some within the cluster had morphed into something contextually-relevant and valuable. Although university staff remained as friends and mentors who could be called upon for advice, a self-sustaining learning community had evolved. Presentations by combined school coalitions became the norm, and the role of critical friend and confidante added a uniquely powerful dimension and further value for this diverse group of teaching professionals. Several entries in my learning journal demonstrate my view of this productive collaboration:

There were so many people within the 2003 cluster group that supported my learning journey. They opened up new perspectives, pointed to new possibilities, encouraged and believed in me. It is just great, that many of us still meet. I really look forward to the sharing that continues to occur.

I look back at my experiences as an IDEAS cluster member, and realize what a significant part of my professional development occurred within the safety of this group. I developed leadership skills and facilitation skills that I had no idea I possessed. The trust and responsibility given to me by my principal and my peers was an honor—at times a burden. However, I learned not to use my insecurities as an excuse, but rather as a challenge to learn more. Our cluster group is bonded with lingering ties never to be broken.

CONCLUSION

Even though each context was unique, the shared understandings through involvement in the revitalization process created a common cluster language or meaning system, which allowed for collective comprehension and the quick uptake of new knowledge. The key to knowledge creation is a sense of collective responsibility resulting in effective pedagogical reform, and the capacity for sustainable school improvement (Andrews & Crowther, 2002; Crowther et al., 2009).

School personnel within the cluster found that the changes within leadership, and the decision-making structures had a direct influence on the culture of each school. Transparent decision-making practices, adherence to professional conversation protocols, and the establishment of an inclusive culture, engendered a sense of empowerment within staff. Over a period of time, cluster contact and interaction was a major contributor to growth in teacher efficacy.

The effectiveness of teacher leaders as facilitators was clearly established, and this further supports the notion that:

> Traditional leadership approaches have had little, if any, direct or sustained impact on organizational effectiveness. The notion of the leader as a visionary champion, who is able to drive through change and improvement is one that has been shown to be fundamentally flawed. (Harris, 2003, p. 76)

Shared leadership has the potential to achieve outstanding and long-lasting results, which are not dependent on one champion. This is best illustrated through the concept of parallel leadership, where the teacher leaders and administrative leaders collaborate through "three intersecting processes—namely holistic professional learning, distinctive culture-building, and schoolwide pedagogical development" (Crowther et al., 2009, p. 54).

The emergent strength within the cluster, as individuals increasingly sought each others' professional company, illustrates a theory of professional development that begins to debunk the myths of difficulty and complexity, which surrounds the ongoing dilemma of organizing effective professional development for teachers. In spite of the differences between schools and individuals, the lived experiences as presented in this chapter, herald the possibility of an explanatory model of professional development, characterized by continual individual and collective strengthening.

A reciprocity of growth, capturing what has been, and creating anew with the increasing ease of ebbing and flowing during "reflection-in-action" (Schon, 1983, p. 62), further awakens the place that reflection-in-action plays, in clarifying the meaning and enabling the possibilities for shared understandings to be made in a collaborative environment. As individuals are brought to a realization of how to reflect-in-action, the higher levels of shared meaning, in a collective sense, become more apparent. In so doing, individuals select to use a shared language, enabling others to see their meaning, share their experiences, accept critique, and further evaluate their new knowledge. This ultimately transforms collegial understandings and relationships, while presenting opportunities for individual growth and school improvement.

Within schools, teachers were reassured by the fact that their facilitators (their colleagues) really knew the joys and strains of teaching in their context. Within the school cluster, the professionalism of the group inspired admiration, and lasting professional connections. Between the schools and the university, a culture of collegial trust and hope emerged. This dissipated the myths of the external expert/researcher collecting data to meet the needs of his/her own agenda, and never adding value to the school. Overall, the strength of the cluster, as a vehicle for creating connections of professional worth for school and university communities, cannot be underestimated. In the quest to improve student outcomes, the schools-university partnership proved an effective means of transforming school cultures by developing teacher leadership, building collegial relationships, making meaning, and sharing responsibility for school revitalization.

ACKNOWLEDGMENTS

The authors wish to thank the many teachers who have contributed to this chapter. Their engagement in meaningful conversations about their journeys of discovery have enlightened and enriched our lives, with the hope that other teachers might seek collective responsibility for new ways of thinking and acting as 21st century professional teachers.

REFERENCES

Agee, J. (2002). "Winks upon winks": Multiple lenses on settings in qualitative educational research. *International Journal of Qualitative Studies in Education, 15*(5), 569–585.

Andrews, D., Conway, J. M., Dawson, M., Lewis, M., McMaster, J., Morgan, A., & Starr, H. (2004). *School revitalisation the IDEAS way* [ACEL Monograph Series 34]. Melbourne: ACEL.

Andrews, D., & Crowther, F. (2002). Parallel leadership: A clue to the contents of the "black box" of school reform. *The International Journal of Educational Management, 16*(4), 152–159.

Andrews, D., & Lewis, M. (2007). Transforming practice from within: The power of the professional learning community. In L. Stoll & K. Seashore Louis (Eds.), *Professional learning communities: Divergence, depth and dilemmas* (pp. 132–147). New York: McGraw Hill Open University Press.

Block, J. H., & Hazelip, K. (1995). Teachers' beliefs and belief systems. In L. Anderson (Ed.), *International encyclopedia of teaching and teacher education Queensland* (pp. 161–186). Cambridge, UK: Cambridge University.

Bryk, A. S., & Schneider, B. (2002). *Trust in schools: A core resource for improvement*. New York: Russell Sage Foundation.

Connolly, F. M., & Clandinin, D. J. (Eds.). (1999). *Shaping a professional identity: Stories of educational practice*. New York: Teachers College Press.

Conway, J. M. (2009). *Collective intelligence in schools: An exploration of teacher engagement in the making of significant new meaning*. Saarbrucken: VDM Verlag Dr Muller.

Crowther, F., Andrews, D., Dawson, M., & Lewis, M. (2002). *Innovative designs for enhancing achievements in schools: Facilitation folder*. Toowoomba, Qld: LRI.

Crowther, F., Ferguson, M., & Hann, L. (2009). *Developing teacher leaders* (2nd ed.). Thousand Oaks, CA: Corwin Press.

Day, C., Sammons, P., Stobart, G., Kington, A., & Gu, Q. (2007). *Teachers matter: Connecting lives, work and effectiveness*. Maidenhead, UK: Open University Press.

Edge, K., & Mylopoulos, M. (2008). Creating cross-school connections: LC networking in support of leadership and instructional development. *School Leadership & Management, 28*(2), 147–158.

Erwee, R., & Conway, J. M. (2006). Cocreation of knowledge: Roles of coresearchers in research teams. *The Educational Forum, 70*(2), 171–184.

Hargreaves, A., & Fink, D. (2003). Sustaining leadership. *Phi. Delta Kappan, 84*(9), 693–700.

Harris, A. (2003). Teacher leadership and school improvement. In A. Harris, C. Day, M. Hadfield, D. Hopkins, A. Hargreaves, & C. Chapman (Eds.), *Effective leadership for school improvement* (pp. 72–83). London: RoutledgeFalmer.

Hattie, J. (2003). *Teachers make a difference: What is the research evidence?* Paper presented at the annual conference of the Australian Council for Educational Research, Melbourne, Victoria.

Holden, G. (2008). Knowledge-building and networking: The leadership for learning case. *School Leadership & Management, 28*(4), 307–322.

Hord, S. (1997). *Professional learning communities of continuous inquiry and improvement*. Austin, TX: Southwest Educational Development Lab.

Isaacs, W. N. (1999). *Dialogue and the art of thinking together*. New York: Currency.

Johnson, D. W., & Johnson, R. T. (1999). Making cooperative learning work. *Theory into Practice, 38*(2), 67–73.

Johnson, D. W., & Johnson, R. T. (2004). This issue. *Theory into Practice, 43*(1), 3–5.

Lanigan, R. L. (1992). *The human science of communicology: A phenomenology of discourse in Foucault and Merleau-Ponty*. Pittsburgh, PA: Duquesne University Press.

Moran, M. J. (2007). Collaborative action research and project work: Promising practices for developing collaborative inquiry among early childhood preservice teachers. *Teaching and Teacher Education, 23*(4), 418–431.

Mulford, B. (2007). Building social capital in professional learning communities: Importance, challenges and a way forward. In L. Stoll & K. Seashore Louis (Eds.), *Professional Learning communities: Divergence, depth and dilemmas* (pp. 167–180). New York: McGraw-Hill Open University Press.

Schon, D. A. (1983). *The reflective practitioner*. New York: Basic Books.

Seashore Louis, K., & Marks, H. M. (1998). Does professional community affect the classroom? Teachers' work and student experiences. *American Journal of Education, 106*(4), 532–575.

Senge, P. M. (1990). *The fifth discipline: The art and practice of the learning organization*. New York: Currency Doubleday.

Swann, M., McIntyre, D., Pell, T., Hargreaves, L., & Cunningham, M. (2009). Teachers' conceptions of teacher professionalism in England in 2003 and 2006. *British Educational Research Journal, 36*(4), 549–571.

van Manen, M. (1997). *Researching lived experience: Human science for an action sensitive pedagogy* (2nd ed.). London, Ontario: The Althouse Press.

Wenger, E. (1999). *Communities of practice: Learning, meaning, and identity*. Cambridge, UK: Cambridge University Press.

CHAPTER 14

LINKING PEDAGOGICAL DOCUMENTATION TO PHENOMENOLOGICAL RESEARCH

Laurie Kocher

Douglas College, New Westminster, British Columbia, Canada

INTRODUCTION

The original research for this chapter was based on the case study of a teacher, Ann, who was located in Seattle, Washington. The teacher worked with the practice of pedagogical documentation, a way of making visible the learning processes of children and teachers through narrative forms of observation, developed in the early childhood programs of Reggio Emilia. The Reggio Emilia practice of observing and documenting in pre-schools is described by Reggio pedagogue Rinaldi (2006) as a "listening made visible as traces of the learning event in written notes, photographs, and videos, and so forth" (p. 68). The documentation serves as a way of publically sharing the learning experiences of teachers and children, as well as a form of teacher research.

Creating Connections in Teaching and Learning, pp. 177–189
Copyright © 2011 by Information Age Publishing

Seeking to understand what enabled the teacher to embrace this documentation work within her own American context, I explored the following research question: Do some teachers demonstrate particular attributes that foster a disposition to document? As I worked closely with Ann, I recognized that much in the way she described her experience as a documenter resonated with the work of Canadian phenomenologist Max van Manen (1991, 1997, 2002). I discovered that Ann's documentation of her lived experience with children, in the day-to-day encounters of her classroom setting, and the ways in which she talked about how that experience affected her meshed well with van Manen's description of the work of the phenomenological researcher.

IN THE BEGINNING

I was first introduced to the early childhood programs of Reggio Emilia through viewing the travelling exhibition *The hundred languages of children* (Municipality of Reggio Emilia Infant-Toddler Centers and Preschools, 1996). The pre-schools of Reggio Emilia are recognized internationally with the popular press magazine *Newsweek* (Kantrowitz & Wingert, 1991) acclaiming them as "the best in the world." This grand exhibit is a visual documentary of the pedagogical approach developed in this town in northern Italy, and weaves together experiences, reflections, debates, theoretical premises, and the social and ethical ideas of many generations of teachers, children, and parents. The exhibit, which itself is a collection of pieces of pedagogical documentation, presented primarily in the form of large panels, consists mainly of photographs "depicting moments of teaching and learning, explanatory scripts and panels (many containing texts of children's words), and samples of children's paintings, drawings, collages, and constructions" (Edwards, Gandini, and Forman, 1998, p. 10). Through this encounter with the pedagogy of Reggio Emilia, I was impressed by the way the educators seemed to know their children so intimately and how they had such passion for their work with them.

Inspired by this work and by my study of the ever-evolving Reggio Emilia philosophy of education, I chose to focus my doctoral research on the impact of the practice of pedagogical documentation on a particular teacher (Ann), working at a children's centre in Seattle, Washington. I was curious to know what, if anything, sustained this passion in educators. The question I set out to investigate was: Do some educators demonstrate particular attributes that foster a disposition to document?

The methodology for this study included my immersion as a participant-observer over a number of months in Ann's classroom. This gave me the opportunity to understand more fully the rhythms and routines of the day and the relationships that were built amongst the children and the families.

It also meant that I could have first-hand experience of a number of the instances that were documented by Ann and shared them with her co-teachers and the children's families. Ann had amassed a great archive of documented daily vignettes, in addition to dozens of history books that documented longer-term project work. All of this was made available to me, as were the personal journals created by Ann, of a number of children. Given this reference of immersion into the working of the classroom and having read so much of Ann's documentation, I was then able to have a series of four, 2 hour long interviews with her. These interviews which were transcribed by me, gave an additional opportunity to revisit what Ann had to say about her work. In those conversations, which were loosely structured around some "grand tour" questions, a number of significant themes emerged. These helped me to understand Ann's passion for pedagogical documentation more fully. Much of what is included in this chapter comes from those substantive conversations.

Along the pathway of my doctoral journey, I discovered the work of Canadian phenomenologist Max van Manen (1991, 1997, 2002). As I delved into his work, I identified some connections between my personal experiences of working with pedagogical documentation, the stories teachers such as Ann told me about their practice of documentation, and the way that van Manen writes about phenomenology. Put simply, van Manen (1997) writes that "phenomenology aims at gaining a deeper understanding of the nature or meaning of our everyday experiences" (p. 9). This, I have come to believe is what Ann is doing as she uses pedagogical documentation to make children's learning visible. These are the connections that I want to highlight throughout this chapter.

In what follows, I will briefly describe the fundamental principles of the Reggio Emilia approach. I will also more fully explain what pedagogical documentation is and how it is rooted in an understanding of what Reggio educators call "a pedagogy of listening" (Dahlberg & Moss, 2005, p. 97). Further, I will explain briefly what phenomenological methodology is and why it is relevant to this study. I will highlight the connections via the interweaving of Ann's voice with van Manen's observations of the phenomenological researcher, leading to how I determine that, in Ann's case, pedagogical documentation can be thought of as a phenomenological act.

FUNDAMENTAL PRINCIPLES OF THE REGGIO EMILIA APPROACH

The Reggio Emilia approach to early childhood education is based on a comprehensive philosophy that is underpinned by several fundamental guiding principles. These principles should be considered a tightly woven, integrated, systemic philosophy in which each principle reflexively influences and is influenced by all of the other principles (Gandini, 1998). The key tenets of the Reggio Emilia approach are not carved in stone but rather should be considered as essential guidelines to the underlying Reggio Emilia philosophy. The following six principles represent a synopsis of what has been named by the educators in Reggio Emilia, as the philosophy's fundamental guidelines: the child as a protagonist, collaborator, and communicator; the teacher as a partner, nurturer, guide, and researcher; co-operation as the foundation of the educational system; the environment as the "third teacher"; the parent as a partner; and documentation as communication (Cadwell, 2003; Edwards et al., 1998; Gandini, 1993; Spaggiari, 1998).

In several empirical studies of the early 1990s, researchers (Gandini, 1993; Katz, 1990; Malaguzzi, 1993; New, 1990) agreed that the Reggio Emilia philosophy was based primarily on relationships. Katz (1990) provided first hand qualitative observations and research insights in her description of the origins of the Reggio Emilia approach, educational results generated in Italy, and implications regarding successful adaptation in other cultures. She explained that Reggio Emilia pre-schools are part of a public system that strives to serve children's welfare and the social needs of families, while supporting children's fundamental right to grow and learn in favorable environments, with key relationships that include co-operative peers and caring, professional adults. As part of this co-operative effort, Reggio Emilia educators teach together for many years with different groups of children, discuss experiences in their classrooms, share documentation, and plan future classroom experiences. Children are taught by a pair of teachers and remain in the same classroom for 3 years in a looping arrangement which provides time and continuity of experience, in trusting supportive environments for teaching and learning (Moran, 1998).

In 1991, *Newsweek* magazine proclaimed the pre-schools of Reggio Emilia, Italy, to be "the best in the world" (Kantrowitz & Wingert, 1991). It was claimed that the three tenets of communication, exploration and problem solving complement one another and are paramount in these schools. Together, they form the underpinnings of a robust and collaborative early-childhood education paradigm.

PEDAGOGICAL DOCUMENTATION

The educators of Reggio Emilia recognized early in their history that documenting their work with children in a systematic way would simultaneously serve three vital functions. Edwards, Gandini and Forman (1998) explain that it would provide:

- the children with a concrete and "visible" memory of what they said and did, and this could then serve as a jumping-off point for the next steps in learning;

- the educators with a tool for research;
- parents and the public with detailed information about what happens in schools, potentially eliciting their support. (pp. 10–12)

This practice of pedagogical documentation, then, refers to the process of an educator's observing, recording and, individually and collectively with colleagues, interpreting encounters, discoveries, exchanges, and ordinary moments selected from classroom practice. This could include children's conversations, children's work, and teachers' dialogues with children. Documentation is understood as "making learning visible" (see Giudici, Krechevsky, and Rinaldi, 2001)—for the educators, for the families, for the public, and for anyone who has an interest in education and young children. Educators see themselves as observers and researchers in their everyday work with children and in the pedagogical documentation they create as a component of their research. They regularly, throughout the day, make careful observations, documenting their observations with notes, photographs, audiotapes, videotapes, diaries, and other narrative forms. This practice is considered an essential part of their teaching; it is not considered an additional or onerous task. The process is ongoing and cyclical, and it is based on the art of critical reflection by a community of learners that includes researchers, educators, children, and their families (for further reading, see Kocher & Pacini-Ketchabaw, 2011).

Dahlberg, Moss, and Pence (2007) describe pedagogical documentation as two related subjects: a process and important content in that process. The content includes material which records what the children are saying and doing, and how the teacher relates to the children and their work. The process involves the use of the documented material as a means to "reflect upon the pedagogical work and to do so in a very rigorous, methodical and democratic way" (pp. 147–148).

PEDAGOGY OF LISTENING

At the very heart of the educational approach of Reggio Emilia is the art of listening. Listening is understood quite particularly in Reggio Emilia to be a complex and multi-faceted concept, based on an active relationship that is "dialogic and interpretive" (Dahlbert & Moss, 2005, p. 99). Close listening is so highly valued that practitioners coined the term "pedagogy of listening." Carlina Rinaldi (2001) defines her understanding of listening as:

listening not just with our ears, but with all our senses ... welcoming and being open to differences, recognizing the importance of the other's point of view and interpretation ... an active verb that involves interpretation, giving meaning to the message and value to those who offer it ... requiring a deep awareness. (pp. 79–80)

One of the primary tasks of pedagogical documentation is to make the pedagogy of listening visible, through producing traces or documents that show the learning of both children and educators. It is a narrative form with many similarities to the view of pedagogy that Readings (1996) calls "an infinite attention to the other" (p. 16).

PHENOMENOLOGICAL METHODOLOGY

It is van Manen's (1997) perspective that "pedagogy requires a phenomenological sensitivity to lived experience ... and pedagogy requires a way with language, in order to allow the research process of textual reflection to contribute to pedagogical thoughtfulness and tact" (p. 2). This is the essence of what pedagogical documentation does.

Phenomenology studies the structure of various types of experience, ranging from perception, thought, memory, imagination, emotion, desire and volition, to bodily awareness, embodied action and social activity, including linguistic activity. The structure of these forms of experience typically involves intentionality; that is, the directedness of experience toward things in the world, the property of consciousness that it is a consciousness of or about something. Thus, phenomenology leads from conscious experience into conditions that help to give experience its intentionality (Smith, 1997).

The term *phenomenology* is a compound of the Greek words *phainomenon* and *logos*. It signifies the activity of giving an account, a logos, of various phenomena, of the various ways in which things can appear (Sokolowski, 2000). In other words, the researcher tries to identify the lived experiences of participants directly involved with the phenomena under investigation. Phenomenology has been applied in two ways: first, in a philosophical sense where one tries to understand it as a logical process of thinking about the world, and second as a methodology "that attempts to use the attitude of phenomenology to construct patterns of research that reveal lived formations of meaning" (Brown, 1991, p. 18). Van Manen (1997) suggests that phenomenology may also be considered a profoundly reflective inquiry into human meaning: "The aim of phenomenology is to transform lived experience into a textual expression of its essence—in such a way, that the effect of the text is at once a reflexive re-living and a reflective appropriation of something meaningful" (p. 36).

The focus of phenomenology is toward illuminating details and seemingly trivial aspects within experience that may be taken for granted in our lives, with a goal of creating meaning and achieving a sense of understanding (Wilson & Hutchinson, 1991). According to Smith (1997), this is a "research methodology aimed at producing rich textual descriptions of the experiencing of selected phenomena in the life-world of individuals that are able to connect with the experience of all of us collectively" (p. 80). From the identification of the experience of the phenomena, a deeper understanding of the meaning of that experience is sought. This occurs through increasingly deeper and layered reflection by the use of rich descriptive language.

Hermeneutic phenomenology can be understood as a process of co-creation between the researcher and participant (Hertz, 1997). The very production of meaning occurs through a circle of readings, reflective writing, and interpretations. In the case of pedagogical documentation, this co-creation takes place between documenter/writer and reader. Hermeneutic research demands self-reflexivity, an ongoing conversation about the experience while simultaneously living in the moment, actively constructing interpretations of the experience, and questioning how those interpretations came about (Hertz, 1997). Pedagagogical documentation, as described above, is one way in which a hermeneutic circle can be engaged, moving back and forth between the parts and the whole of the text. It is this approach that is captured in the story of Ann.

FINDING CONNECTIONS

Van Manen (1997) suggests that phenomenological inquiry cannot be separated from the practice of writing. This is, to put it simply, where the primary connection between pedagogical documentation and the work of the phenomenological practitioner becomes evident. In terms of pedagogical documentation in the working of writing and reading text, one could ask with van Manen (1997), "How can we invent in the text a certain space, a perspective wherein the pedagogic voice which speaks for the child, can let itself be heard?" (p. 153).

As I worked alongside Ann in this research study, it became apparent that something moving and profound does happen in the act of phenomenological writing. This was particularly apparent in the writing that she does as a documenter. As van Manen (1997) explains, phenomenological writing "encourages a certain attentive awareness to the details and seemingly trivial dimensions of our everyday educational lives. It makes us thoughtfully aware of the consequential in the inconsequential, the significant in the taken-for-granted" (p. 8). Whether it is recording some of the ordinary moments that together create a picture of life lived in community in the children's center, or the documentation that follows the unfolding of project work, it is this attentive awareness to detail that draws the reader/observer into the experience.

It is important to point out that Ann expresses comfort with the skill of writing, saying "it is my natural language." Still, it is also helpful to be reminded that phenomenological writing is based on the idea, that no text is ever perfect; no interpretation is ever complete; no explication of meaning is ever final; no insight is beyond challenge. Merleau-Ponty (1973) speaks of phenomenological writing as a poetizing project, a language that "sings the world" (p. 186). Elsewhere, Merleau-Ponty (1962) shows that turning to the phenomena of lived experience, means re-learning to look at the world by "re-awakening the basic experience of the world" (p. 8). Thus, no meaning can be understood as absolute, but rather continually open to new and unfolding understanding.

INTERWEAVING IDEAS

By interweaving quotes from van Manen (1997) and Ann, I now make connections between the practice of pedagogical documentation and the orientation of a phenomenological researcher. To illuminate this connection, the evocative tone of pedagogical documentation is illustrated in Exhibit 14.1, which also captures the essence of lived experience in the phenomenological sense.

In one of our interviews, Ann describes her documentation work and how she finds it nourishing, on both intellectual and emotional levels:

> My work with children and families fills a big piece of my life and my heart. I am deeply nourished by the relationships with children, families, and co-workers that are at the center of my days at school, relationships full of joy, honesty, belly laughter, and soulfulness. My writing about teaching also feeds me; the act of articulating the thinking and feeling that shapes my work, deepens my awareness and my practice.

The theoretical practice of phenomenological research stands in the service of the mundane practice of pedagogy; it is a "ministering of thoughtfulness" (van Manen, 1997, p. 12). This attentive practice of thoughtfulness emerges in Ann's pedagogical documentation. She continues by saying:

> It's hard to even find words for it because it's such a heart-level experience … it is exactly what I want to be doing, and if I can't be doing that, then I don't want to be doing this work.

Exhibit 14.1. Example of pedagogical documentation displayed in Ann's classroom.

> *So much tenderness and joy today as children reveled in their friendships back from winter break. Kids excitedly showed each other treasures from Christmas—a new backpack, a Scooby-Doo umbrella, a stuffed unicorn, a stuffed horse. They hugged each other with joyful exuberance, often ending up on the floor rolling over and over each other like puppies. Kids told each other, "I missed you!" And "I'm glad to see you," and "Let's hurry up and play!" Children played this morning with dear friends as well as with folks they do not usually hang out with—just relishing each other's company and their community of relationships. At nap time this afternoon, Melia said, snuggling into her blankets, "I'm tired out from all that fun today." That's just how the day felt—a full-hearted, physical, joyful celebration of relationships and love. ~Ann*

There is a sense of resonance, a heart-felt connection with Ann's experience of living and working with children in an authentic, intentional way. Van Manen's (1997) seminal work, *Researching lived experience*, comes to mind here again as he describes phenomenological research:

> to know the world is to profoundly *be in the world* ... the act of researching ... is the intentional act of attaching ourselves to the world, to become fully part of it, or better, to become the world. Phenomenology calls this inseparable connection to the world, the principle of "intentionality." (p. 5, emphasis added)

The vehicle of pedagogical documentation is what makes this principle of intentionality visible and shareable. And this intentionality, according to Ann, helps to frame her way of being in the world.

Ann describes her documentation practice with passion and intensity, using expressive terms like it "feeds me" and "nourishes me." Her animation and engagement come through in the following interview excerpt:

> One way that I experience the power of this little being called documentation is finding myself invited to be nourished, to be challenged to be a close observer, and to be really present in the world ... what that's all about for me is the practice of staying intimately present to the children, present with delight and curiosity, and readiness to reflect on what they're doing ... In large part, the reason I know them intimately, I think, is because of this practice.

Ann, as a documenter, writes as an educator, who is oriented in a strong way to the world of real children, who has a fascination with real life. The meanings of the lived sense of phenomena are not exhausted in their immediate experience, but rather live on in her documentation. Her narratives retrieve what is unique and particular from an experience, the dialogic nature of which requires a response from the reader:

> A hope that I have is that documentation engages a reader on many levels, so it's not just watching something but getting curious side-by-side with the writer of this piece, some invitation to be engaged or to be in relationship with what happened ... the process or way of being in the world is really a way of understanding our work, or understanding our relationships with children and with each other, that is about mindful presence and authentic engagement and curiosity and delight. How that all gets lived out or made tangible is the form of this thing. Documentation means a way of being with children—a habit of paying attention, watching and listening closely, reflecting together about what we see, planning from our reflections and understandings, and telling the stories in ways that enrich our communities.

This sense of living in relationship with children and families, this intimate way of being with children that Ann experiences (in large part through her pedagogical documentation), embodies a phenomenological perspective that brings to light her passion and her pedagogy in the lives of children. This kind of thinking guides both the educator and the audience from theoretical abstraction to the reality of lived experience.

PEDAGOGICAL DOCUMENTATION AS A PHENOMENOLOGICAL ACT

For Ann, whose thoughts are expressed here, pedagogical documentation has certainly had an impact on the way she sees herself as a professional and as a researcher, honing her disposition of intellectual commitment, curiosity, and passionate engagement with her work. As a documenter, her written work puts into symbolic textual form what she is seeing in the children's experiences. Ultimately, phenomenological reflection affects a more direct contact with the experience as it is lived—as Ann said earlier when describing her documentation, "I feel the contact of it."

As I have listened closely to Ann speak of her experience as a teacher-researcher and documenter, I have been impressed again and again by the similarities between the ways in which she describes her orientation to this work and the way that Max van Manen (1997) writes about phenomenology as researching lived experience. The documented ordinary moments or anecdotes that Ann has collected provide a launching point for thoughtful reflection and deconstruction. Phenomenological description is not intended to develop theoretical abstractions that are separate from the reality of tangible, lived experience, but rather "phenomenology tries to penetrate the layers of meanings of the concrete by tilling and turning over the soil of daily existence" (van Manen, 2007, p. 119).

CONCLUSION

Ann expresses a desire for her writing to serve pedagogy. Pedagogical documentation is a way in which a conversational relation is sustained; it is a discourse about our pedagogic lives with children. Van Manen (1997) provokes one even to wonder, whether ordinary conversational discourse is adequate to address the nature of pedagogy. He asks, "What form of writing is needed to do justice to the fullness of pedagogy and pedagogic experience?" (p. 111). My response is that pedagogical documentation, as modeled after the early childhood project of Reggio Emilia and enacted by Ann, is just that form of writing.

What Ann is doing in her everyday practice appears to be, indeed, unnamed phenomenological research of the lived experiences of a teacher and the children she teaches. I have sought to discover if Ann has particular attributes that foster a disposition to document. I have found that she embodies the disposition of a phenomenological researcher, as portrayed by van Manen (1991, 1997, 2002), who wonders, imagines, speculates, and thinks deeply about the nature of her work with children.

REFERENCES

Brown, R. (1991). *Toward a phenomenology of curriculum: The work of Max van Manen and T. Tetsuo Aoki.* Unpublished doctoral dissertation, Baton Rouge, Louisiana: Louisiana State University.

Cadwell, L. (2003). *Bringing learning to life.* New York: Teachers College Press.

Dahlberg, G., & Moss, P. (2005). *Ethics and politics in early childhood education.* London: RoutledgeFalmer.

Dahlberg, G., Moss, P., & Pence, A. (2007). *Beyond quality in early childhood education and care: Languages of evaluation.* London: RoutledgeFalmer.

Edwards, C., Gandini, L., & Forman, G. (1998). Introduction: Background and starting points. In C. Edwards, L. Gandini, & G. Forman (Eds.), *The hundred languages of children: The Reggio Emilia approach—Advanced reflections* (pp. 5–25). Greenwich, CT: Ablex.

Gandini, L. (1993). Fundamentals of the Reggio Emilia approach to early childhood education. *Young Children, 49*(1), 4–8.

Gandini, L. (1998). Educational and caring spaces. In C. Edwards, L. Gandini, & G. Forman, (Eds.), *The hundred languages of children: The Reggio Emilia approach to early childhood education – Advanced reflections* (pp. 161–178). Norwood, NJ: Ablex.

Giudici, C., Krechevsky, M., & Rinaldi, C., (Eds.) (2001). *Making learning visible: Children as individual and group learners.* Reggio Emilia, Italy: Reggio Children.

Hertz, R. (1997). *Reflexivity and voice.* Thousand Oaks, CA: Sage.

Kantrowitz, B., & Wingert, P. (1991, December 2). The best schools in the world [Electronic version]. *Newsweek*, pp. 60–64. Retrieved from http://www.news-week.com/1991/12/01/the-best-schools-in-the-world.html

Katz, L. (1990). Impressions of Reggio Emilia preschools. *Young Children, 45*(6), 11–12.

Kocher, L., & Pacini-Ketchabaw, V. (2011). Destablizing binaries in early childhood education: The possibilities of pedagogical documentation. In W. Midgley, M. A. Tyler, P. A. Danaher, & A. Mander (Eds.), *Beyond binaries in education research* (pp. 46–59). New York: Routledge.

Malaguzzi, L. (1993). For an education based on relationships. *Young Children, 49*(1), 9–17.

Moran, M. J. (1998). *Reconceptualizing early childhood pre-service teacher education: A pedagogy of collaborative inquiry.* Unpublished doctoral dissertation, Durham, New Hampshire: University of New Hampshire.

Merleau-Ponty, M. (1962). *Phenomenology of perception.* London: Routledge and Kegan Paul.

Merleau-Ponty, M. (1973). *The prose of the world.* Evanston, IL: North-Western University Press.

Municipality of Reggio Emilia Infant-Toddler Centers and Preschools. (1996). *The hundred languages of children: Catalogue of the exhibit.* Reggio Emilia, Italy: Reggio Children.

New, R. (1990). Excellent early education: A city in Italy has it. *Young Children, 45*(6), 4–10.

Readings, B. (1996). *The university in ruins.* Cambridge, MA: Harvard University Press.

Rinaldi, C. (2001). Documentation and assessment: What is the relationship? In C. Giudici, C. Rinaldi, & M. Krechevsky (Eds.), *Making learning visible: Children as individual and group learners* (pp. 78–89). Reggio Emilia: Reggio Children.

Rinaldi, C. (2006). *In dialogue with Reggio Emilia: Listening, researching, and learning.* London: Routledge.

Smith, D. (1997). Phenomenology: Methodology and method. In J. Higgs (Ed.), *Qualitative research: Discourse on methodologies* (pp. 75–80). Sydney, NSW: Hampden Press.

Sokolowski, R. (2000). *Introduction to phenomenology.* Cambridge: Cambridge University Press.

Spaggiari, S. (1998). The community-teacher partnership in the governance of the schools: An interview with Lella Gandini. In C. Edwards, L. Gandini, & G. Forman (Eds.), *The hundred languages of children: The Reggio Emilia approach to early childhood education—Advanced reflections* (pp. 99–112). Norwood, NJ: Ablex.

van Manen, M. (1991). *The tact of teaching: The meaning of pedagogical thoughtfulness.* London, ON: Althouse Press.

van Manen, M. (1997). *Researching lived experience: Human action for an action sensitive pedagogy.* Albany, NY: SUNY Press.

van Manen, M. (2002). *The tone of teaching.* London, ON: Althouse Press.

Wilson, H., & Hutchinson, S. (1991). Triangulation of qualitative methods: Heideggerian hermeneutics and grounded theory. *Qualitative Health Research, 1*(2), 263–276.

CHAPTER 15

JUGGLING RESEARCH WITH TEACHING: BUILDING CAPACITY IN A UNIVERSITY RESEARCH TEAM

Margaret Baguley and Helmut Geiblinger

University of Southern Queensland, Springfield,
Queensland, Australia

INTRODUCTION

This chapter utilizes the methodology of narrative inquiry to describe the strategies used to form a research team in a Faculty of Education at an Australian regional university. Although there has been considerable research undertaken on academic life in the university sector (for example, Barlow & Antoniou, 2007; Malcom & Zukas, 2009), little attention has been given to the challenges faced by active early career researchers, who undertake the responsibility of leading a research team. This chapter will examine the formation of a research team to enhance research productivity. The account is from the joint perspective of the team leader (an early career researcher who was newly appointed to the university and as such was initially unaware

Creating Connections in Teaching and Learning, pp. 191–206

191

of the politics and interpersonal connections which would inevitably shape the team's dynamics), and one of the members of the team.

The chapter will discuss the types of strategies which were implemented to increase research productivity in the team, describe how intrinsic and extrinsic factors affected the team, and consider the complexities of collaboration along with some of the concerns for active early career researchers, who are required to mentor other researchers. A number of issues will be considered, including academic identity, the complexities of involvement in a collaborative group, the pressure that universities and ultimately academics are facing in relation to raising research productivity, and the types of institutional support that can enhance or hinder such endeavors.

CONTEXTUAL FACTORS

The methodology of narrative inquiry is used by the research team leader to provide insights into the complexities and challenges involved in establishing a research group predominantly composed of academics with low research productivity. This member of the team has taught for the past 6 years in the tertiary sector, after 14 years as a teacher in primary and secondary schools.

The second co-narrator of this chapter has taught for 30 years in tertiary education, at three different universities. He has undertaken extensive research, specifically in the area of sports science and was an invited researcher, conducting applied research at the Sports University in Cologne for 4 months. He was also a competitor, coach, judge, and scientific investigator at five different World Gymnastics Championships.

Shortly after arriving at her new university and taking up a post as senior lecturer, the future team leader was made aware that funding was available for research teams on a competitive basis as part of an approach to enhance research productivity. The success of the proposal she submitted provided funding for a research team consisting of predominantly early career researchers and some experienced researchers, who taught across most of the key curriculum areas, including the arts, English, health and physical education, mathematics, science, technology, and studies of society and the environment. To date, the research output of the team members had been minimal due to the interplay of a number of variables, such as the relative research inexperience of team members, high teaching loads, and the challenges posed by the demands of a newly established campus. The successful proposal for research team funding, including its aims and the strategies implemented to fulfill them, and the subsequent progress of the team provide the basis of this chapter.

Although there are many texts, particularly in management, which describe group work strategies (for example, McDermott, 2002; Toseland & Rivas, 1998), it is only recently that the human aspect of collaborative working environments has received emphasis from researchers (Paulus & Nijstad, 2003; Winer & Ray, 2000). Many traditional texts, such as *Organizational behaviour* (Hellriegel, Slocum, and Woodman, 1992) and *Basic group-work* (Douglas, 2000), provide factual information about groups, including how and why they are formed and the different types of dynamics that may emerge in particular environments. However, they do not tackle the more problematic issue of the intensity of the relationship evident in groups that are fully engaged in collaborative processes. This intensity can create a vibrant and collegial environment, but it can just as likely demand a subsumption of the individual ego, that some may find impossible (Pullen, Baguley, and Marsden, 2009).

In 2008, the arrival of the Excellence in Research for Australia initiative, which will assess research quality within Australia's higher education institutions (Australian Government, 2008), ensured that the formation of the research team was both timely and politically sensitive. In this charged environment, a number of complex factors exerted a considerable influence on the team. These included the varied motives underpinning individual decisions to join such a team, which may have been as simple as a fear of being ostracised, the willingness of team members to avail themselves of informal leadership and mentoring opportunities, and the team's preparedness to accept the leadership of a relative newcomer without an institutionally recognized authoritative position (Churchman & King, 2009; McDermott, 2002).

ACADEMIC IDENTITY

Even though academics working in education faculties may have had substantial teaching experience prior to their university appointment, the transition can often be a stressful and difficult process (Murray & Male, 2005; Sinkinson, 1996, 1997). Zeichner (2005) contends that this is due to the assumption that, if new academics specializing in education are perceived to be competent school teachers, then their transition into the role of a university teacher will be seamless. Murray and Male (2005) describe the importance for teacher educators to move from being "first-order practitioners" to "second-order practitioners" (p. 126), in order to acquire the new skills and knowledge, which they require in order to be able to teach future teachers. As Geiblinger (2010) notes, the challenges faced by teacher educators in various roles increases their levels of knowledge of their own practice over time and this can be passed on subsequently to pre-service teachers.

However, there are many pressures on new academics. They need to teach, research, and contribute to community service as well as deal with the effects of globalization and increasing demands for efficiency, accountability and evaluation (Åkerlind, 2005; Churchman & King, 2009). The business model approach has also affected the identity of academics who as Jauhiainen, Jauhiainen, and Laiho (2009) contend, may now be working in an environment in which competition is seen as a natural state, an anathema to the culture of collaboration in what was, in this case, an eclectic group with very different career journeys.

Although academic teaching has increasingly become more visible in an era of accountability (Harris, 2005; Weimer, 2006) and can be used as an instrument of power, it appears that research is more highly valued (Jauhiainen, Jauhiainen, and Laiho, 2009; Tien, 2000). This tension can affect the identity of an academics with low research productivity, especially if he/she has been successful in a previous school teaching career.

PRESSURE TO RESEARCH

Dollery, Murray, and Crase (2006) argue that the new corporate ethos adopted by Australian universities has resulted in institutions being seen as quasi-commercial, competitive enterprises. This view is supported by Harland, Tidswell, Everett, Hale, and Pickering (2010) who cite a similar situation in New Zealand. The pressure on academics to publish has become increasingly intense as has the implementation of strategies to increase research productivity.

Sinkinson (1996, 1997) proposes that the most significant difficulty, particularly for beginning university teachers, is the requirement to conduct research in addition to teaching. Promotion has also been cited as a way in which higher education institutions can influence faculty research behavior, by manipulating the requirements to achieve particular rankings (Fox, 1985; Tien, 2000). However, Scott, Farh, and Podsakff (1988) found that a combination of intrinsic (satisfaction of curiosity, a sense of mastery, joy of involvement) and extrinsic rewards (personal income increase, peer recognition, respect from students, upward mobility within the university system) produces a significant increase in research performance.

Grbich (1998) argues that collaborative, team research is an important way for academics to start and to feel supported in their research, and that this also creates strong links between the individual, the department, and the institution. Several studies have shown that structural factors, when combined with personal variables, determine the levels of research productivity (Bland & Ruffin, 1992; Ramsden, 1994). However, Grbich also reveals, that there are important characteristics of successful researchers, including knowledge of their area, research skills, previous socialization and mentoring toward academic life, an established publishing record, outside networks, being involved in more than one research project at a time, and spending an average of 40% of the time on research. The pressure to research, therefore, can affect academics either in positive or negative ways, depending on a range of structural and personal variables.

INSTITUTIONAL SUPPORT

Institutional pressure to research is reliant on academics having the characteristics stated in the previous section, or being willing to foster these as part of their role in academia. It is also a responsibility of the institution to provide mentoring and support, to enable the academics to achieve increased research productivity. Grbich (1998) argues that, if a supportive nurturing environment is put in place, there is an expectation that the individual will "achieve an acceptable professional profile in the minimum time" (p. 69). However, if this does not eventuate, institutions may impose structural factors, such as increasing teaching workloads and/or providing financial incentives for research, to provide the necessary motivation (Fox, 1985; Tien, 2000). Malcom and Zukas (2009) describe a clear dislocation between the official and academic view of the work the academics undertake, evidenced in work allocation forms which fragment teaching, research, community service, and administration into discrete elements of practice.

It appears that previous socialization in other education environments, such as through work as an academics and/or through obtaining a research higher degree, results in an increased ability to conform to the expectations of an academic role (Grbich, 1998; Malcom & Zukas, 2009). Additionally, the service component of education has resulted in less focus on research outcomes and more emphasis on teaching. Education faculties are generally an important element of the financial structure of the universities in which they exist, due to the number of students enrolled and limited requirements for expensive equipment, such as that needed, for example, in the sciences. Proportionally, therefore, it could be expected that universities with faculties which are contributing heavily to their financial projections, could receive commensurate support, in relation to enhancing the research productivity of the academic staff with a higher staff/student ratio.

METHODS AND TECHNIQUES

In order to examine the experiences of a newly formed research team, the authors have utilized the qualitative narrative inquiry method. Narrative inquiry uses a storytelling method in order to describe, through reflection and discussion, why the subject of the inquiry has acted in a particular way (Chase, 2005; Clandinin, 2007). This results in an opportunity for the readers to develop an understanding of the different ways, in which the individuals have been affected by various events in their lives (Dunn, 2003; Trzebiński, 2005). As Leavy (2009) notes, narrative inquiry requires participants to be engaged in the unfolding stories they share, which "they restory or replot through their own reflective process and with the passing of time" (p. 27). Webster and Mertova (2007) argue that people make sense of their lives through engaging in narrative, and their stories are constantly restructured, because they do not exist in a vacuum but are shaped by life's experiences.

Polkinghorne (1988) notes that, even though each of us has direct access to our own cognitive processes of meaning-making, they are not directly observable to others. Therefore, the narrative composed through this methodology has enabled the authors to construct, re-construct and ultimately make sense of their experience, in leading and being part of a research team in the university context. This allows others to engage with the events described in these narratives, and to connect with them according to their personal and professional experiences. The narrative is interspersed with references to theoretical sources, which provide an opportunity for the authors to reflect on the events which occurred, and to demonstrate an awareness of how the narrative can contribute to research in this area. The narrative inquiry method was utilized in this study, in order to investigate the complex challenges involved in creating a research team at the university level, with the mandate to create, foster, and sustain connections with its community.

VALIDITY AND RELIABILITY IN NARRATIVE RESEARCH

Narrative research generally does not tend to utilize the same criteria as those applied to more traditional qualitative and quantitative methodologies (Huberman, 1995; Polkinghorne, 1988). The validity of the data in narrative research is concerned with it being well grounded and supported. In this respect, it does not provide results that produce generalizable truths (Clandinin, 2007; Leavy, 2009). The dependability of the data is referred to as reliability in narrative research, and is achieved in this chapter by the trustworthiness of the data being used (Leavy, 2009; Webster & Mertova, 2007). The measures of access, honesty, verisimilitude, authenticity, familiarity, transferability, and economy have also been proposed by Huberman (1995) to determine validity and reliability in narrative research.

In this study, access has been granted to readers, through the narrative of establishing a research team by the team leader and participation in the team by the second author. In addition, extracts of this narrative are included to provide the reader with first-hand accounts of the experience, on which the authors have based their findings. Honesty has been achieved by the responsiveness of the researchers to the narrative, by seeking to understand the complexity of the phenomenon under investigation, through constant clarification and exploration of responses. Verisimilitude has been achieved by utilizing a common experience for many people of working in groups. In this way, the reader may also experience these events as being plausible and may recognize a similar event or generate new understandings of the experience being explored.

Webster and Mertova (2007) reveal that authenticity is often intertwined with verisimilitude. The authors have sought authenticity in this study by ensuring that the narrative is coherent and has been written with integrity through reflection on how the events have affected the researchers. In this chapter, transferability is provided by providing enough detail and accessibility to readers, so that that they could create a similar study in another setting. An efficient and economical approach has been applied through reflection on, and incorporation of, the experiences of the researchers into a short narrative without compromising the integrity of the data or the findings.

THE NARRATIVE

It is astonishing that an industry ostensibly committed to encouraging research allows its efforts to be so regularly demonised, at all levels, by the ubiquitous phrase *publish or perish*. In the minds of both neophyte and more experienced researchers, the phrase establishes a construct that neither nurtures nor encourages. It merely exacerbates the perception of compulsion, irrespective of competing career demands. The thoughtfully named Excellence in Research for Australia initiative, being implemented by the Australian Research Council can, in the eyes of some, be dismissed as a means by which some will publish and others may well perish.

There is an expectation in a senior lecturer role to continue to enhance personal research productivity, as well as to support others in this endeavor. The establishment of a research team appeared to be the perfect vehicle for such an initiative. The co-narrator of this paper had also fulfilled the role of a senior lecturer at a previous university. However, an interstate move had caused him to accept a position at the lower level of lecturer. His previous role had socialized him into the importance of research and the importance of collaboration to increase research productivity.

Shortly after arriving at her new campus, the future team leader was delighted to learn that research funding was available for research teams.

She considered forming a team based on her discipline speciality; however, it became evident that the other people based in the education faculty at the campus were understandably very keen to be part of a proposal which was inclusive of the entire department. Time constraints, which demanded that conception through to final proposal was confined to a mere 5 days, and the unwieldy nature of a 10 person group, saw a series of hurriedly time tabled meetings to ascertain the aims and objectives of the team.

As most of the members were early career researchers with all but one having been awarded a doctorate, the primary underpinning element in the conceptualization of the proposal became their status as early career researchers, who were intent on building a profile. The ultimate aim was to formalize a research team among colleagues in the faculty at the particular campus in order to enhance research, to promote the distinctiveness of the university's regional focus, and to more broadly work with and inform the community, about the team's educational expertise. This aim was linked to various objectives, including building and fostering links with schools in the local area with a particular emphasis on whole-school approaches; examining the way that schools engage with the multi-cultural diversity of their local community; examining how the campus prepared pre-service teachers to become critical agents of change with links to the school and wider community; providing mentoring in qualitative and quantitative research methodologies, and enhancing the research productivity of team members.

The proposal was successful and successive planning sessions were implemented in order to fulfill the stated aims. As with all successful grants, there is an initial morale boost which provides important energy and focus to engage with the hard realities of undertaking and completing the range of activities, outlined in the proposal. Efforts to create a research culture were hampered by the team's general lack of experience, a shortcoming particularly evident in a stated lack of awareness of the existence and potential impact of the impending Excellence for Research in Australia initiative. This inexperience was compounded by the ever present spectre of perishing, a fear that made it difficult for team members to be discerning in their research choices. The importance of aiming for top tier journals or ensuring that conference papers were refereed was always a secondary consideration to being active as researchers. Attempts to emphasize the funding ramifications of these decisions were perceived as obstructionist by some members of the team, and this was made even more difficult by the nebulous and ambiguous nature of the team leader's mandate.

After considering these factors, the team leader felt the best approach was for the team members to consider their research stories and how these had impacted on, and resulted in the positions they now held. This was a similar approach to the one used by her mentor, at her previous university.

The mentor had encouraged her to utilize research stories and this worked exceedingly well. She believed that the motivation and encouragement to move from the familiar to the unfamiliar, a concept encouraged in teaching, had actually helped to increase her research productivity and to pave the way for her promotion to senior lecturer, over longer serving staff members.

As Unrath and Kerridge (2009) state, "reflection fosters accountability" (p. 283), and it appeared to both researchers, that the often competing demands of teaching, research and community service had given way predominately to a teaching focus on the campus. This observation appeared to support Robinson and McMillan's (2006) contention that many teacher educators initially identify themselves more as teachers than as academics, conveniently but to their ultimate career peril, ignoring the expectation to be actively involved in research. Statements made by team members, such as needing a break of 12 months after the submission of a PhD, revealed a lack of understanding about such issues as the critical five year publishing period as an early career researcher.

In addition, it appeared that many team members were utilizing the research days as a means of ensuring dedicated time to complete marking and teaching preparation. The obvious result of these choices was a further barrier to achieving quantifiable research outputs. This also had the unfortunate consequence of reinforcing the view that teaching loads made research difficult, if not impossible. This was supported anecdotally in the perception among some of the group, that the absence of institutional mentoring had hampered their development as researchers. When allied to increasing demands for research output, this sense of professional abandonment created an environment in which the less prolific researchers might have seen the creation of a team not as an opportunity, but as a threat which would demand quantifiable achievement in an area which they appeared to have hitherto avoided.

The team leader, also an early career researcher, had immersed herself in research at her previous university and had been socialized into understanding the importance of research in an academic career. Grbich (1998) contends that this socialization process enables the academics moving to other universities, to easily fit in with the expectations of their new institution and to accelerate their research production. However, Barley and Redman (1979) argue that fairly experienced early career researchers who take the responsibility for those less experienced can only slow down their own development to the detriment of their particular department or faculty.

Introducing narrative methodology became the focus of early team meetings, which also complemented some of the team members' own methodological research interests. Conscious of the difficulties of organizing a group larger than the team leader had envisaged, she set up partnerships between people who had utilized narrative research and those who had not, in order to create mutually supportive groups within the team and to ensure that it was a collaborative effort, not entirely dependent on one or two individuals. Her newness to the faculty was exposed almost immediately, when one of the members informed her about an unwillingness to work with the assigned partner. This resulted in some changes being made, to ensure that team members were comfortable with those they were working with.

Over the next few months, the research team continued to shape the research papers for an international education conference in Australia. This early period of preparation proved to be rewarding as the group began the initial process of sharing their stories. This sense of purpose was matched by substantial faculty funding and a 20% time allocation for each member. When considering the characteristics of productive researchers, Bland and Schmitz (1986) emphasize the importance of a supportive environment, which recognizes research through time allocation, praise and rewards.

Despite the sense of being supported by the faculty, this sense of purpose could not mask the general inexperience of the team or the team leader's slowness in recognizing, just how entrenched some members had become in their daily routine of teaching and marking. Having previously worked at a regional university, she was cognizant of the importance of networking. She organized, through connections at her previous university, to send the abstracts of the team's papers to an international theorist in narrative research methodology, who had agreed to mentor the group and wished to meet through video-conference. This was a very important meeting and a strategic networking opportunity for the group; however, given the time difference, the meeting began at 7.30 am. The team leader had not factored in the reticence of some members to alter work routines to permit their attendance at what they may have mistakenly dismissed as one of dozens of meetings they might attend in the course of a semester. This sense of missed opportunity was heightened by just how valuable the feedback was. Additionally, there was no recognition that her attendance at an international conference to meet the same researcher and an invitation to present a seminar at the researcher's university had grown out of such an opportunity provided to her, while a member of a research team 3 years before.

The research team shaped proposals for six conference papers in order to form a symposium for the conference. As the initial brain storming discussions were consigned to the past and the more precise and demanding work of shaping a conference paper began in earnest, the eclectic nature of the group ceased to be the strength and became a major limitation. At this point, it was revealed that four of the team did not wish to submit conference papers for a variety of reasons. Having previously worked in what appeared to be a research vacuum and having only a cursory knowledge of conference etiquette, some team members were not fully aware of the lead-in time that was required for alterations to their papers. Although the team leader was initially a part of the symposium, one of the team members, who had initially opted out found that circumstances had changed, and now wished to submit. The leader felt that she would need to accommodate this change, so she rewrote the proposal, gave the team member her place, and made arrangements to present two individual papers.

Further difficulties included the travel plans of one team member precluding their attendance and the rejection of one of the papers. This sense of fluidity, in what should have been a firm proposal, created a situation about which the team leader had no previous experience. As a result, she had not prepared a contingency plan. Possibly due to the inexperience of the team, only the co-author and the team leader submitted their papers on time, and this created logistical difficulties with the organizers and with the research team's preparations. Though not one of these issues created an insurmountable problem of itself, the issues were indicative of the inexperience and eclectic career paths of the team members. Although the leader felt that the timeline created a structure for the team's activities, it proved insufficient as an organizational device. As Bernstein (cited in Middleton, 2008) noted, knowledge is an "inner dedication" rather than something which can be externally regulated (p. 134). Even if it could be externally regulated, the team leader's position made it impossible for her to offer such external regulation.

Another aspect of the research team's proposal was to work with schools, in order to examine whole school approaches to value education, with a particular emphasis on the inclusion of students from different cultural backgrounds. The team agreed to structure their research around each of the key curriculum areas, with which they were involved. Though there was a clear consensus concerning this approach, this did not last beyond the first challenge. After the team leader prepared the ethics application with the required attachments and emailed it as a model to all of the team members, many of whom had little or no experience in this vital step of the research process, some of the team members reassessed their earlier commitment or acquiescence to the project parameters.

The team leader interpreted this as being indicative of the lack of personal ownership of this research specifically, and of the aims of the research team more generally. As the public face of the research team, she was well aware of the implications of failing to fulfill the aims of a funded initiative; she felt keenly that such an impasse would have career implications for all involved. As a result of a work place issue and her belief that the team members were expressing a preference for greater autonomy than the parameters of the proposal could in good faith allow, she handed the leadership over to the senior academic on campus. She was fortunate that, at the same time, another opportunity arose, which would allow the fulfillment of the research proposal.

However, this initiative, due to its discipline specific nature, could only involve three members of the group, which reflected her initial preference for a smaller, more cohesive group. Though this project was concluded successfully, it remained subject to many of the same pressures as the parent group. As it was based on a national initiative which placed artists in three low socio-economic schools to ascertain how the arts engage children in their learning, it was a very suitable complement to the initial proposal.

Even though a supportive environment had been established for the research team, the elements of a non-supportive environment described by Bland and Schmitz (1986) remained an ever-present challenge. Though being part of a group offered opportunities unavailable to an individual researcher, it also had the unintended potential to limit personal account-ability. The frustration which the team leader and co-author felt keenly was due to the difficulty of placing disparate personalities together, some less willingly than others, into a collaborative environment which existed para-doxically within a competitive paradigm weighed down by the almost crip-pling moniker *publish or perish*. Any group cohesion was likewise hampered by being compelled to move at a speed which was inherently a compromise. Some members were threatened by the speed of developments, while others were threatened by what they perceived as lethargy, or more danger-ously, obstructionism.

CONCLUSION

In hindsight, it is clear that there was a number of issues, both structural and personal, which impacted on the journey of the research team and its members. Even though the majority of the team had begun their careers at other universities, it does not appear that they had been socialized into the type of research culture demanded by the Excellence for Research in Australia initiative. The predominance of early career research-ers also meant that there were significant gaps in their awareness of what might be considered fundamental knowledge for those actively engaged in research.

In addition, the size of the group often precluded all the members from being available to attend whole team meetings due to timetabling con-straints. One member, who had sought out membership the most actively of all, did not attend any of the meetings. Winer and Ray (2000) recom-mend that up to fifteen people are ideal for group work. However, Farrell (2001) found that within groups, people often split and work in dyads, using this more intimate relationship to explain and examine their ideas before bringing them back to the group. The team leader utilized this approach when team members were working on their conference papers and it proved, as the co-author concurs, to be a more effective approach, than the ostensibly more inclusive whole team meetings.

In addition, the immediate rewards for membership, such as time release and the public recognition of a faculty team, were powerful motivators. Yet they were not matched by a commensurate acknowledgment, that the institution was indeed offering considerable support. The fact that all members received equal funding and were able to access a day each week as dedicated off-campus release time created a sense that this was an alteration to everyone's working conditions, more akin to one across the board pay rise rather than an investment in quantifiable research outcomes.

It became possible, without an inherent sense of contradiction, to discuss the use of substantial institutional funding and the time tabling of meetings to fit in with study days as well as to question the perceived lack of institutional support. Research has shown that universities can use the creation of teams as a cover story (Connelly & Clandinin, 1999) to be used in official and public capacities as though the creation of a team will inevitably increase research capacity. Yet, an area worthy of further research is the complicity of team members in this process, a situation exacerbated by large-size teams and some members being involved in several teams, which can result in a dilution of commitment and time availability.

It also appeared that some team members may have been experiencing the *imposter syndrome*, which refers to "individuals' feelings of not being as capable or adequate as others perceive or evaluate them to be" (Brems et al., 1994, pp. 183–184). The literature also suggests that feelings of inadequacy are more prevalent in women, due to expected stereotypical maternal behavior, such as being supportive and nurturing (Overall, 1997; Studdard, 2002), which can contradict and inhibit the stereotype of professional identity. More than half of the team were women and they may have experienced the associated pressures described by Vasil (1996) as experienced by female academics—greater isolation, higher levels of stress, and a lower sense of self-efficacy and self-confidence. Aisenberg and Harrington (1988) propose that female academics also have more difficulty in establishing relationships with colleagues.

There are many advantages to working collaboratively, particularly in the university sector, where this arrangement can enhance research productivity, provide important connections with other academics, and provide support and guidance. Where collaboration has been successful, it has provided both intrinsic and extrinsic rewards to the participants. However, many people engage in the collaborative process, without being fully aware of the depth of commitment required. A thorough understanding of the participants' backgrounds and cultures is most beneficial during the early stages. As Mattessich, Murray-Close and Monsey (2004) note, "collaboration thrives on diversity of perspective and constructive dialogues between individuals, negotiating their differences while sharing their shared voice and vision" (p. 6). Due to the short time frame in forming the research team, it was not possible to comprehend the range of interpersonal dynamics and prior relationships which ultimately affected the leadership of the team. However, as a leader it is simply not feasible or advisable to have all of the responsibility and limited authority in advising team members of actions, which do not support the performative storying of the university.

REFERENCES

Aisenberg, N., & Harrington, M. (1988). *Women of academe: Outsiders in the sacred grove*. Amherst, MA: University of Massachusetts Press.

Åkerlind, G. (2005). Academic growth and development—How do university academics experience it? *Higher Education*, 50(1), 1–32.

Australian Government. (2008). *New ERA for research quality* [Media release]. Retrieved from http://www.arc.gov.au/media/releases/media_26Feb08.htm

Barley, Z., & Redman, B. (1979). Faculty role development in university schools of nursing, *Journal of Nursing Administration*, 9(5), 43–47.

Barlow, J., & Antoniou, M. (2007). Room for improvement: The experiences of new lecturers in higher education, *Innovations in Education and Teaching International*, 44(1), 67–77.

Bland, C., & Ruffin, M. (1992). Characteristics of a productive research environment: Literature review. *Academic Medicine*, 67(6), 385–397.

Bland, C., & Schmitz, C. (1986). Characteristics of the successful researcher and implications for faculty development. *Journal of Medical Education*, 61(1), 22–31.

Brems, C., Baldwin, M., Davis, L., & Namyniuk, L. (1994). The imposter syndrome as related to teaching evaluations and advising relationships of university faculty members. *The Journal of Higher Education*, 65(2), 183–193.

Chase, S. (2005). Narrative inquiry. In N. Denzin & Y. Lincoln (Eds.), *The Sage handbook of qualitative research* (3rd ed., pp. 651–679). Thousand Oaks, CA: Sage.

Churchman, D., & King, S. (2009). Academic practice in transition: Hidden stories of academic identities. *Teaching in Higher Education*, 14(5), 507–516.

Clandinin, D. J. (Ed.). (2007). *Handbook of narrative inquiry: Mapping a methodology*. Thousand Oaks, CA: Sage.

Connelly, F., & Clandinin, D. (Eds.). (1999). *Shaping a professional identity: Stories of educational practice*. New York: Teachers College Press.

Dollery, B., Murray, D., & Crase, L. (2006). Knaves or knights, pawns or queens? An evaluation of Australian higher education reform policy. *Journal of Education for Teaching*, 31(1), 47–62.

Douglas, T. (2000). *Basic groupwork*. New York: Routledge.

Dunn, D. S. (2003). Teach me about your life: Narrative approaches to lives, meaning, and transitions, *Journal of Social and Clinical Psychology, 22*(5), 604–606.

Farrell, M. (2001). *Collaborative circles.* Chicago: The University of Chicago Press.

Fox, M. (1985). Publication, performance, and reward in science and scholarship. In J. C. Smart (Ed.), *Higher education: Handbook of theory and research.* (Vol. 1, pp. 255–282). New York: Agathon Press.

Geiblinger, H. (November 29–December 3, 2010). *"Tumbling" through life ... and expecting a safe landing: A narrative journey of an educational research.* Paper presented at the Australian Association for Research in Education Annual Conference, Canberra.

Grbich, C. (1998). The academic researcher: Socialisation in settings previously dominated by teaching. *Higher Education, 36*(1), 67–85.

Harland, T., Tidswell, T., Everett, D., Hale, L., & Pickering, N. (2010). Neoliberalism and the academic as critic and conscience of society. *Teaching in Higher Education, 15*(1), 85–96.

Harris, S. (2005). Rethinking academic identities in neo-liberal times. *Teaching in Higher Education, 10*(4), 421–433.

Hellriegel, D., Slocum, J., & Woodman, R. (1992). *Organizational behaviour* (6th ed.). St Paul, MN: West Publishing Company.

Huberman, M. (1995). Working with life-history narratives. In H. McEwan & K. Egan (Eds.). *Narrative in teaching, learning and research* (pp. 127–165). New York: Teachers College Press.

Jauhiainen, A., Jauhiainen, A., & Laiho, A. (2009). The dilemmas of the "efficiency university" policy and the everyday life of university teachers. *Teaching in Higher Education, 14*(4), 417–428.

Leavy, P. (2009). *Method meets art.* New York: The Guilford Press.

McDermott, F. (2002). *Inside group work.* Crows Nest, NSW: Allen & Unwin.

Malcom, J., & Zukas, M. (2009). Making a mess of academic work: Experience, purpose and identity. *Teaching in Higher Education, 14*(5), 495–506.

Mattessich, P., Murray-Close, M., & Monsey, B. (2004). *Collaboration: What makes it work* (2nd ed.). Saint Paul, MN: Amherst H. Wilder Foundation.

Middleton, S. (2008). Research assessment as a pedagogical device: Bernstein, professional identity and education in New Zealand. *British Journal of Sociology of Education, 29*(2), 125–136.

Murray, J., & Male, T. (2005). Becoming a teacher educator: Evidence from the field. *Teaching and Teacher Education, 21*(2), 125–142.

Overall, C. (1997). Feeling fraudulent: Some moral quandaries of a feminist instructor. *Educational Theory, 47*(1), 1–13.

Paulus, P., & Nijstad, B. (Eds.). (2003). *Group creativity: Innovation through collaboration.* Oxford: Oxford University Press.

Polkinghorne, D. (1988). *Narrative knowing and the human sciences.* Albany, NY: State University of New York Press.

Pullen, D., Baguley, M. & Marsden, A. (2009). Back to basics: Electronic collaboration in the education sector. In J. Salmons & L. Wilson, (Eds.), *Handbook of research on electronic collaboration and organizational synergy* (Vol. 1, pp. 205–222). Hershey, PA: Information Science Reference (IGI Global).

Ramsden, P. (1994). Describing and explaining research productivity. *Higher Education, 28*(2), 207–226.

Robinson, M., & McMillan, W. (2006). Who teaches the teachers? Identity, discourse and policy in teacher education. *Teaching and Teacher Education, 22*(3), 327–336.

Scott, W., Farh, J., & Podsakoff, P. (1988). The effects of "intrinsic" and "extrinsic" reinforcement contingencies on task behaviour. *Organisational Behaviour and Human Decision Processes, 41*(3), 405–425.

Sinkinson, A. (1996). From teaching mathematics to training teachers. *Mathematics Education Review, 7*, 17–24.

Sinkinson, A. (1997). Teachers into lecturers: An agenda for change. *Teacher Development, 1*(1), 97–105.

Studdard, S. S. (2002). Adult women students in the academy: Imposters or members? *Journal of Continuing Higher Education, 50*(3), 24–37.

Tien, F. (2000). To what degree does the desire for promotion motivate faculty to perform research? *Research in Higher Education, 41*(6), 723–752.

Toseland, R., & Rivas, R. (1998). *An introduction to group work practice* (3rd ed.). Boston: Allyn & Bacon.

Trzebiński, J. (2005). Narratives and understanding other people. *Research in Drama Education, 10*(1), 15–25.

Unrath, K., & Kerridge, D. (2009). Becoming an art teacher: Storied reflections of two preservice students. *Studies in Art Education, 50*(3), 272–286.

Vasil, L. (1996). Social process skills and career achievement among male and female academics, *Journal of Higher Education, 67*(1), 103–114.

Webster, L., & Mertova, P. (2007). *Using narrative inquiry as a research method*. Abingdon, Oxon: Routledge.

Weimer, M. (2006). *Enhancing scholarly work on teaching and learning*. San Francisco, CA: Jossey-Bass.

Winer, M., & Ray, K. (2000). *Collaboration handbook*. Saint Paul, MN: Amherst H. Wilder Foundation.

Zeichner, K. (2005). Becoming a teacher educator: A personal perspective. *Teaching and Teacher Education, 21*(2), 117–124.

CHAPTER 16

SHARING JAPANESE AND AUSTRALIAN CULTURE: A CASE STUDY IN SECOND LANGUAGE LEARNING

Junichi Hatai, *St Joseph's College, Toowoomba, Queensland, Australia;*
Robert D. White, *University of Sunshine Coast, Sippy Downs, Queensland, Australia*

INTRODUCTION

The focus of this study was the experiences of 12 Japanese students, who were visiting Australia in 2007, learning English as a second language. The research, conducted in three rounds of interviews, investigated how cultural topics created conversational and relational connections. The investigation was particularly interested in the students' use of cultural topics which the Japanese students knew well (for example, school life and Japanese food). A prima facie case emerged that practising speaking in English when studying their own traditional Japanese culture enables Japanese students to converse more easily with native English speakers in general, and about Japanese life and culture specifically.

Creating Connections in Teaching and Learning, pp. 207–219
Copyright © 2011 by Information Age Publishing
All rights of reproduction in any form reserved.

English is an international lingua franca, "a way of referring to communication in English between speakers who have different first languages"
(Jenkins, 2008, p. 5), and an important subject in Japanese schools. About
2 billion people in the world speak English, but only about 320–380 million are native speakers of English (Yano, 2004). Approximately 300–500
million people in English-speaking countries use English as a Second Language (ESL), and 500–1000 million people living in non-English speaking
countries use English as a Foreign Language (EFL).

The Australian domestic students form the third largest number of
students studying Japanese (Japan Foundation, 2008). Many sister city or
sister school partnerships between Japan and Australia exist, and these are
an ideal way for students of both countries to enhance their second language skills. Japanese students are familiar with the more popular aspects of
their own culture, and Japanese culture in general is increasingly familiar to
many people around the developed world. Therefore, there exists an opportunity to enhance conversation skills and exchange cultural knowledge in
the target languages of Japanese and English. Kawano (1999) stated that
"Japanese learners of English ... must learn culture to communicate with
non-Japanese efficiently" in classrooms and other environments.

LEARNING ENGLISH IN JAPAN

Japan has a 150 year old history of studying the English language. However, it has been noted that Japanese people's English speaking skill has
not improved a great deal in that time. In addressing this issue, Morioka
(1988) argues that English study in Japan has concentrated on reading and
writing, rather than speaking and listening. A survey conducted by the
Japanese Ministry of Education, Culture, Sports, Science, and Technology
(2003) concluded that junior high school students generally could not
understand complicated English sentences because they did not have
enough training or practice in speaking English. Scores from the Test of
EFL also demonstrate that many Japanese learners of English are struggling (Sawa, 1999). The *World competitiveness yearbook* (IMD International,
2007) indicates that Japan was placed 55th compared to the other Asian
countries in English proficiency.

There is also evidence that Japanese people find it difficult to answer
questions about Japanese culture when they travel internationally. A greater
knowledge of their own culture and a stronger ability to talk about it in
English could enhance the personal and social benefits of their interactions
with native English speakers. The level of English proficiency among

1st year Japanese university students continues to be of significant concern (Ministry of Education, Culture, Sports, Science, and Technology, 2003). Nevertheless, schools' curriculum frameworks do not promote using Japanese cultural content to teach English. Classes continue to concentrate on aspects of Western culture such as Easter, Thanksgiving, American civil rights, and Shakespearean literature.

The research described in this chapter proposed that, if Japanese learners know and practice discussing and explaining aspects of their own culture in English, they could increase their English proficiency and confidence. Additionally, greater familiarity with their culture could lead to a continuing cycle of practice and increasing proficiency. Connections can be created with native English speakers, if students can develop the confidence to take the initiative in conversation, by explaining their own cultural and/or favorite topics.

As this research was exploratory in nature and sought prima facie evidence for its hypothesis, this chapter initially describes the exploratory phase of the study, and then discusses relevant literature and the nexus of the two. Japanese students' experiences of their interactions with the Australian students provided an opportunity to observe the potential for change in the Japanese students' views of studying English. The findings suggest that the proposed changes could enhance the learning of English in Japan.

THE STUDY

The study was situated within an annual sister school exchange program, during which 12 Japanese students spent two weeks in the homes of Australian students. The study used mixed methods to measure and test vocabulary acquisition and proficiency. For example, correlation analyses of gains in vocabulary scores have been demonstrated to produce valid outcomes (Proctor, Dalton, and Grisham, 2007), while increasing knowledge of the world leads to increasing vocabulary knowledge, increasing language use, and vice versa (Nation & Waring, 1997). Given these precedents, the study used a mixed approach to examine the nexus between vocabulary gain and knowledge of the world (in this instance, knowledge of Japanese society and culture).

Data were collected from interviews with the Japanese students before and after an English Study Tour (EST), as well as during group interaction activities with Australian students during the tour and 2 months after their return to Japan. The students' speech was analyzed to measure their improvement in English speaking ability. The number of English words spoken by the participants in the pre-English Study Tour (pre-EST) and post-English Study Tour (post-EST) interviews and during five group inter-actions was compared. In the pre-EST and post-EST interviews, command of English language, confidence in speaking English, and confidence in speaking about Japanese life and culture were explored by posing four requests:

1. Please talk about Japan in English for 2 minutes;
2. Please rank your level of confidence of speaking English from 1 (bad)—5 (good);
3. Please rank your knowledge about Japanese culture from 1 (limited)—5 (extensive);
4. Please rank your level of English from 1 (limited)—5 (strong).

This technique of self-assessment, while subjective, enabled the examination of the students' lived experience. The subjectivity was off-set by the observations and multi-lingual expertise of the researcher, a teacher of both Japanese and English.

Follow-up interviews, which posed a different set of questions to the Japanese students, were also conducted. These asked:

• Was the time in Australia useful for you to improve your English? Why?
• What was most helpful to improve your English?
• What did you learn about Australia? Tell me in English for example, food, festival, seasons, arts, and school.
• Can you please tell me what kind of advice/tip you would give to the next group of students, in order for them to improve their English speaking skills?
• How do you think about your knowledge of Japan in English?
• Does this knowledge enhance your speaking or not? Why?
• Did you make friends with the Australian people?
• What topics did you talk about in Australia?
• What helped you obtain more confidence in speaking English?

These follow-up questions were asked first in English and then again in Japanese. This enabled the students to respond and express themselves more freely and fully for the purpose of obtaining richer data. This technique of self-assessment, while subjective, enabled the examination of the lived experience of those experiencing the phenomenon under investigation. The subjectivity was off-set by the observations and multi-lingual expertise of the researcher, a teacher of both Japanese and English.

WHAT WAS DONE

Twelve female Japanese students, 16–17 years of age, participated in the study. Participation in this EST and research were voluntary, and the students were keen to gain better English communication skills. Interviews and interactions were recorded by video camera and transcribed for analysis. The group interactions involved groups of three Japanese students and two Australian students, discussing five topics: Japanese food, festivals, school life, seasons, and the arts. Each group discussed a different topic in the class on five different occasions. The participants had significant opportunities to practice listening to and speaking in English during these group interactions. By holding the follow-up interview 2 months after the students' return to Japan, the participants had time to reflect on their experiences and learning.

As measures of proficiency, the number of English words spoken by the Japanese students were counted (that is, vocabulary was measured), and the students also did a self-assessment of their command of English, confidence in speaking English, and confidence in speaking about Japanese culture. The place, significance, and importance of English vocabulary acquisition in developing the English language proficiency of ESL students are well established (Jaén, 2007; Nation & Waring, 1997; Wisconson Department of Public Instruction, 2009).

HOW IT WAS DONE

While the questions asked were qualitative in nature, both qualitative and quantitative techniques were used to analyze the lived experience of the students. Quantitative analysis of the data examined the statistical frequencies and dispersions of word use and placement; qualitative analysis examined participants' self-perceptions and self-beliefs and interrogated the meaning of the quantitative analysis.

Small sample sizes permit only simple statistical analysis. However, statistical trends in small samples can suggest prima facie support for a hypothesis. This type of analysis is inherently problematic (Weiss, 1989), and Kelly (2004) cautions about the search for causality. With that in mind, the primary data was analyzed relative to three dependent variables. It is noted that small sample pilot studies are limited in the range of their exploration and generalizability can only be inferred from a logical basis (Wiersma & Jurs, 2005). They can infer or point to other factors and variables which may warrant further study. It is within this caveat that this study chose the variables to be analyzed.

THE QUANTITATIVE ANALYSIS

Four variables were investigated: (1) word count (the number of English words used in conversation); (2) participants' self-assessment of command of English language; (3) participants' self-assessment of speaking English; and (4) participants' self-assessment of their knowledge of Japanese culture. All showed increases between the pre-EST and post-EST interviews.

The comparative information shown in Figs. 16.1–16.4 suggests a positive change in the variables over the period of the participants' EST in Australia. The lines of best fit indicate the pattern of response dispersion relative to the mean of the responses represented by the straight lines. The changes of position and shape of these lines give a picture of the trend of the change in the students' proficiency.

The figures demonstrate that, although there is a significant improvement in the variables for the sample as a whole, the dispersion of individual plots indicates that improvement is much more varied for individual students. Individual changes varied from significant to relatively little. This could reasonably be expected from any sample–people are different, and these figures depict that.

While the figures collectively suggest a correlation between the independent variables and improvement in the three dependent variables, it must be remembered that "correlation is not causation" (Weiss, 1989,

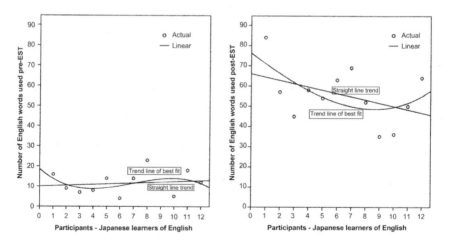

Figure 16.1. Comparative means of the numbers of English words used by participants pre- and post-English study tour

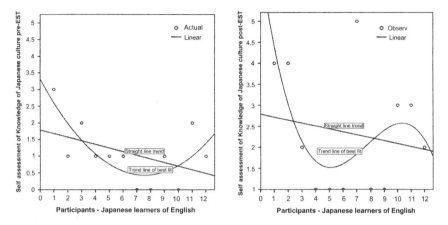

Figure 16.2. Comparative means of self-assessments of participants' English skill (command of language) pre- and post-English study tour

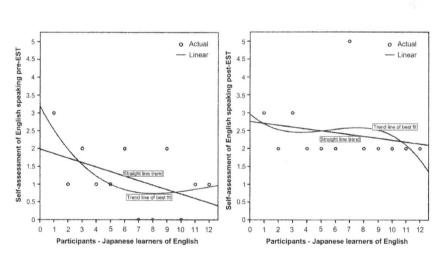

Figure 16.3. Comparative means of self-assessments of participants' English speaking ability pre- and post-English study tour

p. 528). Correlation on its own does not prove a causal link; there may be another unidentified factor to which all four variables are causally linked. Nevertheless, on the strength of this data, we can infer that there was a statistically significant improvement in the Japanese students' English language ability over the course of the EST period.

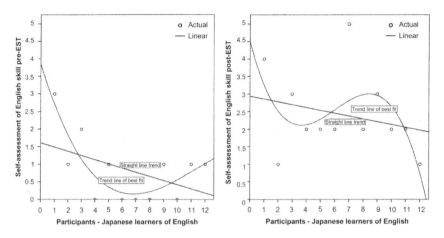

Figure 16.4. Comparative means of self-assessments of participants' knowledge of Japanese culture pre- and post-English study tour

THE QUALITATIVE ANALYSIS

The sample comprised academically proficient, female Japanese secondary students. They claimed that they did not know enough about their own Japanese culture to explain it well to others and most of them felt they should have studied more about Japanese culture before they visited Australia. Students reported that during the EST their self-confidence increased and that they learnt how to identify and adopt linguistically appropriate words from the Australian students who were native speakers of English. Their facial expressions changed positively and the volume of their voices increased.

However, the Japanese students reported that they could not understand the Australian students' speech well, and they had difficulty replying to the Australian students' questions. In group interactions, the Japanese students were able to speak some English, but they mostly used simple English nouns and verbs; their conversation as a whole was a blend of these simple English words and many untranslated Japanese words. Two things became apparent from these observations. Firstly, junior high school English was enough for basic communication by these Japanese students. Secondly, they needed preparation in English for trans-cultural conversation.

The four Japanese teachers who were involved in the exchange program had mixed views about the Japanese students' English ability as evidenced during the EST. Two teachers reported that students' English responses were quicker and more competent and more engaged, while two teachers felt that the students' English competence had not improved. However, all four concurred that students had become more outgoing and engaged and exhibited more initiative in English speaking and conversation, and that using learning about Japanese culture to practice speaking English would assist the students' overall English competence.

In the light of the teachers' views, the videos of group interaction between the Japanese and Australian students were interesting. The Japanese students struggled to translate many Japanese words into English, even when speaking about their favorite topics. From observation of the video data, it appeared that the students were keen to explain Japanese culture and daily life, but they were frustrated by the limits of their English competency. Their self-efficacy in relation to English language is evidently important to analyze. Why are these students not proficient English speakers? Do they need to learn more about Japanese life and culture in order to use that knowledge as a basis for conversation with the native English speakers? These questions form a part of the final discussion.

THE ISSUE IN THE LIGHT OF THE FINDINGS

When Japanese people encounter native English speakers, they have opportunities to speak in English and about their own culture. People's respective cultures are a common topic for facilitating conversation between people of difference languages. Japanese students may struggle to answer questions about their culture because of insufficient knowledge of their culture, and they may lack sufficient training and vocabulary to adequately communicate in English. This appeared to be the case with this study's sample.

Based on what participants said, we propose three reasons why it would be helpful for Japanese students to learn about their own culture as a means to learn other languages. Firstly, even when students' second language skills are not strong, familiarity with their culture is necessary for their personal development and efficacy. Secondly, students are likely to be asked about Japanese life and culture when they meet people from other cultures. Thirdly, practice and experience in second language conversation can enhance second language speaking skill, self-confidence, and self-efficacy. Although the study is based on participants' views and self-assessments, it indicates that this approach to English language learning has the potential to benefit English language learners and to improve their learning outcomes.

People communicate to exchange information and opinions, and students studying foreign languages need conversational ice-breakers to help them overcome people's natural hesitance towards initial conversational openness. Topics familiar to one or all parties in a conversation are effective ice-breakers and the life and culture of one's home country are often the most interesting to others and the easiest to talk about. The ability to initiate and enjoy conversations facilitates the use of such ice-breakers, an ability that improved among the study's participants over the period of the EST.

Communication must be a two-way process; Japanese people must not only benefit from Australian people, but they should also find their own identity and offer something Japanese for the benefit of Australians. This is a fundamental aspect of a global perspective of life and trans-cultural interaction and communication (Kato, 1988).

Communication involves an exchange not only of words, but also of body language. Body language includes facial expressions, head and body movements, and gestures; it also includes proxemics (distance between conversationalists), prosody (such as rhythm, intonation, pitch, and sentence stress), and norms of interaction which operate subconsciously (Barraja-Rohan, as cited in Liddicoat, Crozet, and Lo Bianco, 1999). These factors were observed in the study, and the participants demonstrated interactional competence with initiative by using gestures and onomatopoeia in the interaction when they talked about Japanese life and culture. The interactional topics needed to suit both parties in the interaction. It was that common topical interest that the participants found to be a vehicle for interaction in English with the Australians.

Cultural content learning enhances communication and motivates language learning. It provides more opportunities for students to assess their own learning strategies (Honna, 1995). Some theories endorse the use of cultural content in second language learning. Teachers can use language that reflects the topics that the learners might want to talk about, and are relevant to their interests (Littlewood, 1990). Krashen (1988) has theorized that second language (L2) and first language (L1) acquisition are similar, but that learning cannot produce speech without monitoring L1 acquisition which occurs in natural (informal) settings. In contrast, L2 acquisition most often occurs in more formal settings by collecting and knowing words. If teachers can facilitate and challenge students' understandings with what Krashen (1988) has also theorized as comprehensible input, students' L2 learning can be enhanced. Students can also transfer their knowledge from their native tongue L1 into the target language conversation (Cummins, 1981).

Talking about Japanese life and culture by the Japanese students facilitates their speaking of English; this helps when they interact with native English speaking students. This was the experience of the study's participants. They experienced improvement in their overall command of English as their conversational confidence grew and conversational topics with Australians increasingly involved Japanese and Australian life and culture. This is consistent with

Vygotsky's (1978) concept of the socially situated nature of learning. Speaking ability can be built systematically, beginning with non-verbal communication, followed by one word responses, two-three words responses, phrase responses, sentence responses and ultimately, complicated conversations (Richard-Amato, 1996). Knowledge of familiar topics can help Japanese students to develop their speech systematically, reduce worry, and increase self-efficacy and self-confidence.

CONCLUSION

As this chapter has indicated, Japanese students often find it challenging to understand what native English speakers say and how to reply. According to Yokoyama (2004), "comprehensible input" is not sufficient to enhance language acquisition, but "pushed output" is necessary (p. 2). It is because listening cannot enhance precise understanding, but speaking can, because "output" makes learners notice the gap between what they learn and what they want to say. These strategies can be taught and developed in preference to receiving teachers' instruction, rote-practice, copying correct sentences, and memorizing. For learning English, some Japanese students could benefit from a more interactive approach, including the English speaking opportunities that occur during exchange programs. It was those opportunities during the participants' EST in Australia which contributed to the improvement in their command of English.

We posit that more opportunities to practice speaking and listening skills would help some of the Japanese students to communicate more proficiently in English. The use of native English speakers or teachers in class would also be expected to facilitate English speaking practice. Patterned practices, such as reading together and repetition of sentences pronounced by English teachers, are still popular in Japanese schools. However, it has been argued that this is not an effective pedagogical technique and it is not sufficient for learning to speak English, because the content and exercises do not replicate authentic English conversation (Hirashima, 2007). Practice could be enhanced by the use of cultural conversation content, and Suzuki (1999) advocates that Japanese high school students should learn how to speak about Japanese culture in English.

Discussing one's own culture and life style in another language can help make conversation smoother and more effective. As a vehicle for English language study, the study of Western culture is arguably one-sided and not the most beneficial to cultural exchange. This research study found that, during an EST to Australia by Japanese students, Australian students used their knowledge of Japan and the Japanese language (learnt in Australian classes) to help Japanese English language students to talk about Japanese cultural topics in English. The Japanese students' self-assessments of their command of English language improved, their fear of speaking English was reduced, and their motivation to speak English grew. However, they felt that had they visited Australia with a greater knowledge of the life and culture of their own country, they could have spoken English with even more confidence.

Despite the qualifications discussed earlier, it can be said that creating cognitive and social connections between second language learners through the use of common interests and familiar topics is helpful and beneficial to their learning. The students, who participated in this study, now have the potential to become more competent English speakers because of their improved understanding of how to use English words correctly and their knowledge of what to talk about with Australian students. The pedagogical implications of these results suggest that a more effective approach to helping Japanese students to learn to speak English is readily available. A vocabulary built on cultural knowledge in both first language and target language could facilitate the creation of connections between Japanese students of English and native English speakers by stimulating mutual understanding and motivating learning.

It is now technologically possible for students to communicate with people in other parts of the world, creating mentally close connections. In the present global era, access to knowledge and the means to communicate are unprecedented and ubiquitous. The time and circumstances are well suited to using knowledge of one's own culture as common ground for creating trans-lingual connections between people.

REFERENCES

Cummins, J. (1981). The role of primary language development in promoting educational success for language minority students. In California State Department of Education (Ed.), *Schooling and language minority students: A theoretical framework* (pp. 3–49). Los Angeles: National Dissemination and Assessment Center.

Hirashima, R. (2007). Pattern practice to enhance communication skill. *Journal of Foreign Language Education and Research, 13*, 79–95.

Honna, N. (1995). English in Japanese society: Language within language. In J. C. Maher & K. Yashiro (Eds.), *Multilingual Japan* (pp. 45–62). Philadelphia, PA: Multilingual Matters.

IMD International (2007). *World competitiveness yearbook*. Retrieved from http://www. imd.ch/research/publications/wcy/wcy_book.cfm

Jaén, M. M. (2007). A corpus-driven design of a test for assessing the ESL collocational competence of university students. *International Journal of English Studies, 7*(2), 127–147.

Japan Foundation. (2008). *Present condition of overseas Japanese-language education summary: Survey report on Japanese language education abroad 2006* (Report No. 19JE925). Tokyo, Japan: Japan Foundation.

Jenkins, J. (September 11–13, 2008). *English as a lingua franca.* Paper presented at the JACET 47th Annual Convention, Waseda University, Waseda, Japan. Retrieved from http://www.jacet.org/2008convention/JACET2008_keynote_jenkins.pdf

Kato, J. (1988). *Cultural exchange in Japan.* Tokyo, Japan: The Simul Press.

Kawano, M. (1999.) *Teaching culture in English class in Japan.* Retrieved from http://www.cdu.edu.au/ehs/caesl/staff/kawano/kawano5.html

Kelly, A. (2004). Design research in education: Yes, but is it methodological? [Electronic version]. *Journal of the Learning Sciences, 13*(1), 115–128.

Krashen, S. (1988). *Second language acquisition and second language learning.* New York: Prentice Hall.

Liddicoat, J. A., Crozet, C., & Lo Bianco, J. (1999). *Teaching languages, teaching cultures.* Melbourne, Victoria.: Applied Linguistics Association of Australia.

Littlewood, W. (1990). *Communicative language teaching.* New York: Cambridge University Press.

Ministry of Education, Culture, Sports, Science and Technology, (2003). *Regarding the establishment of an action plan to cultivate "Japanese with English ability."* Retrieved from http:/www.mext.go.jp/english/

Morioka, K. (1988). *Kotoba no kyouiku (Education of languages).* Tokyo, Japan: Meiji Shoin.

Nation, P., & Waring, R. (1997). Vocabulary size, text coverage and word lists. In N. Schmitt, & M. McCarthy. (Eds.), *Vocabulary: Description, acquisition and pedagogy* (pp. 6–19). Cambridge: Cambridge University Press.

Proctor, C. P., Dalton, B., & Grisham, D. L. (2007). Scaffolding English language learners and struggling readers in a universal literacy environment with embedded strategy instruction and vocabulary support. *Journal of Literacy Research, 39*(1), 71–93.

Richard-Amato, P. A. (1996). *Making it happen: Interaction in the second language classroom* (2nd ed.). White Plains, NY: Longman.

Sawa, T. (1999, October 18). Cramming cripples. *The Japan Times,* 20.

Suzuki, T. (1999). *Why Japanese people cannot speak English?* Tokyo: Iwanami Shinsho.

Vygotsky, L. S. (1978). *Mind and society: The development of higher mental processes.* Cambridge, MA: Harvard University Press.

Weiss, N. A. (1989). *Elementary statistics.* Reading, MA: Addison-Wesley.

Wiersma, W., & Jurs, S. G. (2005). *Research methods in education: An introduction.* (8th ed.). Boston: Pearson Education.

Wisconson Department of Public Instruction. (2009). *English language proficiency levels. Serving English language learners.* Retrieved from http://dpi.wi.gov/ell/pdf/elp-levels.pdf

Yano, Y. (2004). *The bulletin of the graduate school of education of Waseda University, 14,* 176–195. Retrieved from http://ci.nii.ac.jp/naid/110004668862/en

Yokoyama, N. (2004). Role of input and output in language acquisition. *Japanese International Centre Journal, 14,* 1–12.

SECTION IV

MAKING VIRTUAL CONNECTIONS

CHAPTER 17

A NEW ZEALAND TERTIARY EDUCATOR'S ONLINE JOURNEY

C. E. Haggerty

Whitireia Community Polytechnic, Porirua, New Zealand

INTRODUCTION

This chapter follows the author's journey of learning while designing and developing an online tertiary course for a specialist group of nurses in New Zealand. Working as an educator within a tertiary institution, I was approached to develop a course for nurses, who were adult students and were working in a specialist community context. The nurses were working across the country, and the cost associated with having them travel to a tertiary institution to access a course was prohibitive for their employer. It seemed appropriate, therefore, to consider online delivery as a viable option. However, creating an online course from the beginning was something that neither I nor my colleagues were confident with. This would be a journey of discovery for us all.

This chapter explores this journey, what decisions were made along the way, and the literature that supported our learning. Through researching

Creating Connections in Teaching and Learning, pp. 223–232
Copyright © 2011 by Information Age Publishing

the issues of online access and use within a postgraduate nursing program, I highlight connectedness and engagement as key issues for the educators to understand and consider. The end result was the design, development, and delivery of a quality course that met the needs of students as well as industry. The journey also provided key principles to support this type of design and development, and a framework which has become an exemplar for the organization as a whole. The lessons learnt from this journey have wide application to tertiary teaching.

THE JOURNEY BEGINS

Our first challenge was to design a course that would engage the nurses by distance and support the development of their specialty practice. The first questions we asked ourselves were: Where would we start? What help would we need along the way?

The first step was to understand who our students would be. They would be registered nurses with a variety of educational qualifications, and some may not have studied for many years. Some literature (for example, Clark, 2000; Laurillard, 1993; Rouda & Kusy, 1996) states that, without having completed a sound analysis upfront, the educators cannot effectively design or develop a teaching and learning environment that is pedagogically sound, appropriate for the students, and supports their connection with each other, educators and the content. This may require accessing experts in instructional design, as well as expertise in the technical and pedagogical aspects of teaching and learning online (Billings, 1999; Blood-Siegfried et al., 2008; Palloff & Pratt, 2000).

We (the educators) did need some expert instructional design assistance, and an external person was contracted to provide this support. Although there were clear advantages in using an instructional designer, there was a feeling among the education team that we were losing control of the process, and that our educational expertise was not being recognized. Primarily, the focus seemed to be on what could be done with the technology, rather than on what the technology could do for the course.

Adams and Morgan (2007) discuss this notion, stating that a technology-driven focus, when developing online learning, can create further barriers for the academic staff. They identify this as the first generation e-Learning, as opposed to second generation e-Learning, which is pedagogy driven. Both the generations have a role, and need to be considered up-front when designing and developing online learning. In this instance, this was not happening, with the instructional designer introducing a framework that we were expected to follow without deviation. Although the framework was useful, the strict adherence to its stages was both confusing and frustrating.

Our focus was on the pedagogical considerations of the course, the learning outcomes and how these would be assessed, and the content and how we would teach this from distance. It was not helpful to be constantly being told, "You cannot focus on that now; you need to focus on the activities you will use in your teaching and the resources you will need." Unfortunately, this placed us in a situation where we allowed the instructional designer to take the lead role, while we felt that we were just along for the ride.

Literature (for example, Anderson, 2009; Burke, 2008; Gibson, Harris, and Colaric, 2008; Johnson, 2008; Thompson, 2004) tells us that the role adjustments for educators can be stressful, and that they can potentially create a barrier to implementing online learning. This was indeed what was happening in our situation, and after a few weeks we actively limited the external instructional designer's ongoing involvement. We took over control of the process, by working more closely with an internal educational technologist and Web editor. This allowed the educational pedagogy to become central to the process.

However, the framework that the instructional designer had introduced did have some positive aspects, and it was further modified into a tool to better support both the pedagogical and technological components of online course design and development. The new framework, based on Moore and Hunt's (2005) work, had a more logical and sequential flow, and was developed into the LATAR framework (Haggerty, 2009). The LATAR framework provides a structure for planning the components of a course and is initially completed as an outline, with more specific details included, as the design and development progress.

The LATAR framework has five domains:

L—Learning outcomes: This component contains the approved learning outcomes for the course, and is the foundation of the framework. As learning outcomes are central to any course development, these are identified first, and all other domains of the framework flow from there.

A—Assessments: This is an outline of how the learning outcomes will be assessed during the course. How many assessments will the course have? What type of assessments will be used? Will the assessments be formative or summative? When will they be due? And what weightings will they be given? These are key questions to explore early in the design and development phase of any course.

T—Topics: These are the contents of the course, or what will be taught. This section provides an opportunity to list core content for the course and to group the topics into teachable modules of learning. What is "need to know" and what is "nice to know" should be clearly differentiated.

A—Activities: These are the learning activities that will be used during the course to teach the content and to promote pedagogically-sound learning. These can be in the form of written content, readings and asynchronous interactions, such as voice-over PowerPoints, forum discussions and group activities, through to synchronous activities like video-conferencing and chat rooms.

R—Resources: This component identifies the resources that are required to enact the previous components of the framework. Resources can include Web links, PowerPoints, audio, written lecture content, Skype, links to databases, and any other specific resources, that need to be planned or developed as part of the course.

To encourage the use of second generation e-Learning (Adams & Morgan, 2007), the LATAR framework incorporated prompts to assist the educators to remember student-centered best practice principles, when designing and developing online learning environments. These prompts were created by Chickering and Gamson (1987), and they were adapted for e-Learning by Bangert (2004) into seven principles of good practice:

- Encourage engagement with the educator, other students, and the content;
- Provide prompt feedback to students, setting clear timeframes for feedback and responses;
- Provide clarity of expectations through exemplars and criteria for assessment;
- Encourage time on task through the use of time-tables, study plans, and learning agreements, when required;
- Promote active learning that is challenging and achievable, and is situated within the context of the course content;
- Promote reciprocity and co-operation through the use of collaborative activities, problem-based learning and shared assessments;
- Respect diversity and different ways of learning, and provide multiple opportunities to demonstrate proficiency (Based on Bangert, 2004, pp. 222–227).

Bangert's principles became the focus for the development of the course, and they are incorporated into the discussion for the remainder of this chapter.

DECISIONS ALONG THE JOURNEY

The connection between student and faculty as well as content is critical to engagement, no matter what the context, and this was a particular focus for us, as we developed the course. A positive sense of social connection and community will support the students to develop the knowledge, skills, and attitudes necessary for them to be successful (Bangert, 2004, 2005; Blair & Hoy, 2006; Gunawardena & Zittle, 1996; Mahoney, 2006; Pelz, 2004; Woods, Baker, and Hopper, 2004).

The experience of undergraduate nursing students in an online learning environment was investigated by Holloway and Wilkinson (2002). They identified specific issues such as access and the challenge of getting (as well as being) online, perceived lack of tutorial support, and limited contact with classmates. Haggerty (2007) found that postgraduate nursing students also identified access and use, facilitator presence, sense of community, interactivity, and structure as issues to be considered when designing, developing, and facilitating online learning. Gunawardena and Zittle (1996) noted that online students need to adjust to new ways of acquiring knowledge and using technology that they may not be comfortable with, while interacting with the instructor, other students, and the content. These interactions require a student to be technologically sound, self-motivated, and able to work collaboratively, as well as to have independent learning skills.

The students' ability to engage will vary, depending on their experience of education in the past, as well as their technical skill and computer literacy (Garrison, 2004), and computer literacy, access, and technical issues can be barriers to the establishment of a virtual community of practice (Haggerty, 2007; Moule, 2006; Williams, Gunter, and Nichols, 2006). Therefore, to support the students' engagement, we negotiated a one day face-to-face orientation for the students, so that the teaching staff was introduced, and the students were orientated to the learning management system, the program, and the supports available to them. Students left the orientation day knowing the educators, their fellow students, what was expected of them, and what they could expect in return. This provided a strong platform for engagement. In hindsight, I do not believe the course would have been so successful, without this initial face-to-face interaction.

Engaging students with their peers, as well as with the content was something that we were aware needed to be developed throughout the course. To do this, we considered how to best situate the teaching within the students' contexts (Bangert, 2004; Gunawardena & Zittle, 1996; Hung & Chen, 2001; Jonassen, 1998; Moule, 2006; Rovia, 2002). Pelz (2004) discusses this as interactivity, which includes students working collaboratively to facilitate learning. Developing a sense of community through the face-to-face orientation and ongoing discussion forums, with topics directly related to the clinical practice of the students, was the way we promoted the active learning, reciprocity, and co-operation that Bangert (2004) discussed. According to the literature (Gillespie, 2005; Hollis & Madill, 2006), interactivity positively impacts on educational outcomes in professional nursing programs, with students wanting to collaborate more with their lecturers and peers, as part of their online learning experiences (Haggerty, 2007).

Maintaining time on task was something that we, as educators, needed to consider for the students, as well as for ourselves. A common problem in nursing curriculum is content overload (Dalley, Candela, and Benzei-Lindley, 2008). This has the potential to create excess work for students, and to increase content writing and assessment marking for academic staff. Therefore, the content that was developed for the course was enough to stimulate learning, but not so much as to overwhelm.

The content introduced a topic and suggested readings. We then added questions that promoted cognitive dissonance, thus causing imbalance in the students who then needed to critically reflect and develop new perspectives to restore equilibrium (Ruland & Ahern, 2007). Adams and Morgan (2007) describe this as engagement through provocation, by incorporating questions that promote dissonance, and using reflective practice to assist the individual to re-establish balance. Johnson (2008) argued that the focus of the online environment should be on asking the questions, rather than purely delivering content, thus promoting critical thinking skill development in nursing students. This is what we were keen to utilize in the course, allowing the students to create meaning and to develop knowledge and skill, through asynchronous discussion and reflection on their own practice. Reflection is seen as an important component of learning, particularly in relation to professional practice through the promotion of deep learning (Adams & Morgan, 2007; Lautenbach & van der Westhuizen, 2003; Morgan, Rawlinson, and Weaver, 2006; Ruland & Ahern, 2007).

For these cognitive strategies to be effective, prompt feedback, and guidance from the educators was critical to ensure that the students remained engaged. This feedback was given through the electronic medium, by summarizing discussion forums weekly, and e-mailing students directly with suggestions for further learning. From time to time, we needed to contact the students by telephone to provide additional support. It is argued that one of the benefits of online environments is the ability to provide instant feedback; however, this can place high demands on faculty workload (Anderson, 2004; Blair & Hoy, 2006; Fox & MacKeogh, 2003; Karber, 2001). It was therefore important, that clear expectations around timeframes for feedback and responses were established with the students during their face-to-face orientation day, so that students and educators had clear expectations of each other.

Another challenge we faced in developing this online course was asking ourselves what were the important components to assess. For us, the important learning would occur within the discussion forum, and therefore the students' participation in this forum was critical to learning. To this end, we chose to grade the students' participation within the discussion forum as 60% of the students' overall result, with the summative written assessment constituting only 40% of the total grade. Gulati (2008) states that grading participation risks not engaging the students and increasing the potential to promote only surface interaction to meet grading requirements. Cognizant of this risk, we were determined to provide formative feedback to the students on their participation for the first three modules of the course, in preparation for summative grading in the fourth module. This allowed the students to develop confidence in the online environment and to understand what was expected of them before being graded.

Finally, we needed to consider cultural diversity when designing the online program, particularly with respect to Māori and Pacific Nations students. New Zealand literature (for example, Koloto & Associates Limited, 2006; New Zealand Council for Educational Research, 2004) states that Māori students' low participation rates in Internet activities is due to a cultural preference for face-to-face contact, and that mixed mode delivery is a better option. In both Māori and Pacific Nations cultures, there is a strong connection to the *whanau*/family concept, and this sense of community needs to be actively promoted within the online environment (Neal & Collier, 2006). Porima (n.d.) discusses this in relation to the Māori concept of *whanāungatanga*, which loosely translated refers to connectedness, interaction, and mutual support. She goes on to state that Māori students can feel isolated in the online environment and recommends that interactive material is included in the course work materials.

Haggerty (2007) identifies a number of key issues for Māori and Pacific Nations postgraduate nursing students, such as orientation to the online learning management system (access), and the support provided to remain connected (use). No other significant differences in satisfaction were reported between the Māori, Pacific Nations and European students, once the access issues were addressed. Both the face-to-face orientation day and the interactivity built into the course were appropriate and effective in promoting engagement for all the students enrolled in the course, regardless of ethnic origin.

CONCLUSION

What was learnt along the way? Although instructional design is a specialized skill, it can and indeed should be part of the repertoire of all educators. Educators are the content experts and any specialist input should provide support to educators rather than control the process. Educators are the keepers of the curriculum and all that this entails. Thus we needed to think through the pedagogical issues associated with design, and then utilize the expertise of the instructional designer and educational technologist to enact this pedagogy.

This process supported the development of sound strategies, with the course design and development being pedagogically, not technologically, driven. The use of less technology worked best for us in this instance, making sure that the use of technology was appropriate to the content, the course and the teaching philosophy, as well as not overwhelming the students or the educators. Another key lesson learnt was that this process could be applied to any teaching and learning situation. Bangert's (2004) seven principles of good practice can be applied to any context, as can the LATAR framework.

Teaching in the online environment can be rewarding both for educators and students. This chapter has provided insights into our journey in the development, design, and facilitation of an online course for postgraduate nurses. The LATAR framework, underpinned by Bangert's (2004) principles, provided a basis for design and development. Creating connections within an online environment does have its challenges. However, when the connection is made, the satisfaction both for students and educators is high. Online learning in the applied sciences such as nursing remains in its infancy, with more research required to understand its place further into the future.

REFERENCES

Adams, J., & Morgan, G. (2007). "Second generation" e-learning: Characteristics and design principles for supporting management soft-skills development. *International Journal on E-learning, 6*(2), 157–185.

Anderson, J. (2009). The work-role transition of expert clinician to novice academic educator. *Journal of Nursing Education, 48*(7), 203–208.

Anderson, T. (2004). Toward a theory of online learning. In T. Anderson & F. Elloumi (Eds.), *Theory and practice of online learning* (pp. 45–74). Edmonton, Canada: Athabasca University. Retrieved from http://cde.athabascau.ca/online_book/ch2.html

Bangert, A. (2004). The seven principles of good practice: A framework for evaluating on-line teaching. *The Internet and Higher Education, 7*(3), 217–232.

Bangert, A. (2005). The seven principles of effective teaching: A framework for designing, delivering, and evaluating an internet-based assessment course for nurse educators. *Nurse Educator, 30*(5), 221–225.

Billings, D. (1999). *Program assessment and distance education in nursing. Journal of Nursing Education, 38*(7), 292–293.

Blair, K., & Hoy, C. (2006). Paying attention to adult learners online: The pedagogy and politics of community. *Computers and Composition, 23*, 32–48.

Blood-Siegfried, J., Shot, N., Rapp, C., Hill, E., Talbert, S., Skinner, J., & Goodwin, L. (2008). A rubric for improving the quality of online courses. *International Journal of Nursing Education Scholarship, 5*(1), 1–13.

Burke, M. (2008). The incidence of technological stress among baccalaureate nurse educators using technology during course preparation and delivery. *Nurse Education Today, 29*(1), 57–64.

Chickering, A., & Gamson, Z. (1987). Seven principles for good practice in undergraduate education. *American Association of Higher Education Bulletin. 39*(7), 3–7.

Clark, D. (2000). Instruction system design: Analysis phase. Retrieved from http://www.nwlink.com/~donclark/hrd/sat2.html

Dalley, K., Candela, L., & Benzei-Lindley, J. (2008). Learning to let go: The challenge of de-crowding the curriculum. *Nurse Education Today, 28*(1), 63–69.

Fox, S., & MacKeogh, K. (2003). Can elearning promote higher order learning without tutor overload? *Open Learning, 18*(2), 121–133.

Garrison, D. R. (2004). Students' role adjustment in online communities of inquiry: Model and instrument validation. *JALN, 8*(2), 61–74.

Gibson, S., Harris, M., & Colaric, S. (2008). Technology acceptance in an academic context: Faculty acceptance of online education. *Journal of Education for Business, 83*(6), 355–359.

Gillespie, M. (2005). Student-teacher connection: A place of possibility. *Issues and Innovation in Nursing Education, 52*(2), 211–219.

Gulati, S. (2008). Compulsory participation in online discussions: Is this constructivism or normalisation of learning? *Innovations in Education and Teaching International, 45*(2), 185–192.

Gunawardena, C., & Zittle, R. (1995). *An examination of teaching and learning processes in distance education and implications for designing instruction* [ACSDE Research Monograph No. 12]. Research Symposium, Pennsylvania State University.

Haggerty C. (2007). *Students' experiences of the online learning environment: Working toward improvement.* Unpublished research report, University of Southern Queensland, Toowoomba, Queensland.

Haggerty, C. (2009). Developing an online course: Reflections on the process. *Whitireia Nursing Journal, 16*, 8–17.

Hollis, V., & Madill, H. (2006). Online learning: The potential for occupational therapy education. *Occupational Therapy Internationals, 13*(2), 61–78.

Holloway, K., & Wilkinson, J. (2002). *The experience of an online learning environment: Undergraduate nursing students and faculty perspectives.* Unpublished research report. Whitireia Community Polytechnic, Porirua, New Zealand.

Hung, D. W. L., & Chen, D. T. (2001). Situated cognition, Vygotskian thought and learning from the communities of practice perspective: Implications for the design of web-based e-learning. *Educational Media International, 38*(1), 3–12.

Johnson, A. (2008). A nursing faculty's transition to teaching online. *Nursing Education Perspectives, 29*(1), 17–22.

Jonassen, D. (1998). Designing constructivist learning environments. In C. M. Reigeluth (Ed.), *Instructional theories and models* (2nd ed., pp. 215–239). Mahwah, NJ: Erlbaum.

Karber, D. (2001). Comparisons and contrasts in traditional versus on-line teaching in management. *Higher Education in Europe, 26*(4), 533–536.

Koloto & Associates Limited (2006). *Critical success factors for effective use of e-learning by Pacific learners* [Report]. Auckland: Author.

Laurillard, D. (1993). *Rethinking university teaching: A framework for the effective use of educational technology.* London: Routledge.

Lautenbach, G., & van der Westhuizen, D. (2003). Staff development for e-learning: Community building as a change agent, In D. Lassner & C. McNaught (Eds.), *Proceedings of world conference on educational multimedia, hypermedia and telecommunications 2003* (pp. 1994–1997). Chesapeake, VA: AACE. Retrieved from http://www.editlib.org/p/11154

Mahoney, J. (2006). Do you feel like you belong? An on-line versus face-to-face pilot study. *Visions: The Journal of Rogerian Nursing Science, 14*(1), 16–26.

Moore, M., & Hunt, K. (2005). *OTARA framework.* Wellington, NZ: EFest. Conference presentation. Retrieved from http://www.efest.org.nz/2005/speakers/bio_moorehunt.html

Morgan, J., Rawlinson, M., & Weaver, M. (2006). Facilitating online reflective learning for health and social care professionals. *Open Learning, 21*(2), 167–176.

Moule, P. (2006). E-learning for healthcare students: Developing the communities of practice framework *Journal of Advanced Nursing, 54*(3), 370–380.

Neal, T., & Collier, H. (2006). Weaving kaupapa Māori and e-learning. *He Puna Korero: Journal of Maori and Pacific Development, 7*(2), 68–73.

New Zealand Council for Educational Research. (2004). *Critical success factors and effective pedagogy for e-learning in tertiary education: Background paper for ITP New Zealand.* Wellington: Author.

Palloff, R., & Pratt, K. (2000). *Making the transition: Helping teachers to teach online.* Paper presented at EDUCAUSE annual conference. Nashville, TN. Retrieved from http://net.educause.edu/ir/library/pdf/EDU0006.pdf

Pelz, B. (2004). (My) three principles of effective online pedagogy. *JALN, 8*(3), 33–46.

Porima, L. (n.d.). *Understanding the needs of Māori learners for the effective use of eLearning.* Wellington: Tertiary Education Commission.

Rouda, R., & Kusy, M. (1996). Development of human resources. Part 2: Needs assessment: The first step. *Tappi Journal, 78*(4), 263–265.

Rovia, A. (2002). Building sense of community at a distance. *The International Review of Research in Open and Distance Learning, 3*(1), 1–16.

Ruland, J., & Ahern, N. (2007). Transforming student perspectives through reflection. *Nurse Educator, 32*(2), 81–88.

Thompson, M. (2004). Faculty self study research project: Examining the online workload. *JALN, 8*(3), 84–88.

Williams, P., Gunter, B., & Nichols, D. (2006). Health education online: Issues arising from the development and roll-out of a pilot distance education programme for NHS staff. *Health Education, 106*(3), 210–226.

Woods, R., Baker, J., & Hopper, D. (2004). Hybrid structures: Faculty use and perception of web-based courseware as a supplement to face-to-face instruction. *The Internet and Higher Education, 7*(4), 281–297.

CHAPTER 18

CONNECTING LEARNERS IN VIRTUAL SPACE: FORMING LEARNING COMMUNITIES

Lyn Brodie and Peter Gibbings

University of Southern Queensland, Toowoomba,
Queensland, Australia

INTRODUCTION

Facilitated by the scope and the speed of advances in technology, the higher educational landscape is changing rapidly. For example, with enhanced broadband availability and with the ongoing development of learning management systems that better enable the use of Web 2.0 technology, universities worldwide are moving increasingly to external (distance) markets and online delivery of courses. These changes have led to expanded markets and increased competition for universities. Traditional delivery of lectures, practicals, and tutorials now has a major competitor in the alternatives that are on offer through distance and online education. Online students are becoming an entirely new cohort of higher education learners (Diaz, 2002).

Distance education is a growth area, providing the flexibility necessary for many students to undertake higher education. However, students'

Creating Connections in Teaching and Learning, pp. 233–248
Copyright © 2011 by Information Age Publishing

233

diverse educational backgrounds, life experiences, and existing skills and knowledge are not always recognized, particularly when studying entirely in virtual space, where study may be an isolating and lonely experience. Students studying by distance education are generally older than their traditional counterparts, and are interested in learning that can be done at home and fitted around work, family, and social obligations (Bates, 2000). Many mature students are motivated by professional advancement and external expectations. The paradox is that the rapidly changing technological advances that provide the flexibility to allow students to study off-campus are the same technologies that make them nervous about succeeding in higher education, because many may not have kept abreast of recent technological developments (Howell, Williams, and Lindsay, 2003).

In Australia, the delivery of online courses can be a major factor in addressing the national priority of increasing access to and participation in higher education. *The Bradley review of Australian higher education* (Australian Government, 2008) recommended an additional 284,000 student places for the 25–34 age group. The latest advances in technology will play a vital role in increasing access to higher education for many of these additional students.

This chapter reports on the development of a virtual learning community with a diverse group of engineering and surveying students, studying through problem-based learning (PBL) activities conducted in the distance mode. The students became active participants in the learning process through reflective thought and dialogue with others. These are critical to transformative learning and the social construction of knowledge.

ISSUES IN DISTANCE AND ONLINE EDUCATION

While some students relish the independence and flexibility of distance or online education, they can also be disadvantaged by the isolation and the lack of classroom community, opportunities for discussion, debates and sharing of knowledge, and the general social aspects of a more traditional university education. However, most of the research suggests that appropriately designed, delivered and supported Web-based, and online education can be at least equivalent to traditional face-to-face education (Russell, 1999). A significant aspect of this design, delivery, and support concerns the appropriate use of technology to facilitate the development of learning communities.

Discussions in these communities are beneficial to learning as they encourage learners to develop and clarify their thought processes. Learning communities provide an opportunity for exposure to cognitive dissonance which is critical to intellectual growth (Anderson, 2004). Students, who do not possess advanced knowledge, benefit from communication with more knowledgeable peers (Brook & Oliver, 2003; Misanchuk & Anderson, 2001; Rovai, 2002; Wallace, 2003). The nature of these discussions and their role in facilitating student understanding is central to the development of lasting knowledge that can be used by the students in solving future problems (Innes, 2007).

These sorts of collaborative learning methods are suited to constructivism. In accordance with the ideas of Dewey (1938), collaborative learners are afforded the opportunity to develop useful knowledge, through co-operative inquiry within a community of practice. Sustained two-way communication also enables the social construction of knowledge among learners at a distance (Jonassen et al., 1995). This is a constructive effect, often called social constructivism (Jonassen, 1998; Vygotsky, 1978), which occurs in learning environments when learners negotiate ideas with others and reflect on what has been learned. The existence of this social construction aspect to students' learning in communities was also recognized by Pea (1993) who noted that the acquisition of knowledge can be socially constructed when there is a collaborative effort toward a shared goal, and that this can occur through dialogue prompted by differences in individuals' perspectives. The development of effective communities of practice is critical to collaborative learning in virtual space.

In the case of PBL, the communities of inquiry at the base level are essentially the PBL teams themselves. Given the increase in online education, much of this dialogue occurs in virtual space, and hence the term virtual teams. A virtual team is one whose members share a common purpose or goal, and work independently of other teams. The team members are often separated by distance and therefore perhaps by time and culture, as well as by organizational and international boundaries. Their common theme is often that they are linked only by communication technologies (Lipnack & Stamps, 1997; Noe, 2002; Robey, Koo, and Powers, 2000). They are often assembled virtually to work on a specific project with a finite lifespan, and the team members may never physically meet.

The increasing popularity of virtual teams in the industry has given rise to a parallel growth in research. However, in reviewing the literature, care must be taken not to confuse virtual teams with virtual or networked organizations, virtual communities, or forms of teleworking, which do have different characteristics, processes, and outcomes from a true team. Today, virtual teams are acknowledged as playing an increasing role in organizations. Similar to distance education, the growth of virtual teams in industry is made possible by advances in technology. E-mail, discussion boards, the Internet (wikis and Web pages), text-based chat, and voice over the Internet are facilitating the formation and growth of virtual teams.

USE OF VIRTUAL TEAMS IN EDUCATION

The research surrounding virtual teams covers the adoption and use of technology as well as socio-emotional processes, task processes, and outcomes. Much of the published literature focuses on comparisons of virtual and traditional teams; however, little published literature is available surrounding virtual team work that bears relevance to the topics of PBL and education. In industry, it is acknowledged that communication channels adopted by teams have a major effect on the relationships formed among members.

Literature describing the communication channels used by virtual teams covers true electronic communication technology, such as e-mail, chat, and discussion board, and also sensory communication devices like telephone, telephone conferences, and audio/visual conferences (Lau, Sarker, and Sahay, 2000; Pauleen, 2001). Pauleen and Yoong (2001) concluded that telephones (audio connections) were the most important relationship-building communication channel available, as the inclusion of voice intonation and facial expressions for visual links give substantial non-verbal clues and extra subconscious information to the participants. Not surprisingly, then Pauleen and Yoong's research goes on to state that setting up a communication channel, for example a videoconference, between geographically separated members is essential in building trust, which is a major factor in the success of a virtual team.

Most of the research agrees that working with electronic communication technologies alone is problematic without having first established personal relationships and trust within the team. If face-to-face meetings are not possible then many researchers argue that, at a minimum, more sensory modes of communication such as videoconferencing must be utilized (Furst, Blackburn, and Rosen, 1999; Pauleen & Yoong, 2001; Townsend, DeMarie, and Hendrickson, 1998; Warkentin & Beranek, 1999). In contrast, however, work by Brodie (2009) and Gibbings and Brodie (2008) has demonstrated that, in a distance education context, virtual teams have developed into high performance teams without videoconferencing, instead using a variety of non-sensory communication technologies. This has been achieved through careful and considered use of appropriate technology, scaffolding, and appropriate pedagogy and assessment. The pedagogy has been developed by incorporating theories on problem-solving, reflective practice, traditional face-to-face teamwork, distance education, and learning communities.

AIM AND BACKGROUND

The aim of this paper is to describe how virtual teams were used to form learning communities that address the educational needs of distance education students, studying in virtual space within the context of an engineering PBL course. The University of Southern Queensland is a regional Australian university that has developed an international reputation for distance and online education, with approximately 75% of its students studying in these modes. The Faculty of Engineering and Surveying within the University offers a number of undergraduate programs (2–5 years), all fully articulated across nine majors. Due to multiple entry pathways and the range of programs, there is a diverse student intake and different required outcomes, dependent upon major and program. In 2000, the Faculty revised the curriculum to integrate a number of graduate attributes such as teamwork, communication skills, problem-solving, and lifelong learning skills required by professional accreditation bodies. The first of four PBL courses was introduced in 2001. This course is undertaken by all students of the faculty and all course resources are accessible by on-campus and distance students.

While PBL has been incorporated effectively into a wide range of professional studies (Boud & Feletti, 1997), its application to distance education is not well documented. There are limited references to PBL in the distance mode, and the cited examples mostly require a facilitator and some face-to-face interaction within the teams. Brodie (2009) describes the adaption of Anderson's (2004) model as a foundation for online PBL, and the use of technologies, in this case a learning management system. The learning management system delivers resources and the content required to support teamwork in a virtual environment and individual student learning in a learning community.

A learning community can be described as a cohesive community that "embodies a culture of learning in which everyone is involved in a collective effort of understanding" (Rogers, 2000, p. 384). An essential characteristic of a learning community is that, learning is shared among group members including the facilitator. Each member can contribute existing skills and knowledge to the group to further the final outcome. It is suggested that this type of collaborative learning leads to a better or deeper understanding of processes and content for the group members (diSessa & Minstrell, 1998). If these collaborative activities are applied to authentic, real life scenarios, then the similarity to PBL emerges.

DEVELOPMENT OF A LEARNING ENVIRONMENT

In the introductory PBL course, students are allocated to a team of eight members, all of whom communicate via the learning management system. Teams are formed randomly, but a skills audit of students prior to allocating to a team is used to ensure there is a sufficient skill basis in the team for peer assistance and mentoring to take place (Gibbings & Brodie, 2008). All teams are allocated a member of the teaching team to act as a facilitator, and a discussion board, and wiki pages are established specifically for each team. The team members have the ability to interact through a number of discussion and chat forums.

Assessment in the course is a mixture of team tasks, covering team process and outcomes, peer- and self-assessment of individual effort and participation, and individual portfolios. The initial assessment tasks and most of the facilitator interaction with the team are focussed on forming a learning environment for the students to tackle the subsequent open-ended, contextualized, engineering problems, or projects. The first individual assessment is a portfolio covering the setting of individual learning goals based on prior knowledge and experience and aligned with the course specifications. This caters for the diverse student cohort with wide-ranging work, life, and educational experiences. This skill and experience mixture is further explored and developed in the first team task.

The first team assessment is to develop a team code of conduct and responsibilities, a peer- and self-assessment strategy, a communication, and team-work strategy to suit all communication constraints within the team (time, location, and technology), and a project management plan and peer assistance plan which will help all students meet their individual learning goals set in the portfolio. Further individual portfolios over the course of the semester require reflective analysis on individual learning, team participation, and interaction on combined discussion forums. The facilitation of each team and at times individual students, discussion forums, electronic chat rooms, and the carefully structured assessment items help the students to form their own learning communities, both on a team level and on a course level.

METHODOLOGY

Numerous investigations and analyses of student learning and behavior which contributed to the formation of a virtual learning community have been undertaken since the course was introduced. Results from a number of investigations have been analyzed and validated through triangulation. The data has been collected from student self-perception surveys, a thematic analysis of student reflective portfolios, student usage of the resources, and interaction through the learning management system, and a phenomenographic study.

Student Self-Perception Surveys

Three main course surveys were implemented from 2005–2008, covering 12 offers of the course to both on-campus and distance students. During this period, 1427 students completed the course and 847 students responded to surveys (a response rate of 59.4%). The surveys formed the basis for a longitudinal study on student perceptions and learning. Two of the surveys were modified from the standard university student evaluation question-naires that are used to monitor the quality and effectiveness of teaching mate-rials and delivery. The modifications reflected the different teaching strategy and were more applicable to the pedagogy and philosophy of the course. The third survey investigated the student perceptions of their learning and covered the main objectives of the course, such as teamwork, communication, problem-solving, and prior knowledge of self and peers. Answers were multi-ple choice (Likert scale) and short written responses to open-ended questions. A thematic analysis of reflective portfolios was used to validate the findings.

Thematic Analysis of Student Portfolios

Portfolio entries can fall into two main categories: product and process. Product entries respond to a specific stimulus or task, while process entries are more reflective in nature and are not necessarily in response to a par-ticular or specific prompt. In the course, both types of artefacts were ana-lyzed. Emergent patterns or themes were identified, coded, and classified. The thematic analysis yielded recurrent themes across the two portfolio types: teamwork, communication, technical skills and knowledge, conflicts, self-knowledge and learning, and professional development. Each of the thematic categories was divided into sub-categories, pertaining to specific dimensions of the broader thematic category.

Use of the Learning Management System

Statistics was gathered from the learning management system for:

- number and frequency of postings per student and per team;
- student time spent on the learning management system;
- use of resources;
- communication systems used by the student teams and their effec-tiveness.

Phenomenography

Phenomenography is a well accepted and documented interpretative qualitative research method that focuses on the essence of an experience, or what remains constant or is common to different forms of experience (Marton, 1984). The basic premise of the approach was that analyzing students' responses to appropriate questions would reveal a "limited number of qualitatively different ways" (Marton & Booth, 1997, p. 31) of experiencing PBL in virtual space, and that this would be possible even if the differences were grounded in reflective thought and not necessarily in the immediate physical experience (Marton & Booth, 1997; Pang, 2002). The project concentrated on developing a representation of the variation in students' interpretations, of how they did PBL in virtual space within the context of the course and sorting these into conceptual categories (called categories of description for the research data or conceptions in a general sense). The categories of description and the structure linking them become the primary outcome of research, and are commonly called the *outcome space* (Marton, 1981, 1984).

Five categories of description were identified and reported in the outcome space (Gibbings, Bruce, and Lidstone, 2009b): a necessary evil for program progression; developing skills to understand, evaluate, and solve technical engineering and surveying problems; developing skills to work effectively in teams in virtual space; a unique approach to learning how to learn; and enhancing personal growth. Each of these categories represents a qualitatively distinct manner in which people voice the way they think about or experience PBL in virtual space. Many aspects of this outcome space provide insight to the formation of learning communities in virtual space.

Part of the outcome space from the phenomenographical study was *dimensions of variation*, and these have been reported in Gibbings (2008). These are essentially elements of awareness that may be held relatively constant over any particular category of description but may be experienced qualitatively differently in each category of description. Together, the referential aspects of the discovered categories of description and the dimensions of variation provide a rich source of information relevant to learning in virtual space. As will be seen in the following section, these elements of the phenomenographical study provided triangulation for the results discovered by other methods.

FINDINGS

Figure 18.1 indicates that 72.2% of the respondents agreed that the social aspects of the course—the interaction via discussion forums and the team work—assisted their transition to the university, their learning in this course and in concurrent courses, and anticipated study in future courses. The survey results are corroborated by analysis of individual and team reflections and postings to discussion forums. Students reported that:

> I also found that it was easy to communicate within a group via e-mail and the Internet. I enjoyed this part of the course, as it allowed members to

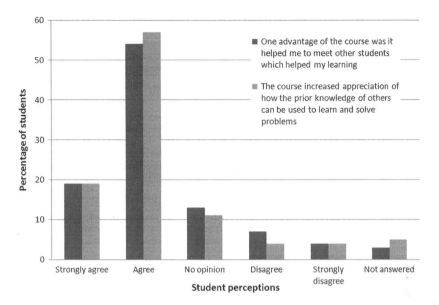

Figure 18.1. Student self-perceptions of the course's social aspect and use of student diversity in learning and problem-solving

join in discussions at different times of the day and this suited the group, as we all work different hours and have a range of Internet access times available to us.

We all have a lot of fun together even though we have never met face-to-face. Our team has found common interests, and all show a genuine concern for each others' welfare.

Having other students who can mentor can be a lot less stressful. I guess, being in a team, there is sense of connection between the members, and so they feel happier to help those they know. I've found just by having people there to talk with, a lot of stress is reduced and the feeling of being alone with no one to help is diminished.

The importance of social learning with respect to learning in general has been well documented in the literature (for example, Brown & Duguid, 2000; Salmon, 1993; Smith, 2003) and is highlighted by the comments from students. There is evidence of the formation of learning communities within the teams and that learning by the students moved away from an individual constructivist focus, as described by Piaget (1952), to social learning in a community. In contrast to Brown and Duguid (2000), evidence from the course indicates that this social aspect to student learning is occurring in the online environment, and it is being improved by the judicious use of the communication features of the learning management system. This ability of the Internet, used appropriately to significantly improve the learning experience in virtual space, is a view supported by Tu and Corry (2002) and Reushle (2006).

Student diversity and prior knowledge and skill are effectively utilized in the course, and help to build the learning community. Students reflect on their own prior knowledge, skills, and experience which they bring to the course. These are shared with team members and through peer assistance, they help the team and individuals meet learning goals. Peer assistance is encouraged and rewarded through the assessment scheme. Figure 18.1 shows that, by the end of the course, the majority of students appreciated how prior knowledge can be successfully utilized in a team environment in virtual space to enhance learning. As one student stated:

> The diversity of the team is one of its greatest strengths; subsequently, suggestions and comments always vary due to our different backgrounds, experience, and individual viewpoints. This should result in a wide range of alternatives to always consider and be advantageous to all of us.

Mentoring within the team has resulted in students learning from each other and valuing the diversity of the team. As recognized by Brown and Duguid (2000), this has allowed the teams to produce more creative solutions, than would be possible from an individual. The sense of community within the teams has led to true collaboration, since it involves the sharing of creation, understanding, and discovery (Schrage, 1990). Students commented that:

> Diversity works for the team because we solve a problem using different viewpoints, use each others' skills to increase the team's output, and learn skills from one another.
>
> With so much interaction between other students in this course, it is hard not to learn a great deal. Each person has a large amount of useful information and this combined into a team environment, the collective information can almost seem endless.

Schrage (cited in Kilpatrick, Barrett, and Jones, 2003) sees this collaboration as essential, because our society is so complex and its intricacies cannot possibly be understood without accepting the contributions of peers.

The data from the learning management system indicated that, during any semester and depending on the total enrolments, between 16,000 and 18,000 postings were made to the discussion forums. The distribution of postings between on-campus and distance teams is shown in Figure 18.2. Early in the semester, distance teams had significantly more postings than

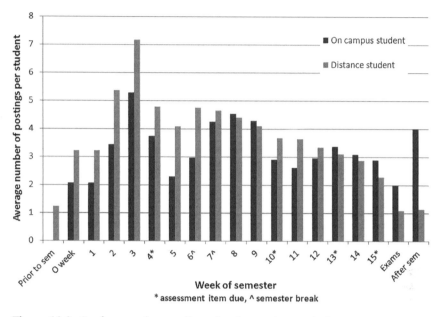

Figure 18.2. Student postings to discussion forums in a typical semester

on-campus teams, as the members of these teams were establishing communication, building trust, and getting to know the team members. However, toward the end of the semester, the on-campus students were using the discussion forum at a similar rate to distance students, even though they had the ability to meet face-to-face.

Figure 18.3 shows typical student usage of the learning management system in terms of the total average time per student for each week of the semester. Distance students spent more time on the learning management system establishing their learning community than the on-campus students, who had the opportunity to do this in face-to-face meetings and timetabled tutorials, at least at the beginning of the semester.

LEARNING IN VIRTUAL SPACE

As already discussed, learning in virtual space provided the context for the phenomenographical research study reported in Gibbings et al., (2009). Lindsay, Naidu, and Good (2007) noted that learning in virtual space is a pedagogically-different learning experience from the traditional face-to-face experience. There is not just a physical separation, but a psychological separation as well. This has been shown to affect student learning, since it

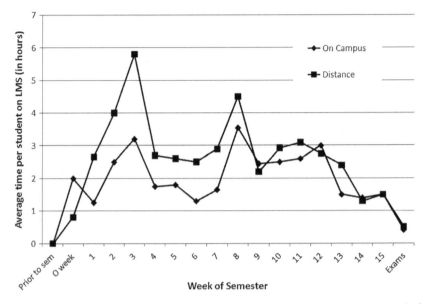

Figure 18.3. Student usage of the learning management system in a typical semester

changes the context in which students construct their knowledge (Lindsay et al., 2007). It is not surprising, then, that it was discovered that students saw this aspect of learning in a virtual environment differently in each of the five conceptions identified as a part of the phenomenographical study. The five conceptions are worthy of further consideration, in light of the earlier discussion surrounding the learning communities.

The conceptions provide insights into the ways in which students related to their team in the context of a learning community, and how they operated and interacted with their team. This ranged from conception one, where students were carrying out basic operational aspects of the course that are necessary to pass the assessment items, through to conception five, where students experienced a deep personal satisfaction from successfully studying in virtual space. In conception one, students worked largely as individuals and did not see themselves as an integral part of the team. Students recognized the team but regarded it as a necessary component of the course to gain assessment marks.

In conceptions two and three, students recognized that being able to work in teams in virtual space was a skill that would be useful in their future workplace. The team work, though, was still at the superficial level. Little effort was put into mentoring in the teams, and there was no evidence of true collaboration or sharing of innovations. Students saw themselves as individuals first and the team was a secondary consideration. Although they identified with the team, their learning was an individual enterprise.

In conception four, students understood that the learning in virtual space was quite a different experience from on-campus study. They were aware of the importance of their expanding community of practice, and they saw themselves as part of a learning community. There was evidence of co-operation, collaboration and mentoring, and students showed a strong awareness of the value of sharing dialogue and interacting with others from outside the team. The students saw themselves as team players, and they often discussed issues with their team to evaluate and synthesize their new understandings.

In conception five, students displayed similar characteristics to conception four with respect to mentoring and helping within the team, but they displayed deeper appreciation of the knowledge building process within the team. In this conception, there was evidence of true knowledge building, as a result of interactions within the learning community. Debates and consensus often preceded team decisions, demonstrating that students were not just sharing new understandings, but were using the team discussions to synthesize and test their own knowledge. There was recognition that, with respect to collective knowledge and experience, the team as a whole was greater than the sum of the individual parts.

CONCLUSION

In a rapidly changing world, it is soft skills such as teamwork, communication skills, lifelong learning, and problem-solving, which will enable the students to respond to the changing technology and demands of the global workforce. This globalization and a multi-cultural workforce require future graduates to be able to work in a virtual environment, sharing tasks on a round the clock basis, working across time zones and geography, communicating electronically, and solving an array of, as yet, unknown problems. Universities educating the future workforce should respond to these challenges as well as to market demands when catering to the new student demographics in distance and flexible education.

Developing and supporting a learning community working in virtual space meets many of these demands, but the pedagogy and course design must support student learning through this new model. It should not merely continue in the traditional paradigm. In the rush to uptake online education, academics often overlook or misunderstand the concept of a learning community sharing knowledge and skills among members, and acknowledging both shared and different learning goals. Developing a virtual learning community is more than just adding technology. Students must be able to learn through jointly constructing knowledge. By engaging in dialogue with other students in virtual space in a supportive environment, they are active participants in the learning process. This active participation, along with opportunities to critically reflect on their own learning and behaviors to validate new ideas and to use them in new contexts, is in line with adult transformative learning and social construction.

Evidence from the PBL course described in this chapter indicates that this social aspect to student learning is occurring in the online environment, and it is being improved by the judicious use of the communication features of the learning management system. Team members, working in virtual space can indeed transcend geography and form an effective learning community which addresses the needs of distance education students.

REFERENCES

Anderson, T. (2004). Toward a theory of online learning. In T. Anderson & F. Elloumi (Eds.), *Theory and practice of online learning.* (pp. 33–40). Athabasca, Canada: Athabasca University.

Australian Government. (2008). *The Bradley review of higher education* [Report]. Canberra: Author.

Bates, A. W. (2000). *Managing technological change: Strategies for university and college leaders.* San Francisco: Jossey Bass.

Boud, D., & Feletti, G. (1997). *The challenge of problem-based learning* (2nd ed.). London: Kogan Page.

Brodie, L. (2009). eProblem based learning: Problem based learning using virtual teams. *European Journal of Engineering Education, 34*(6), 497–509.

Brook, C., & Oliver, R. (2003). *Designing for online learning communities.* Paper presented at the World Conference on Educational Multimedia, Hypermedia and Telecommunications, Honolulu, Hawaii.

Brown, J. S., & Duguid, P. (2000). *The social life of information.* Boston, MA: Harvard Business School Press.

Dewey, J. (1938). *Experience and education.* New York: The Macmillan Company.

Diaz, D. P. (2002). Online drop rates revisited. *The technology source archives.* Retrieved from http://technologysource.org/article/online_drop_rates_revisited/

diSessa, A., & Minstrell, J. (1998). *Cultivating conceptual change with benchmark lessons.* Mahwah, NJ: Lawrence Erlbaum.

Furst, S., Blackburn, R., & Rosen, B. (1999). Virtual team effectiveness: A proposed research agenda. *Information Systems Journal, 9*(4), 249–269.

Gibbings, P., & Brodie, L. (2008). Assessment strategy for an engineering problem solving course. *International Journal of Engineering Education, 24*(1, Part II), 153–161.

Gibbings, P., Bruce, C., & Lidstone, J. (2009). *Problem-based learning (PBL) in virtual space: Developing experiences for professional development.* Saarbrucken, Germany: VDM Verlag Dr Muller Aktiengesellschaft & Co KG.

Gibbings, P. D. (2008). *Experience of problem-based learning (PBL) in virtual space: A phenomenographical study.* Unpublished Doctor of Education thesis, Queensland University of Technology, Brisbane, Queensland.

Howell, S. L., Williams, P. B., & Lindsay, N. K. (2003). Thirty-two trends affecting distance education: An informed foundation for strategic planning. *Online Journal of Distance Learning Administration, 6*(3). Retrieved from http://www.westga.edu/~distance/ojdla/fall63/howell63.html

Innes, R. B. (2007). Dialogic communication in collaborative problem solving groups. *International Journal for the Scholarship of Teaching and Learning, 1*(1), 1–19.

Jonassen, D. H. (1998). Designing constructivist learning environments. In C. M. Reigeluth (Ed.), *Instructional theories and models* (2nd ed., pp. 189–221). Mahwah, NJ: Erlbaum.

Jonassen, D. H., Davidson, M., Collins, M., Campbell, J., & Banaan-Haag, B. (1995). Constructivism and computer mediated communication in distance education. *American Journal of Distance Education, 9*(2), 7–26.

Kilpatrick, S., Barrett, M., & Jones, T. (2003). *Defining learning communities.* Paper presented at the Australian Association for Research in Education International Conference, Auckland, New Zealand.

Lau, F., Sarker, S., & Sahay, S. (2000). On managing virtual teams. *Healthcare Information Management Communications, 14*(2), 46–53.

Lindsay, E., Naidu, S., & Good, M. (2007). A different kind of difference: Theoretical implications of using technology to overcome separation in remote laboratories. *International Journal of Engineering Education, 23*(4), 772–779.

Lipnack, J., & Stamps, J. (1997). *Virtual teams: Reaching across space, time, and organizations with technology.* New York: John Wiley & Sons.

Marton, F. (1981). Phenomography: Describing conceptions of the world around us. *Instructional Science, 10*, 177–200.

Marton, F. (1984). Phenomenography—A research approach to investigating different understandings of reality. *Journal of Thought, 21*(3), 28–49.

Marton, F., & Booth, S. (1997). *Learning and awareness.* Mahwah, NJ: Lawrence Erlbaum Associates.

Misanchuk, M., & Anderson, T. (2001). Building community in an online learning environment: Communication, cooperation and collaboration. Retrieved from http://www.mtsu.edu/~itconf/proceed01/19.html

Noe, R. (2002). *Employee training and development* (2nd ed.). New York: McGraw-Hill.

Pang, M. F. (2002, November). *Two faces of variation: On continuity in the phenomenographic movement.* Paper presented at the International Symposium on Current Issues in Phenomenography, Canberra, Australia.

Pauleen, D. J. (2001). Facilitators' perspectives on using electronic communication channels to build and manage relationships with virtual team members. In C. Crawford, D. A. Willis, R. Carlsen, I. Gibson, K. McFerrin, J. Price, & R. Weber (Eds.), *Society for Information Technology and Teacher Education International Conference 2001* (pp. 2913–2918). Norfolk, VA: AACE.

Pauleen, D. J., & Yoong, P. (2001). Facilitating virtual team relationships via internet and conventional communication channels. *Internet Research: Electronic Networking Applications and Policy, 11*(2), 190–202.

Pea, R. D. (1993). Distributed intelligence and designs for education. In G. Salmon (Ed.), *Distributed cognitions: Psychological and educational considerations* (pp. 47–87). Cambridge, UK: Cambridge University Press.

Piaget, J. (1952). *The origins of intelligence in children*. New York: International Universities Press.

Reushle, S. E. (October 13–17, 2006). *A framework for designing higher education e-learning environments*. Paper presented at the World Conference on E-Learning in Corporate, Government, Healthcare, and Higher Education, Honolulu, Hawaii.

Robey, D., Koo, H., & Powers, C. (2000). Situated learning in cross-functional virtual teams. *IEE Transactions of Professional Communication, 43*(1), 51–66.

Rogers, J. (2000). Communities of practice: A framework for fostering coherence in virtual learning communities. *Educational Technology & Society, 3*(3), 384–392.

Rovai, A. (2002). Building a sense of community at a distance. *International Review of Research in Open and Distance Learning, 3*(1), 1–16. Retrieved from http://www.irrodl.org/index.php/irrodl/article/view/79/153

Russell, T. L. (1999). *The no significant difference phenomenon*. Raleigh, NC: North Carolina State University.

Salmon, G. (Ed.). (1993). *Distributed cognitions: Psychological and educational considerations*. Cambridge, UK: Cambridge University Press.

Schrage, M. (1990). *Shared minds: The new technologies of collaboration*. New York: Random House.

Smith, B. L. (2003). Learning communities and liberal education. *Academe (TAFE Tasmania), 89*(1), 14–18.

Townsend, A., DeMarie, S., & Hendrickson, A. (1998). Virtual teams: Technology and the workplace of the future. *Academy of Management Executive, 12*, 17–29.

Tu, C. H., & Corry, M. (2002). Research in online learning community. *E-journal of Instructional Science and Technology, 5*(1). Retrieved from http://www.ascilite.org.au/ajet/e-jist/docs/Vol5_No1/chtu_frame.html

Vygotsky, L. S. (1978). *Mind in society*. Cambridge, MA: Harvard University Press.

Wallace, R. M. (2003). Online learning in higher education: A review of research on interactions among teachers and students. *Education, Communication & Information, 3*(2), 241–280.

Warkentin, M., & Beranek, P. M. (1999). Training to improve virtual team communication. *Information Systems Journal, 9*(4), 271–289.

CHAPTER 19

BRIDGING A DISCIPLINE DIVIDE THROUGH THE LENS OF COMMUNITY OF INQUIRY

Petrea Redmond and Christine McDonald

University of Southern Queensland, Toowoomba, Queensland, Australia

INTRODUCTION

There is an increasing number of online and blended courses in higher education. Akyol, Garrison, and Ozden (2009) stated that there is consequently a "need to explore and develop frameworks or models in order to understand the complex nature of teaching and learning in their learning environments" (p. 1834). The Community of Inquiry model developed by Garrison, Anderson, and Archer (2000) is one such framework that has been developed to assist the educators and researchers to explore the dynamics and complexities of online and blended learning environments. Online discussion forums are a common element of teaching and learning within higher education.

Technology has had an impact on teaching and learning in all educational contexts. Boud and Prosser (2002) suggested that improved learning requires educators to explore and respond to "the quality of students'

Creating Connections in Teaching and Learning, pp. 249–263
Copyright © 2011 by Information Age Publishing
All rights of reproduction in any form reserved.

experience using technologies" (p. 237). However, we need to look beyond the technology to the pedagogy, design, and delivery of the learning experience (Ladyshewsky, 2004). It is not about the technology, but about how the educator uses the technology. The introduction of online discussions may not impact on learning. However, what can make an impact are the pedagogical choices made by the educator, regarding how online discussions might be used to promote socially constructed knowledge within higher education.

This chapter argues that effective teaching presence is required to ensure that active online interaction encourages learners to continually share, question, debate, justify, and consider multiple perspectives or solutions, rather than to take a passive role. It investigates connections between disciplines in the use of asynchronous online discussion forums to deepen discipline knowledge. By crossing the divide between the disciplines of mathematics and teacher education, the authors compare and contrast how these two disciplines explore meaning-making within their undergraduate discussion forums.

TECHNOLOGICAL CHANGES IN HIGHER EDUCATION TEACHING

Higher education institutions are no longer bound by the traditional teaching approaches of lecture and tutorial, which are time and place dependent. At the World Economic Forum, Twomey (2009) reported that "education is in a state of transition from a traditional model to one where technology plays an integral role. However, technology has not yet transformed education" (p. 48). The rapid and continuous evolution of technological tools and increased access to information mean that the World Wide Web will continue to enable learning wherever, whenever, and for whomever. Increased internet access, open content repositories, social networking services, and online collaborative tools provide multiple ways of communicating and gaining information. Universities are now embracing these virtual learning resources to provide flexibility in the ways that learners access academic experts, other learners, and "scholarly and research material" (Bradwell, 2009, p. 11).

Increased access provides opportunities for increased engagement and interaction. Twomey (2009) reminded us that "the technology to propel educational achievement can only be value-added if linked with creative pedagogy to educate students with 21st-Century skills and to train teachers to engage actively with students in interactive learning communities" (p. 48). Online learning has "the potential to bring students together and engage them collaboratively in purposeful and meaningful discourse through the creation of sustainable communities of learners" (Garrison, 2009, p. 97).

Boud and Prosser (2002) suggested that in an online environment, educators need to develop pedagogical approaches that promote interaction by focusing on "engaging learners, acknowledging the learning content; challenging learners, and providing practice" (pp. 240–241). They go on to comment that for learners to engage meaningfully they "need to experience a challenge and respond to it, not just be the recipient of an information transfer" (p. 243). Challenge is enhanced through instructional design and pedagogies which scaffold learners to question their prior experiences and promote deep discipline knowledge.

SCAFFOLDING TO PROMOTE IMPROVED LEARNING

Analogous with building construction, cognitive scaffolding implies that support is provided to learners and as progress is made in knowledge construction, the assistance is gradually reduced until the learners achieve independence (Wood, Bruner, and Ross, 1976). Holton and Clarke (2006) defined scaffolding "to be an act of teaching that (i) supports the immediate construction of knowledge by the learner; and (ii) provides the basis for the future independent learning of the individual" (p. 131). Scaffolding can take on different forms, ranging from simply using the right word or question to the provision of tasks, resources or devices to engaging learners in conceptual discourse (Anghileri, 2006; Holton & Clarke, 2006).

Unguided or minimally guided discovery has limited success for novice learners. In fact, there is "compelling evidence that more strongly guided methods that involve demonstrations of problem-solving strategies accompanied by hands on practice exercises with authentic problems and immediate feedback on mistakes are necessary to maximize the learning of most students" (Clark, 2009, p. 6). In a computer-based learning environment, scaffolding can be achieved by providing well structured learning tasks, and may include static questions, and dynamic support sensitive to the needs of individual learners, or computer-based tools to guide the thinking of learners (Azevedo & Hadwin, 2005).

Our expectation is that educators can provide learning experiences and facilitation of online discussion to help learners move from surface learning, which normally produces short term outcomes to a deeper understanding. Henri (1989) revealed that deep learning is achieved "only when the learners translate newly-acquired information into their own terms, connecting it, for example with their lived experience" (p. 130). This requires educators to encourage learners to continually share, question, debate, justify, and consider multiple perspectives or solutions, rather than to take a passive role in their learning.

When learners connect with others through technology, they create networks for and of learning. In his connectivism theory, Siemens (2005) considered learning as actionable knowledge which may be attained through experience. However, this knowledge is strengthened through thinking, sharing, and reflecting, all of which are key elements in the two case studies explored in this chapter.

This chapter investigates connections within and between disciplines in the use of asynchronous online discussion forums to deepen discipline knowledge. Within this virtual space, learners investigated problems, explored and shared possible solutions, and reflected on processes. The online discussion forums were used to connect learners to the instructor, their peers, and the content. The Community of Inquiry model (Garrison et al., 2000) provides a framework for analyzing the level of cognition in online posts. By crossing the divide between the disciplines of mathematics and teacher education, the chapter compares and contrasts how these varied disciplines explore meaning-making and connect theory, and practice within their undergraduate online learning communities.

THE COMMUNITY OF INQUIRY MODEL

Garrison et al.'s (2000) Community of Inquiry model was developed to "articulate the behaviors and processes required to nurture knowledge construction through the cultivation of various forms of 'presence'" (Shea & Bidjerano, 2009, p. 544). Arbaugh et al. (2008) remind us that this framework provides "a collaborative-constructivist perspective to understanding the dynamics of an online learning experience" (pp. 133–134). It values the concepts which parallel the general aims of higher education, including critical thinking, reflection, and discourse.

There are three key presences within the Community of Inquiry framework: social presence, teaching presence, and cognitive presence. Figure 19.1 shows how each of these elements intersect. Social presence is defined by Garrison et al. (2000) as "the ability of participants in a community of inquiry to project themes socially and emotionally, as 'real' people" (p. 94). Cognitive presence is concerned with the "construction of meaning and confirmation of understanding" (Garrison, Cleveland-Innes, and Fung, 2004, p. 63), while teaching presence is "the design, facilitation and direction of cognitive and social processes for the purpose of realizing personally meaningful and educationally worthwhile learning outcomes" (Anderson et al., 2001, p. 5).

These three presences do not necessarily occur independently of one another as all contribute to the educational experience of learners in a semester course of study. In order to develop higher order thinking skills

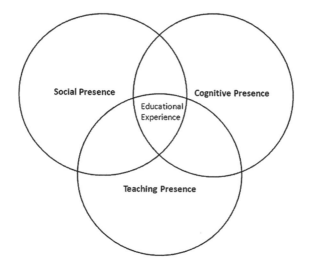

Figure 19.1. The three presences of a Community of Inquiry (based on Garrison & Anderson, 2003)

(cognitive presence) and collaboration in asynchronous online discussion forums, commitment, and participation (social presence) are required (Garrison et al., 2000). To ensure that students move through the phases of cognitive presence effectively, teaching presence provides the necessary guidance (Shea & Bidjerano, 2009), by balancing cognitive and social issues and facilitating discourse and direct instruction (Garrison & Arbaugh, 2007). With an appropriate mix of all three presences, the online asynchronous discussion forum can lead to "fruitful critical inquiry" (Garrison et al., 2000, p. 96).

The primary concern of this paper is with the cognitive presence element. Cognitive presence is "reflective of the purposeful nature of collaborative knowledge construction, inherent in constructivist educational experiences" (Arbaugh et al., 2008, p. 134). It can be partitioned into four phases:

- Triggering: The point at which a problem/issue is conceptualized or realized. Learners feel a sense of dissonance;
- Exploration: Learners search for information and ideas (both experiential and through literature) to clarify/make sense of the problem or issue;
- Integration: The "connecting of relevant ideas capable of providing insight into the dilemma" (Garrison, Anderson, and Archer, 2001, p. 15).

Learners begin to construct tentative solutions to the initial problem or issue;

- Resolution: Learners commit to a solution, testing either vicariously or in an authentic context.

Cognitive presence concerns the construction of meaning and the confirmation of understanding about how knowledge is being constructed by learners. Akyol et al. (2009) commented that cognitive presence incorporates "understanding an issue or problem; searching for relevant information, connecting and integrating information; and actively confirming the understanding in a collaborative and reflective process" (p. 125). As shown in Table 19.1, Garrison and Anderson (2003) identified a set of indicators for each of their four phases of cognitive presence, and these were used to inform the analysis of online discussions, within the two discipline areas of mathematics and teacher education.

Table 19.1. Indicators of Cognitive Presence (based on Garrison & Anderson, 2003)

Triggering event:	recognizing problem/s, puzzlement
Exploration:	divergent thinking, information exchange, making, suggestions, brainstorming ideas and possible solutions, making intuitive leaps
Integration:	convergence of ideas, synthesis of ideas, identifying solutions
Resolution:	applying, testing, defending

METHOD

Within this chapter, case study method is used to investigate the connections between the use of online discussion forums by undergraduate learners in the disciplines of mathematics and teacher education. Merriam (1998) suggested that the benefits of using case study are "in the process, rather than outcomes, in context rather than a specific variable, in discovery rather than confirmation" (p. 19). The study asked two research questions: To what extent are the phases of cognitive presence developed within asynchronous online discussions? And how does the use of asynchronous online discussion forums in undergraduate teacher education and mathematics compare and contrast?

The two case studies describe the learning activities within two different discipline contexts in a regional Australian university. The role of the online discussion forum in both cases was to promote deep learning using the principles of social constructivism. The collaborative learning experiences were designed to assist learners in meaning-making, at both the individual and group level through critical and reflective dialogue focusing on a specific issue or problem.

THE TEACHER EDUCATION CASE STUDY

As part of a teacher education course, learners engaged in an online collaborative project. Within a structured environment, the learners investigated authentic issues of teaching and learning in 21st century classrooms (for example, pedagogical approaches to decrease cyber-bullying, and to enhance the learning outcomes of second language learners and autistic learners). The learning experience was a blended one in that the course was in face-to-face mode; however, the majority of the activities that related to this learning experience were conducted online. The project enabled learners to engage with peers, practising teachers, and academics. The cohort was in the 2nd year of their 4 year education program, and the learners had no, or very limited, previous online learning experiences. Participation in the project was assessed by the learners self-selecting and submitting what they perceived to be their best quality postings throughout the structured experience.

THE MATHEMATICS CASE STUDY

After being provided with information about the aims and mechanics of successful group work, distance learners in a core 1st year mathematics course were divided into groups of 25–30 to participate in collaborative problem-solving in asynchronous discussion forums. Learners were provided with a series of five non-routine problems at 2 week intervals across the semester. Mirroring the on-campus face-to-face experience (see Taylor & McDonald, 2007), discussion of a problem was scaffolded by the educator-initiated forum threads of aim, method, working, and conclusion. These were based on Polya's (1957) heuristic for the problem-solving process (understanding the problem, devising a plan, carrying out the plan, and looking back). The learners were required to participate in online discussions as a part of their assessment; however, they were not evaluated on the quality of their postings.

ANALYZING THE TWO CASE STUDIES

The structure and processes of the educational experience in both the contexts was designed to scaffold the learners. Until the writing of this chapter, however, the educators (who are also the researchers) were unaware that their instructional design intuitively matched the four phases of cognitive presence. Table 19.2 presents the learning activities, and their relation to the phases of cognitive presence for each case.

The archives from online discussion forums in each course form the base data for analysis. The forum posts selected for analysis were from a 5–6 week period, following the establishment of social presence and familiarity

Table 19.2.   Mapping Educational Experiences in Teacher Education and Mathematics Against Garrison & Anderson's (2003) four phases of cognitive presence

Phases	Teacher education context: Activity stages	Mathematics context: Activity stages
Trigger	Stage 1 Stimulus reading was provided to the learners. The stimulus material created a sense of dissonance, where the learners began to see the issues or problems related to teaching in a digital and diverse classroom.	Aim A non-routine mathematical problem was provided to the learners. The learners then presented ideas for what was needed to be achieved and in so doing, they gained an understanding of what the problem was really asking.
Exploration	Stage 2 Learners used the online forums to share experiences; search for and share relevant information and literature; question each other; investigate policy and strategies; and debate differences in perspectives about the issues.	Method Learners presented a variety of ways in which the problem could be approached. To do this they needed to search for relevant techniques, and to determine which might give the best result.
Integration	Stage 3 Learners were joined by practising teachers who acted as experts. The experts provided another informed layer of perspectives and information but more importantly they assisted the learners in integrating the multiple sources of information and seeking multiple solutions.	Working Possible worked solutions were shared and the relative merits of each were discussed.
Resolution	Stage 4 Learners were asked to create an action plan for their future learning, and to reflect on their learning and the learning process of the project.	Conclusion Learners were required to make connections between the aim and solutions.

with the online interface within each group of learners. Content analysis of the postings was conducted using the four phases of cognitive presence, indicated in Table 19.1: triggering, exploration, integration, and resolution. An additional category was added—no category detected—where no cognitive presence could be identified or the posting was unrelated to the purpose of the forum.

A single message or posting is used as the unit of analysis. Where there were two possible phases present in a message, the message was coded up to the higher level in the hierarchy of phases. Each author coded all the postings independently. To improve validity and reliability where there was disagreement between coders, negotiation, and discussion of coding occurred, until a consensus was reached (Garrison et al., 2006).

FINDINGS AND DISCUSSION

The next section of this chapter discusses the findings, which are presented in Table 19.3 and indicate the number and percentages of postings for each case within each phase of cognitive presence.

A chi-square test of independence was used to determine if there were any differences in the distributions of cognitive presence categories within the course online forums for the disciplines. The analysis supported the assertion that there is a difference in the distribution of categories of cognitive presence (chi-square = 22.839, $p < 0.001$), with the mathematics forum containing more than expected integration posts (standardized residual 2.1), and the education forum containing more than expected exploration posts (standardized residual 2.0). This is indicated in Fig. 19.2. The discussion that follows will compare and contrast the relative frequency

Table 19.3. Distribution of Phases of Cognitive Presence by Discipline

Cognitive Presence Phase	Teacher education		Mathematics	
	Number of posts	%	Number of posts	%
Triggering	8	8	12	14
Exploration	55	56	34	39
Integration	14	14	31	35
Resolution	17	18	3	3
No category detected	4	4	8	9
Total Posts	98		88	

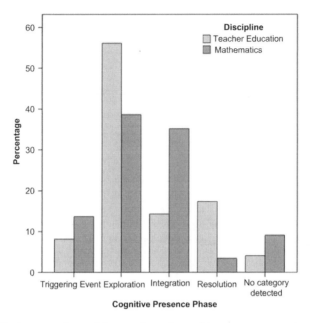

Figure 19.2. A comparison of the number of cognitive presence postings by phase and discipline

of posts at each phase for the cases. The results will be compared with those found in the other published studies.

Triggering Phase

In both the disciplines, a triggering event was initially provided by the instructor (for example, mathematical problem posed, controversial reading provided). At the triggering phase, there was a little difference between the disciplines when analyzing the learners' posts with education having 8% and mathematics having 14% of their postings, at this level. Other researchers have also found that the initial phase, which is used to stimulate the other three phases, has a low percentage of posts (Garrison et al., 2001; Kanuka, Rourke, and Laflamme, 2007; McKlin et al., 2002; Redmond & Mander, 2006).

Exploration Phase

As might be expected, the exploration phase which is characterized by broad searches for information that might assist in finding solutions for the initial dilemma had the largest number of posts in both the disciplines. Teacher education had 56% and mathematics had 39%. This result aligns with the other research, which has found similarly high percentages at the exploration phase (for example, Garrison et al., 2001; Kanuka et al., 2007; McKlin et al., 2002; Redmond & Mander, 2006).

Within the teacher education context, learners' posts in this phase included personal narratives, sharing of literature, and questions of clarification. A reason for an increased percentage of posts in this phase, when compared with mathematics, may be due to the fact that in education there is a larger range of possible suggestions or opinions, and there is rarely one right answer.

The exploration phase within the mathematics context was actioned by learners exploring a range of methods. In their search for a solution, they were encouraged to seek multiple methods to solve the problem. Although there are multiple methods to solve the problem, the number of posts may have been confined because the students were required to arrive at one solution.

Integration Phase

There are significantly more posts in mathematics compared to teacher education in the integration phase with education having 14% and mathematics having 35%. A result of 14% is disappointing in the teacher education context, where you would hope that to derive their best practice, the learners draw from multiple perspectives and sources of information.

The percentage of integration posts in mathematics is noticeably higher than the findings of the other researchers (Garrison et al., 2001; Kanuka et al., 2007; McKlin et al., 2002; Redmond & Mander, 2006). This higher percentage could be linked with the discipline expectations or the design of the activity. During this phase, the mathematics learners were finding or designing their own solution using information and ideas gathered from the posts in the exploration phase. The process of finding a solution required them to integrate ideas from their peers' posts, the text, and other sources. Garrison and Arbaugh (2007) indicated that many researchers have found that learners have "great difficulty moving beyond the information exchange or exploration phase" (p. 162). However, this does not seem to be the case for the mathematics discipline, perhaps because there was a defined answer.

Resolution Phase

At the resolution phase, teacher education had a substantially higher rate of postings (18%) than the mathematics context (3%). The mathematics outcome more closely aligns with the previous research where the percentages ranged from less than 1% (Redmond & Mander, 2006) to 10% (Kanuka et al., 2007).

The cognitive presence process involves "actively confirming the understanding in a collaborative and reflective process" (Akyol et al., 2009, p. 125). As such, when coding resolution in the teacher education context posts, we included posts of a reflective nature. These posts may not have resolved the issue, nor defended our possible solutions; however, they did reflect on the changing nature of the learners' knowledge and future actions in addition to reflecting on the learning process during this time. This is possibly why the percentage of posts at the resolution phase was higher in teacher education than in mathematics.

Within the mathematics context, the resolution phase was deemed to have been the process of learners looking back and checking that they have done what they were asked to do. It goes beyond stating the numerical answer to the question, as the learners were required to link their answer and conclusion back to the aim and context of the initial problem. An explanation of why there was a small number of resolution posts in the mathematics context could be that, once someone had posted a solution and conclusion, there was minimal need for further discussion.

IMPLICATIONS

The differences in distribution of the phases of cognitive presence reflect the differences in the nature of the tasks set for discussion in the different contexts. In the mathematics context, problem-solving involves a considerable amount of integration of ideas in order to arrive at the solution to the problem to reach resolution. In contrast in the teacher education context, the emphasis is on exploration and debate to reach resolution. Through effective teaching presence, the purposeful design and facilitation of learning experiences should provide an opportunity for learners to reach higher cognitive engagement.

The decisions on coding of posts at any particular level can only be made on what learners make visible. Learners' posts do not necessarily represent their private thought processes; they simply represent what they are willing to make public. The cognitive presence phases provide us with a framework to view interactions and to consider how we might improve them at the individual and group level. Educators are able to use this information to review and modify their teaching presence in particular instructional design, scaffolding, and facilitation.

The cognitive presence indicators of the final phase of resolution do not currently include a reflective indicator. Perhaps adding this indicator in the resolution phase may go some way to providing data on learners' meta-cognition, or promoting meta-cognitive activities by the learners. Learners are often asked to reflect on the learning and the learning process, and this will provide coders using the cognitive presence element with an opportunity to explicitly situate these types of postings.

One limitation of this study is that the data was collected from a short segment of the semester. An analysis of discussion postings across a whole semester may result in a different distribution over the phases of cognitive presence. In addition, other artefacts—such as assessment responses—could provide another source of data. It is likely that learners would operate at a higher level of cognition when their efforts contribute to their final result. As with any case study, results are unable to be generalized. These case studies were restricted to two disciplines and two educators in one institution. However, insights gained from the connections established and from the professional conversations between the educators from different disciplines, have proved useful in broadening reflections on teaching practice to develop deep discipline knowledge.

CONCLUSION

The focus of this study was to investigate the quality of cognitive presence within undergraduate online discussions in the two different disciplines of teacher education and mathematics. This study found that, when comparing different disciplines, the context does make a difference. However, teaching presence in the form of course design, scaffolding of learning activities and facilitation of online discussion makes more of a difference on the development of cognitive presence.

It is difficult to look at cognitive presence without considering the impact of teaching presence (and also social presence) on the learning outcomes, and the use of online discussion to encourage the development of deep discipline knowledge. By working with educators in other disciplines and contexts, we are better able to assist our learners and ourselves to become effective contributors to cognitive presence in the online asynchronous learning environment. The lens of the Community of Inquiry framework (Garrison et al., 2000) bridged the perceived divide between two diverse disciplines, creating connections between two academics and opening the pathway to future productive conversations about improving teaching and learning.

REFERENCES

Akyol, Z., Arbaugh, J. B., Cleveland-Innes, M., Garrison, D. R., Ice, P., Richardson, J. C., & Swan, K. (2009). A response to the review of the Community of inquiry framework. *Journal of Distance Education, 23*(2), 123–136.

Akyol, Z., Garrison, R. D., & Ozden, M. Y. (2009). Development of a community of inquiry in online and blended learning contexts. *Procedia Social and Behavioural Sciences, 1*, 1834–1838.

Anderson. T., Rourke, L., Garrison, D. R., & Archer, W. (2001). Assessing teacher presence in a computer conferencing context. *Journal of Asynchronous Learning Networks, 5*(2), 1–17.

Anghileri, J. (2006). Scaffolding practices that enhance mathematics learning. *Journal of Mathematics Teacher Education, 9*, 33–52.

Arbaugh, J. B., Cleveland-Innes, M., Diaz, S. R., Garrison, D. R., Ice, P., Richardson, J. C., & Swan, K. P. (2008). Developing a community of inquiry instrument: Testing a measure of the Community of Inquiry framework using a multi-institutional sample. *Internet and Higher Education, 11*(3–4), 133–136.

Azevedo, R., & Hadwin, A. F. (2005). Scaffolding self-regulated learning and metacognition—Implications for the design of computer-based scaffolds. *Instructional Science, 33*, 367–379.

Boud, D., & Prosser, M. (2002). Appraising new technologies for learning: A framework for development. *Educational Media International, 39*(3), 237–245.

Bradwell, P. (2009). *The edgeless university: Why higher education must embrace technology.* London: Demos.

Clark, R. E. (2009). Translating research into new instructional technologies for higher education: The active ingredient process. *Journal of Computing in Higher Education, 21*(1), 4–18.

Garrison, D. R. (2009). Implications of online learning for the conceptual development and practice of distance education. *Journal of Distance Education, 23*(2), 93–104.

Garrison, D. R., & Anderson, T. (2003). *E-learning in the 21st century: A framework for research and practice.* New York: Routledge.

Garrison, D. R., Anderson, T., & Archer, W. (2000). Critical inquiry in a text-based environment: Computer conferencing in higher education. *The Internet and Higher Education, 2*(2–3), 87–105.

Garrison, D. R., Anderson, T., & Archer, W. (2001). Critical thinking, cognitive presence, and computer conferencing in distance education. *American Journal of Distance Education, 15*(1), 7–23.

Garrison, D. R., & Arbaugh, J. B. (2007). Researching the community of inquiry framework: Review, issues, and future directions. *The Internet and Higher Education, 10*(3), 157–172.

Garrison, D. R., Cleveland-Innes, M., & Fung, T. (2004). Student role adjustment in online communities of inquiry: Model and instrument validation. *Journal of Asynchronous Learning Networks, 8*(2), 61–74.

Garrison, D. R., Cleveland-Innes, M., Koole, M., & Kappelman, J. (2006). Revisiting methodological issues in transcript analysis: Negotiated coding and reliability. *The Internet and Higher Education, 9*(1), 1–8.

Henri, F. (1989). La téléconférence assisté par ordinateur dans une activité de formation à distance. Unpublished doctoral dissertation, Montreal, Canada: Concordia University.

Holton, D., & Clarke, D. (2006). Scaffolding and metacognition. *International Journal of Mathematical Education in Science and Technology, 37*(2), 127–143.

Kanuka, H., Rourke, L., & Laflamme, E. (2007). The influence of instructional methods on the quality of online discussion. *British Journal of Educational Technology, 38*(2), 260–271.

Ladyshewsky, R. (2004). E-learning compared with face to face: Differences in the academic achievement of postgraduate business students. *Australian Journal of Educational Technology, 20*(3), 316–336.

McKlin, T., Harmon S. W., Evans, M., & Jones, M. G. (2002). Cognitive presence in web-based learning: A content analysis of students' online discussions. Retrieved from http://it.coe.uga.edu/itforum/paper60/paper60.htm

Merriam, S. (1998). *Case study research in education: A qualitative approach*. San Francisco: Jossey-Bass.

Polya, G. (1957). *How to solve it*. New York: Doubleday & Anchor.

Redmond, P., & Mander, A. (2006). Online mentoring of pre-service teachers: Exploring cognitive presence. In C. Crawford et al. (Ed.), *Proceedings of the Society for Information Technology and Teacher Education Conference 2006* (pp. 2643–2650). Chesapeake, VA: AACE.

Shea, P., & Bidjerano, T. (2009). Community of inquiry as a theoretical framework to foster "epistemic engagement" and "cognitive presence" in online education. *Computers and Education, 52*(3), 543–553.

Siemens, G. (2005). Connectivism: Learning as network creation. Retrieved from http://www.elearnspace.org/Articles/networks.doc

Taylor, J. A., & McDonald, C. (2007). Writing in groups as a tool for non-routine problem solving in first year university mathematics. *International Journal of Mathematical Education in Science and Technology, 38*(5), 639–655.

Twomey, P. (2009). Summit on the global agenda: On technology and innovation at the World Economic Forum (2009). Retrieved from http://www.weforum.org/pdf/globalagenda.pdf

Wood, D., Bruner, J., & Ross, G. (1976). The role of tutoring in problem solving. *Journal of Child Psychology and Psychiatry, 17*, 89–100.

CHAPTER 20

FINDING THE RIGHT ONLINE LEARNING CONNECTIONS: COMPARING MODELS IN PRACTICE

Tina van Eyk

Learning Designer/eLearning Consultant, Brisbane, Queensland, Australia

INTRODUCTION

Online learning is one way to achieve the goal of flexible lifelong learning. Over the last decade, several "different shades" (Jackson, 2002, p. 1) of e-learning practices have created flexible learning options. Many educational organizations now embrace information and communication technologies to assist learning, whether learning experiences are delivered totally online or via blended approaches where online tools and resources enhance face-to-face instruction. Online learning has become a practical alternative for adults to continue to learn whilst meeting work and lifestyle commitments, as it provides choice for students to study at their own time, place, and pace (Anderson, 2008b).

Creating Connections in Teaching and Learning, pp. 265–279
Copyright © 2011 by Information Age Publishing
All rights of reproduction in any form reserved.

The strategies which work best to create educational connections in online learning are a topic of debate amongst educational professionals. As technologies change and new learning theories "for the digital age" (Siemens, 2004, p. 1) emerge, educational professionals – including teachers, trainers, and designers (educational, learning, and instructional) – must choose how to best use technology to facilitate learning. In particular, this involves making decisions about what theories, themes, strategies, principles, and elements should be used to achieve an engaging online environment that is consistent with the desired learning and teaching outcomes.

This chapter presents reflections on situated learning in practice. It explores my experiences over several years of working in professional online learning environments and reflecting on the characteristics that appeared to work well to encourage adult learning. I reflect on my observations as both a course developer working with a team to design online courses and as a student of online education.

To help guide future online course design, I review adult learning theory and literature, in particular the five themes identified by Gunawardena and Zittle (1996) for effective online teaching and learning. My experiences with very different, and at times competing, models of online learning (Anderson, 2008a) underpin this discussion, which considers why the themes may work well in one context, but not necessarily in another. I identify how the five themes identified by Gunawardena and Zittle (1996) were used and I analyze how they were applied, to highlight the types of educational connections that were made for students, amongst student peers, and between students and teachers. The chapter concludes by suggesting why the themes strategically chosen for one context may not suit other contexts.

LITERATURE REVIEW

The importance of having foundational understandings about adult learning theory for the design and development of learning materials is well documented (Ally, 2008; Anderson, 2008b; Kalantzis & Cope, 2008; Mergel, 1998; Siemens, 2002; Tallent-Runnels et al., 2006). One essential consideration, however, is to decide which adult learning theories are best suited to online learning environments.

The online teaching and learning realm is based on diverse and developing theories, themes, strategies, principles, and elements, alongside rapidly changing technology. Theories of behaviorism (learning through changes in behaviour), cognitivism (learning through changes in thought processes), and constructivism (learning through individual experiences) underpin the design of online materials to cater for learner preferences. Learning and teaching approaches are often combined in different ways to encourage interactive online learning experiences such as, but not limited to, varied interaction with the content and computer interface, providing students with more choice, creating an online social presence, individual learning, and/or peer collaborative learning. Newer theories of connectivism based on "networked and social learning" (Siemens, 2009, p. 1) also help to explain how people are adapting to a digital learning era.

Tallent-Runnels et al.'s (2006) literature review of 76 studies of teaching courses offered online found "no comprehensive theory or model that informed studies of online instruction" (p. 115). This supported Gunawardena and Zittle's (1996) findings that "very few articles provided empirical evidence on the effectiveness of specific teaching strategies" in distance education (p. 59). Despite the age of this work, I have used Gunawardena and Zittle's findings as a foundation for my investigation, as they continue to provide valuable insights into applied online teaching and learning. Reushle, Dorman, Evans, Kirkwood, McDonald and Worden (1999) stated that Gunawardena and Zittle's five themes "seem to permeate successful online teaching and learning," where several "critical elements for online design have emerged" (p. 1). The five themes for effective distance and online learning are:

- interaction;
- cognitive strategies;
- learner-centeredness;
- collaborative learning;
- social presence.

Interaction refers to the way that students communicate online. Four types of interaction are possible to assist learning: learner-content interaction, learner-learner interaction, learner-instructor interaction, and learner-interface interaction (Hillman, Willis, & Gunawardena, 1994). Cognitive strategies are the "mental activities performed by persons" (West, Farmer, & Wolff, 1991, p. 22), where students construct meaning to develop "relationships between key ideas" and to build "hierarchies of knowledge structures" (McDonald & Postle, 1999, p. 7). For example, a carefully designed course framework enables students to build upon their understandings, through exploration of the website content, activities, tools, and resources. Learner-centeredness is a constructivist approach focusing on the student who is encouraged to construct understandings based on experiences. Collaborative learning is "working together to accomplish shared goals" (Harasim, 2000, p. 21), and to construct "coherent knowledge-structures through group communication" (Garrison, 1997, p. 6). The fifth theme, social presence, is the way in which a person is perceived by others online, where a "telepresence" (Gunawardena & Zittle, 1996, p. 54) is created when the

Figure 20.1. A continuum of online learning and teaching experiences

person communicates asynchronously via text or by other means. It could be argued, however, that online learning environments need some, but not all, of the five themes to encourage effective student learning.

Anderson (2008a) described two competing models of online learning. Firstly, he described independent learning, which offers just-in-time, interactive, individual learning where students are guided by the design framework to complete their studies. This enables students to take responsibility for their own learning and to have the freedom to move through study at their own time, place, and pace. Secondly, Anderson suggested that the development of a community of learning offers collaborative learning opportunities using a range of communication technologies, which can provide asynchronous and synchronous discussion. Asynchronous discussion enables students to read, reflect and respond to posts in their own time, whilst synchronous discussion requires the organization of same time learning.

When comparing the two models, it could be argued that the models are at opposite ends of a diverse range of experiences for the online student (see Figure 20.1). Independent learning enables freedom of time, place, and pace learning, whilst a community of learning provides social collaborative learning which "binds learners in time" (Anderson, 2008b, p. 61). Although Anderson described the models as competing, he acknowledged that it is also possible to combine elements of both models to provide "synchronous, asynchronous, and independent study activities in a single course" (Anderson, 2008a, p. 349). This suggests that there is a diverse range of online learning and teaching experiences for the designer to choose from. Figure 20.1 illustrates this point.

REFLECTIONS

In reflecting on my experiences in postgraduate level studies and on my professional experience in online learning, I realize that I have operated in two very different online learning environments. One demonstrates the characteristics of independent learning, whilst the other demonstrates the characteristics of a community of learning. In the discussion that follows, I consider the two environments, which I have called Environment A and Environment B.

Environment A

Environment A was a training organization responsible for the design, delivery, and assessment of training aligned to national competencies. Industry employees had to complete studies every two years to maintain accreditation to work safely with dangerous goods within Australia. The overall training goal was for mastery of skills in the workplace, in particular for the student to know how to resell chemicals competently. I was employed as a course developer, to assist the team to create an engaging, interactive and flexible online learning environment.

Based on education and adult learning design principles, the online course environment was created for remote students who could not afford to be absent from work to attend face-to-face courses. To help structure and organize the creation of the online course environment within project time-lines, the ADDIE (Analysis, Design, Development, Implementation, and Evaluation) instructional design model was applied. It is interesting to note that, although the model is described as "elusive" with unknown origins (Molenda, 2003, p. 1), the ADDIE model has been used by designers and developers for many decades. For Environment A, the design phase involved structuring the course framework, designing the interface and templates, and creating the instructional content, content pages, interactive activities, assessments, and resources, to ensure that relevant learning theories and adult learning principles were embedded. The development phase involved building the content pages, activities, self-assessments, and evaluations, alongside testing and retesting functionality and reviewing and editing content.

The learning environment enabled industry members to study outside of the workplace, and catered for students who preferred to study alone. To tailor resources to meet the needs of the learner group, continuous feedback was obtained from various stakeholders. To ensure quality, industry content experts identified and reviewed materials. Assessments were largely criterion-based, with student performance assessed against the criteria levels required for competence. Some courses were delivered totally online, whilst other courses used a blended approach, where a face-to-face workplace assessment followed the online learning component.

Environment B

Environment B is the university learning environment where I experienced varying degrees of individual and community learning whilst undertaking postgraduate study. Learning was facilitated by a constructivist approach, through asynchronous communication via discussion boards. Computer conferencing, "consistent with higher-order thinking and cognitive development" (Garrison, 1997, p. 5), enabled students to both reflect critically after reading and reflect on and respond to postings to construct their own meanings. Peers shared ideas and teachers monitored progress by providing scaffolding and intellectual support.

Throughout my studies, a constructivist learning approach was used as students were encouraged to tailor their learning experiences with workplace related assessments. Students used their work contexts and experiences to create "authentic and meaningful activities" (Herrington, Oliver, Herrington, & Sparrow, 2000, p. 10). However, the degree of collaborative learning that was required varied from course to course. Of the eight courses I completed as part of my postgraduate study, some used high collaboration with active use of asynchronous discussion; some used a synchronous online meeting tool to organize same time learning; while others used limited collaboration.

Three Questions Considered

In reflecting on the use of Gunawardena and Zittle's (1996) themes throughout my experiences with online environments, I have thought about three questions:

- Were all five themes, which were identified for effective online teaching and learning, essential to facilitate learning online?
- Did the two models of online learning require different strategic themes?
- How did the themes help to create educational connections?

In considering the first question, it would seem that not all of Gunawardena and Zittle's (1996) five themes were essential to facilitate learning online. Different themes were used to suit different learning contexts. Both environments offered a "climate" with "guideposts" (Siemens, 2005, p. 8) to encourage learning. Both used interaction, cognitive strategies, and a learner-centered approach. Content and interface interaction changed learner understanding as students manipulated the computer interface (Gunawardena & Zittle, 1996) to access materials. Cognitive strategies built on knowledge as students articulated their ideas by organizing "their thoughts and information into knowledge structures" (Harasim, 2000, p. 22). It also seemed that students had "individual responsibility and control" (Garrison, 1997, p. 8) to construct meaning based on their experiences.

In Environment A, independent learning required interaction, cognitive strategies, and a learner-centered approach to facilitate learning. Students interacted with the content and interface to complete activities at any time from any online place (learner-centered). Content was provided in small-sized lessons. Interactive activities and instant feedback provided student formative assessment (cognitive strategies) through a range of questioning. Assessments could be retaken to meet the criteria. Due to the self-pacing of independent learning, collaborative learning and social presence did not occur and both learner-content and learner-interface interaction were very high. As stated by Anderson (2003), the "educational experience" is not degraded "as long as one of the three forms of interaction (student-teacher; student-student; student-content) is at a high level" (p. 4).

In Environment B, the community of learning could have used all of Gunawardena and Zittle's (1996) themes. However, not all five were always in use. Of the eight courses I completed as part of my postgraduate study, some offered high levels of social presence to encourage learning together (collaborative learning). One course used a synchronous online meeting tool to build learning networks. Yet, some students still preferred limited peer interaction and continued to lurk with anonymity in the online environment. Asynchronous computer conferencing encouraged critical reflection and idea building, both individually and as a group (cognitive strategies). Using discussion boards and emails, students interacted with peers, teachers, content, and the interface. Other courses followed a more independent learning approach where students addressed questions individually (learner-centered).

For Question 2 (Did the two models of online learning require different strategic themes?), it appeared that the models required the use of different strategic themes suited to their learning context. Learner characteristics and preferences and the types of activities and assessment that were required were major design factors influencing the themes chosen.

In Environment A, an interactive online environment was chosen to provide a flexible alternative for remote students who wanted to study away from face-to-face courses. Students had the freedom to study at any time (learner-control) within their personalized learning timeframe. Learner-content and learner-interface interactions generated independent knowledge. Online workplace activities enabled students to apply their developing skills to real world situations (cognitive strategies and learner-centered) which encouraged and motivated students to take an active role in the learning process.

In Environment B, the university encouraged collaborative learning, which "provides the social glue" to engage and motivate students to participate in a community (Harasim, 2000, p. 21). Where possible, the university also encouraged social presence, "the degree individuals project themselves through the medium" (Garrison, 1997, p. 6). Via asynchronous communication, students read, reflected and responded to online discussion posts to construct their own meaning. Asynchronous discussion boards encouraged knowledge sharing among peers, where the teachers monitored progress by providing scaffolding and intellectual support "in the form of comments, suggestions, feedback, and observations" (Teles, 1993, p. 276). To build "networked and social learning" (Siemens, 2009, p. 1), one course used synchronous online meetings to generate knowledge. However, due to global time and technology differences, some students were not always able to participate. Additionally, some students also expressed preference for asynchronous communication due to meeting time constraints. This experience is consistent with the findings of Rollag (2010), where he describes how the structure of asynchronous discussions enabled students and teachers to "enter and leave the conversation at times of their own choosing" (p. 502). This allowed people "to plan learning and teaching around their other life activities and make contributions from almost anywhere in the world" (p. 502).

In looking at Question 3 (How did the themes help to create educational connections?), it was evident that the two environments used the themes in different ways to create and maintain educational connections. To make the journey real, both environments provided students with "what they want, where they want it, when they want it" (see Taylor, 2001, p. 12), by combining learning with authentic workplace activities (learner-centered).

In Environment A, the primary educational connection was for the learner to discover and build knowledge independently. Students were given control to choose their own content study, as several courses were developed to suit different job roles (learner-control). Students could choose their own learning journey or adventure from a range of course content based on their occupational needs. The PROMOTING mnemonic adult learning principles of Smith and Delahaye (1983) underpinned the environment as an important foundation for adult learning, to build upon knowledge (cognitive strategies) and to ensure a constructivist, learner-centered approach. Similar ideas have been further developed in the work of Kalantzis and Cope (2008).

- P = Primary and recency, where learners recall well those things learnt first and last in a sequence. This was achieved with the welcome orientation home page and the interactive tutorial. Both were designed as learning tools to provide instruction and scaffolding to guide students on how to learn online.

- R = Reinforcement, where rewarded learning is more likely to be retained. Interactive learning tools facilitated teacher presence by providing immediate feedback and reinforcement.

- O = Overlearning, where frequent recall assists learning. In particular, the interactive quiz tool provided opportunities for students to recall knowledge.

- M = Multiple senses learning, where two or more of the senses encourage effective learning. Students were stimulated by using their sight, tactical and hearing senses when keyboard typing, or using the computer mouse to manipulate the learning interface.

- O = Opportunities for feedback. These were achieved by the quiz tools which provided feedback for students to self-assess their learning.

- T = Transfer of training, where study is combined with real life situations. Combining study with work made the journey real. Students reflected on their own experiences in real world settings.

- I = Involve learners actively. This was achieved by providing students with interactive explanations and examples of learning tools and resources, so that they could go beyond the required tasks to further investigate resources as part of their learning experience.

- N = Nibble, where content is provided in chunks. The design of smaller sized lessons prevented information overload and built upon prior knowledge.

- G = Go from the known to the unknown, where new learning is built on previous understandings. To avoid disorientation, the course design guided students to progress step-by-step through the topics. This enabled students to experience known information, which led to the discovery of new understandings (Kalantzis & Cope, 2008).

In Environment B, the primary educational connections were to build knowledge individually and to create knowledge as a networked group. Learning was facilitated by the teacher establishing a supportive community of trust, through encouraging asynchronous conversation and reflective questioning. A constructivist approach facilitated learning through asynchronous communication via discussion boards. The sharing of opinions helped students to reflect and build upon their ideas. This experience is consistent with the online environment study of Wilkinson and Barlow (2010), as most students in my postgraduate studies seemed to experience "educational and professional benefits" of generating knowledge and building networks from their active engagement within the facilitated "online collaborative activities" (p. 8). Students took responsibility for their own understandings, and they were encouraged to use their work context to create authentic experiences. Additionally, synchronous collaborative learning also occurred amongst several peers in one course.

FUTURE EXPLORATIONS

My reflections have focused on two adult learning environments where I have reflected on, analyzed and compared how Gunawardena and Zittle's (1996) five themes for effective teaching and learning were applied. I recognize, of course, that other learning environments, models or modes of online learning may focus on different aspects of learning.

Online learning is changing the way people learn. Over the last decade or so, online learning has had an ever growing influence on our global educational community, by providing flexible study options for the adult worker. To cater for this growing need, educational professionals must choose how to best use technology to facilitate learning. As online learning is, in the words of Tallent-Runnels et al. (2006), "a relatively new frontier in education," further research is needed "to generate information that will guide online instruction design to facilitate" student learning (p. 117).

The design and development of any learning material is a complex process, as the ultimate goal is to transfer knowledge to real life situations. To achieve this goal, the needs of the learner group must be known and considered (Sheinberg, 2001). The designer must also be aware that the characteristics of the learner group may vary. For example, the review findings of Arbaugh (2010) suggest that structured online learning participation may be more of a challenge for undergraduate than postgraduate students, possibly due to their "technological familiarity" (p. 137). Arbaugh suggests that Generation Y students are more comfortable communicating instantly via non-structured and informal mediums such as blogs, so they may find participating via structured asynchronous discussion boards more difficult. Gaining knowledge of the learner group characteristics is one of many ingredients which need to be carefully considered during the design phase, to ensure that the "appropriate mix of student, teacher, and content interaction" (Anderson, 2008b, p. 63) is available for learning.

Another consideration is how adult learning theories can assist the use of technology for learning. As expressed by Laurillard (2002), "design has to be generated from the learning objectives and the aspirations of the course, rather than from the capability of the technology" (p. 22). Figure 20.2 illustrates what can be argued to be the essential design ingredients for guiding future online learning and teaching design, where the learning context determines the overlapping design elements and learning model components. The figure offers an ingredient checklist of what to consider when designing effective online learning environments, based on my

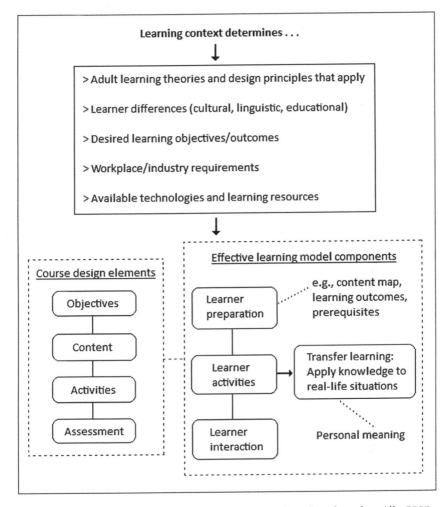

Figure 20.2. Essential design ingredients for online learning (based on Ally, 2008; Reushle & McDonald, 2000; Siemens, 2005)

reflections of my experiences and the work of Ally (2008), Reushle and McDonald (2000), and Siemens (2005).

As Figure 20.2 shows, the components of the learning context should be analyzed first to determine the appropriate learning approach to take. Analysis of the context should also examine learner differences such as culture, language and former educational experiences, to ensure that the choice of learning design matches the desired learning outcomes. Major factors influencing a preferred learning design approach include the workplace and/or industry requirements and resource allocation, including available technologies and learning resources. Such an analysis is part of the first phase of the ADDIE model framework which was discussed previously.

The characteristics of the learning context should influence the course design elements (Reushle & McDonald, 2000) and the learning model components (Ally, 2008). This will determine the appropriate learning objectives, content, interactive learning activities, and assessment which are required to both prepare and engage students to interact within the online learning environment. Ally (2008) suggested that an upfront concept map helps to prepare, motivate and guide learners through a "sequence of instruction" as they complete activities by interacting with the interface and content (p. 36). This is part of the design phase of the ADDIE model, where decisions about how to structure the content and design the interface, content pages, interactive activities and assessments are made to ensure that relevant learning theories and adult learning principles are embedded.

A focus on the learning context, guided by learning and instructional design principles, will guide designers to use the best strategies "to create the right environment for continued learning" (Siemens, 2005, p. 9). Time well spent in the analysis and design phases will guide the development, implementation and evaluation phases. Over time, an effective online learning environment should be improved continuously, by taking into consideration both student and client feedback within changing course content and workplace requirements.

For educators to assist students to continue to learn and work in the digital era as technology continues to rapidly change, we should "adapt existing learning theories" (Ally, 2008, p. 18) and enhance them to suit specific learning environments. Developing learning theories will help educational professionals "to understand that learning is about making connections with ideas, facts, people, and communities" (Anderson, 2008b, p. 49). As professionals, we need to acknowledge that "the web of the future isn't about visiting sites, it's about connecting resources" (Downes, 2009, p. 2).

CONCLUSION

Although successful environments have comparable strategies, my reflections indicate that not all environments require all five of Gunawardena and Zittle's (1996) themes to facilitate effective learning online. From my analysis of the themes in action, it appears that the themes chosen to design online materials are crafted to suit the specific learning context. To encourage learning online, different learning contexts require relevant learning and teaching strategies, which both create and maintain appropriate educational connections for students, amongst peers and between students and teachers.

Purposeful design, learning and instructional tools and resources should be carefully chosen to provide the best possible online learning experiences. Whether the purpose is to build knowledge independently or to create situations where students discover knowledge as part of a networked group, successful online learning environments must be based on relevant adult learning theories and design principles that are suited to the specific learning context.

REFERENCES

Ally, M. (2008). Foundations of educational theory for online learning. In T. Anderson & F. Elloumi (Eds.), *Theory and practice of online learning* (2nd ed., pp. 15–44). Edmonton, Canada: AU Press.

Anderson, T. (2003). Getting the mix right again: An updated and theoretical rationale for interaction. *International Review of Research in Open and Distance Learning, 4*(2). Retrieved from http://www.irrodl.org/index.php/irrodl/article/view/149

Anderson, T. (2008a). Teaching in an online learning context. In T. Anderson & F. Elloumi (Eds.), *Theory and practice of online learning* (2nd ed., pp. 343–365). Edmonton, Canada: AU Press.

Anderson, T. (2008b). Towards a theory of online learning. In T. Anderson & F. Elloumi (Eds.), *Theory and practice of online learning* (2nd ed., pp. 45–74). Edmonton, Canada: AU Press.

Arbaugh, J. B. (2010). Do undergraduates and MBAs differ online?: Initial conclusions from the literature. *Journal of Leadership & Organizational Studies, 17*(2), 129–142.

Downes, S. (2009, July). *gRSShopper: Creating the personal web.* Presentation to the PLE group, Moncton, Canada. Retrieved from http://www.downes.ca/presentation/226

Garrison, D. R. (1997, June). Computer conferencing: The post-industrial age of distance education. *Open Learning, 12*(2), 3–11.

Gunawardena, C. N., & Zittle, R. (1996). An examination of teaching and learning processes in distance education and implications for designing instruction. In M. Beaudoin (Ed.), *Distance education symposium 3: Instruction* (ACSDE Research Monograph, No. 12, pp. 51–63). University Park, PA: Pennsylvania State University.

Harasim, L. (2000). Shift happens: Online education as a new paradigm in learning. *Internet and Higher Education, 3*, 41–61.

Herrington, J., Oliver, R., Herrington, T., & Sparrow, H. (2000). *Towards a new tradition of online instruction: Using situated learning theory to design web-based units.* Retrieved from http://www.ascilite.org.au/conferences/coffs00/papers/jan_herrington.pdf

Hillman, D. C. A., Willis, D. J., & Gunawardena, C. N. (1994). Learner-interface interaction in distance education: An extension of contemporary models and strategies for practitioners. *The American Journal of Distance Education*, 8(2), 30–42.

Jackson, R. H. (2002). *Defining eLearning – Different shades of "online"*. Paper presented at the 8th Hong Kong Web Symposium. Retrieved from http://www.hkwebsym.org.hk/2002/jackson_quote.html

Kalantzis, M., & Cope, B. (2008). *New learning: Transformational designs for pedagogy and assessment*. Retrieved from http://newlearningonline.com/new-learning/

Laurillard, D. (2002). Rethinking teaching for the knowledge society. *Educause*, January/February, 17–25. Retrieved from http://www.educause.edu/ir/library/pdf/erm0201.pdf

McDonald, J., & Postle, G. (1999). *Teaching online: Challenge to a reinterpretation of traditional instructional models*. Paper presented at AUSWEB Conference, Ballina, NSW. Retrieved from http://ausweb.scu.edu.au/aw99/papers/mcdonald/paper.htm

Mergel, B. (1998). *Instructional design and learning theory*. An occasional paper in education technology from the University of Saskatchewan. Retrieved from http://www.usask.ca/education/coursework/802papers/mergel/brenda.htm

Molenda, M. (2003). In search of the elusive ADDIE model. Retrieved from http://www.comp.dit.ie/dgordon/Courses/ILT/ILT0004/InSearchofElusiveADDIE.pdf

Reushle, S., Dorman, M., Evans, P. Kirkwood, J., McDonald, J., & Worden, J. (1999, Dec. 5–8). *Critical elements: Designing for online teaching*. Paper presented at the 16th Annual Conference of the Australasian Society for Computers in Learning in Tertiary Education, Brisbane, Queensland. Retrieved from http://www.ascilite.org.au/conferences/brisbane99/papers/reushledorman.pdf

Reushle, S. E., & McDonald, J. (2000). Web-based student learning: Accommodating cultural diversity. *Indian Journal of Open Learning*, 9(3), 351–359.

Rollag, K. (2010). Teaching business cases online through discussion boards: Strategies and best practices. *Journal of Management Education*, 34(4), 499–526.

Sheinberg, M. (2001). Know thy learner: The importance of context in e-learning design. *Learning circuits* [Webpage]. Retrieved from http://www.astd.org/LC/2001/1001_sheinberg.htm

Siemens, G. (2002). Instructional design in elearning. *elearnspace*. Retrieved from http://www.elearnspace.org/Articles/InstructionalDesign.htm

Siemens, G. (2004). Connectivism: A learning theory for the digital age. *elearnspace*. Retrieved from http://www.elearnspace.org/Articles/connectivism.htm

Siemens, G. (2005). Learning development cycle: Bridging learning design and modern knowledge needs. *elearnspace*. Retrieved from http://www.elearnspace.org/Articles/ldc.htm

Siemens, G. (2009). Connectivism: Networked and social learning. Retrieved from http://www.connectivism.ca/

Smith, B. J., & Delahaye, B. L. (1983). *How to be an effective trainer: Skills for managers and new trainers*. New York: Wiley.

Tallent-Runnels, M. K., Thomas, J. A., Lan, W. Y., Cooper, S., Ahern, T. C., Shaw, S. M., & Liu, X. (2006). Teaching courses online: A review of the research. *Review of Educational Research, 76*(1), 93–135.

Taylor, J. C. (2001, April 1–5). *Fifth generation distance education.* Keynote address presented at the ICDE 20th World Conference, Dusseldorf, Germany.

Teles, L. (1993). Cognitive apprenticeship on global networks. In L. Harasim (Ed.), *Global networks* (pp. 271–281). Cambridge, MA: MIT Press.

West, C. K., Farmer, J. A., & Wolff, P. M. (1991). *Instructional design implications from cognitive science.* Englewood Cliffs, NJ: Prentice Hall.

Wilkinson, S., & Barlow, A. (2010). Turning up critical thinking in discussion boards. *elearning papers.* Retrieved from http://www.elearningpapers.eu/index.php?page=home

CONCLUSION

CHAPTER 21

LINKING THE THREADS: CREATING CLEARER CONNECTIONS

Lindy Abawi, Joan M. Conway, and Robyn Henderson

University of Southern Queensland, Toowoomba, Queensland, Australia

INTRODUCTION

Creating connections in teaching and learning is both what we do as educators and what we aspire to do. The chapters of *Creating Connections in Teaching and Learning* have shown many profound and creative ways in which authors/educators have attempted to do just this, across diverse landscapes and with varying degrees of success. The range of research findings and conclusions emit a cross-chapter resonance that creates powerful messages about the role of educators. In a world of change, connections matter more than ever. This means that there is a need to make links across time, space, cultures, and contexts and to consider new forms of pedagogical practice. In "seeking to illuminate the here and now," as Connors so eloquently phrases it in the Foreword, the contributing authors have accepted the challenge of change. They have openly shared their insights and research

Creating Connections in Teaching and Learning, pp. 283–299

findings, in the hope that their contributions may inform and assist fellow educators, who are also seeking to create connections that enhance teaching and learning.

Beare (2001) clearly identified what we all know to be of paramount importance in education today. This is the need to create interconnected webs of knowledge, where information, process knowledge, and alternate frames of understanding are synthesized into a whole. Although Beare's ideas were written 10 years ago, his desire to challenge our thinking is as pertinent today as it was at the turn of the century. He provokes us to accept the challenge that is faced by educators and the teaching profession—to embrace the quandary of deciding what and how to teach the children who are sitting in our classrooms right now, while preparing them for a future world, which we can only vaguely envisage. In order to challenge teachers' thinking, Beare presented the imagined musings of a 5 year old child called Angelica. Angelica is Beare's "Future's child." She represents any child sitting in a primary or elementary school today. Beare's ponderings as Angelica help us to question our current practices in the light of the ongoing and future educational needs of the students:

> The old way of learning—by steps and stages, by the sequencing of learning into one best path, by the traditional scientific approaches, by having the curriculum divided neatly into subjects—is already passing. Knowledge for me is a web of interconnections where I access interesting information from many angles. (p. 16)

Regardless of the context within which we (the authors) are facilitators of learning—whether it is in relation to early years learning or learning in a tertiary online context—we act as key players within Angelica's world. Each of us spins webs of interconnections, bridging the learning space for both students as learners and for educators as learners. Connors speaks of the *new thinking* that emerges from these pages. This new thinking paints mental pictures of interconnections, neo-pedagogies, and the traversing of new and diverse educational terrains.

EXAMINING THE THEMES

As the editors of *Creating Connections in Teaching and Learning*, we consciously chose to group the chapters according to the resonances to which we had responded. What has emerged is a collection of chapters that are complementary to the creative processes that were undertaken to bring the contributing authors' initial thinking to life. The authors worked independently, and in collaboration in writers' workshops, where thoughts were critiqued and harmonized. Some of the synergies now evident in the book can be attributed to the writing and the review processes which occurred.

Although, as a volume of writings, this is in no way an entirely phenomenological collection of work, nonetheless each chapter captures a sense of unfolding lived experiences. Each chapter represents a journey through the developing understandings of its author/s, educator/s, and researcher/s. As van Manen (2000) observed:

> By naming and renaming experience, we bring it to awareness, (re)interpret it and come to particular understandings or misunderstandings ... finding a language to describe our experience is a critical requisite for addressing and understanding our pedagogical predicaments. (p. 316)

Just as many of the authors have done, we also searched for an appropriate language, with which to explore our understandings of the themes and the research findings that are presented within this volume. The reflections in the next section of this chapter draw heavily on metaphor and imagery in an attempt to capture our understandings. Through these reflections, we suggest how the book as a whole helps to make clearer connections for educators, researchers, and others with an interest in education.

METAPHORICAL REFLECTIONS

Lakoff and Johnson (1980) argued that "metaphorical imagination is a crucial skill in creating rapport and in communicating the nature of unshared experience" (p. 231). With this in mind, we have used metaphor as a tool to convey our understandings, and to create conceptual connections to a variety of author-based experiences. As Lakoff and Johnson emphasized, "metaphor is not merely a matter of language. It is a matter of conceptual structure. And conceptual structure is not merely a matter of the intellect—it involves all the natural dimensions of our experience" (p. 235).

In the first chapter we analyzed some of *what was to come*. Now we give credence to a variety of personal interpretations of *what has been*. We have reframed these as visual metaphors, asking readers to keep in mind that "all research is interpretive; it is guided by the researcher's set of beliefs and feelings about the world, and how it should be understood and studied" (Denzin & Lincoln, 2005, p. 22). The linkages we found are highlighted by the key metaphors, words and images that materialized as we pursued cross-contextual meanings within these pages. Using the metaphoric organizers as the basis, representations of core ideas as produced by *Wordle* (Feinberg, 2009), and the visual symbolism created by one of the editors, are blended to create a number of conceptual connections.

McNaught and Lam (2010) discussed *Wordle* as a "useful tool for pre-liminary analysis, and for the validation of previous findings" (p. 630). However, we are also mindful of the limitations identified by McNaught and Lam and arising from the way that:

> Word clouds treat each word as the unit of analysis. This mechanical manipu-lation of text is fast but at the same time it can be misleading because it neglects the semantics of the words and also the phrases, and even sentences the words are composed of. (p. 641)

With this in mind, we decided to use the word clouds as a validation tool, rather than for the purpose of initial linkage analysis. As each chapter was read, mental montages, indicating the journey of "new thinking" that was being undertaken, emerged.

There was some discussion between the editors as to the validity of pre-senting critical reflections in this montagic way using verbal and visual met-aphors juxtaposed with word clouds. However, the literature provided the resonance and reassurance that was needed. Nonaka and Takeuchi (1995) proposed that figurative language helps to articulate tacit knowledge, and Cook (1981, cited in Denzin & Lincoln, 2005) described montage as using "brief images to create a sense of urgency and complexity. It invites viewers to construct interpretations" (p. 5). Metaphor is seen as one way in which humans make sense of their reality (Jakobson & Halle, 1956; Morgan, 1980; Ortony, 1975). It is often used to simplify the complexities of struc-tures or understandings, thus acting as interpretative paradigms for groups of individuals who are attempting to understand shared multiple realities.

A number of researchers (for example, Alvesson, 2002; Jacobs & Heracleous, 2004, Kövecses, 2005; Steen, 2008; Visser-Wijnveen et al., 2009) have suggested that the power of metaphor lies in its ability to com-municate shared realities and to create cognitive connections. To date, the importance of metaphor in creating pedagogical understandings has still not been explored fully; yet, there are indicators that these cognitive con-nections can trigger pedagogical understandings which in turn trigger changes in practice (Andrews and Associates, 2011).

Visual metaphors are all around us and constitute a primary means of conveying messages to large groups of people. Signs and symbols loaded with meaning have become a taken-for-granted manifestation of a shared social language. Gee (1996) suggested that different social languages "make visible and recognizable different social identities, different versions of *who* one is" (p. 8). For Gee, this raised "the difficult question ... of what ... constitutes our 'core identity', the 'master narrative' that ties our different identities, acted out in different contexts, together into a story that (at least, we think) is unified" (p. 8). It was this search for a master narrative that would tie together the educator/authors' identities and experiences, that directed our mental journeying and led us to the use of metaphor as a means of linking the threads.

The initial organizers—*Connecting within school contexts, Connecting beyond school contexts, Making meaning from lived experiences,* and *Developing virtual connections*—were used as representative of the main threads that emerged from the early work done by the editorial team. Two stages were undertaken to weave the threads together. Stage 1 involved the reading of each chapter and the drawing out of what was considered to be significant points. The most commonly recurrent words and concepts were then placed with individually significant ones (for example, "a pedagogy of listening") into a visual representation about the significance of the messages within a particular theme. Stage 2 saw the text from each set of grouped abstracts uploaded to the *Wordle* processor as "Wordle seems to be particularly useful for studies that involve qualitative/thematic analyses of written or transcribed spoken text" (McNaught & Lam, 2010, p. 631). The resulting word clouds were then used as points of clarification and verification of the linkages, across the chapters and then across the organizers.

The use of this method to verify initial visual metaphors proved very useful, and McNaught and Lam's insights have pointed the way to a new way of thinking about analysis, which is apt in relation to the *new thinking* terrains that our authors have explored. The figures show the synergies between the two forms of interpretation. The messages from each pair were compared, generalized, and analyzed according to the theme.

CONNECTING WITHIN SCHOOL CONTEXTS

What we understood from the images which related to within-school-contexts of learning and teaching (see Figs. 21.1 and 21.2) was a sense of teacher commitment to student-centered learning. We recognized a sense of profound dedication to improving practice, as displayed by teachers who were intent on engaging students in authentic learning experiences. Learning is seen as a powerful positive proactive change facilitator.

The repetition of key words that have places of prominence within this group of chapters and are visible in Figs. 21.1 and 21.2, can be seen as representative of three main within-school-context metaphors:

- The opening of minds to learning captured by the open pages of Fig. 21.1 and by words such as *remove barriers, action, re-engagement,* and *research.*
- A sense of being positive change agents, not in a conscious task driven manner but as a by-product of the requirement to meet student needs is captured by words such as *justice, citizens, gender stereotyping, student voice, connection, world views,* and *inclusive pedagogy.*

Figure 21.1. The visual metaphor for the *Connecting within school contexts* chapters

- The evolution of dynamic learning partnerships is well underway and highlights ways of thinking, learning and teaching necessary for education today, and into the future. A learning environment built of words and conceptual understandings does not remain trapped within the four walls of a learning space, as learning and teaching are built on learning partnerships that are becoming internationally mobile, collaborative and requiring different dynamics, and changing responses from those currently in use.

These three metaphors capture some of what it means to be a *new professional* and they form the foundations for the kind of supported, collaborative risk-taking that leads to neo-pedagogical innovation (Andrews & Crowther, 2006).

Figure 21.2. The *Wordle* word cloud for the *Connecting within school contexts* chapters

CONNECTING BEYOND SCHOOL CONTEXTS

Much of what emerged from the interpretive planes of the beyond-school-contexts has been echoed in the metaphors already described. With recurrent themes becoming apparent through words such as *global*, *off-shore*, *boundaries*, *connections*, *students*, and *partnerships* (see Figs. 21.3 and 21.4), there is resonance with what has come before.

However, new images are emerging from the beyond-school-contexts which can be captured with the following metaphors:

- As educators, we look toward nurturing learning. Before learning can be nurtured it must be created, and then consciously developed and sustained. To nurture implies using pedagogical tact (van Manen, 1991). Therefore, a strengths-based approach to the development of learning experiences that *explore, affirm aspirations, recognize similarities,* and *value difference* is needed. It is these same words that emerge from this analysis (see Figs. 21.3 and 21.4); deficit models are not embraced.

- Contemporary curriculum ecosystems do not look, sound, or feel like each other. They do not deliver the same experiences for all

Figure 21.3. The visual metaphor for the *Connecting beyond school contexts* chapters

Figure 21.4. The *Wordle* word cloud for the *Connecting beyond school contexts* chapters

students, as not all students are the same. Attempts to transpose a package of learning content or a method of learning delivery from one context to another is fraught with danger, as each ecosystem is a delicate network of dependencies and interdependencies (Barab & Roth, 2006). Awareness of this delicate balance is illustrated with two specific examples: the detailed examination of the complexities of supervising doctoral students and the teaching of Western business practices to Chinese students. The authors recognize that the viability of each ecosystem is dependent upon a sharing of ideas, a building of collegial relationships based on trust and respect, and a willingness to make changes that reflect the valuing of individuals and their prior learning journeys.

- The final metaphor that springs to mind under this theme is that of the diverse educational terrains which we now traverse, as both learners and teachers. These terrains involve consideration of both physical and virtual terrains, both of which impact on learning, and both of which have a global aspect to them. This impact is evident by words such as *Internet issues, terrains, contextual factors*, and the need for *critical reflection* to inform practice (see Figs. 21.3 and 21.4), in order to determine the suitability of the vehicles being used to navigate these terrains.

MAKING MEANING FROM LIVED EXPERIENCES

Van Manen (1997) identified the elucidation of lived experience as the means of making significant meaning of situations and interactions within those situations, the focus being on reclaiming lived experience as it is lived, rather than as it is represented in theory. As shown in Figs. 21.5 and 21.6, the essence of the authors *Making meaning from lived experiences*, raised several metaphors that are interrelated around the concept of communicating meaningful messages between participants in the learning process:

- Multiple pathways signposted by multiple narratives depict the entanglement of the lived experiences of educators, how they have chosen to portray their journeys. The narratives form the research signposts captured in Figs. 21.5 and 21.6 in multiple ways, such as *pedagogical documentation, narrative inquiry, listening pedagogy,* exploring *third space,* and articulating *theoretical and philosophical* understandings, while the pathways are the learning journeys that the authors have navigated.
- Cultural and intercultural reflections come to the fore when exploring cross-cultural working and learning relationships, whether they are part of a Japanese student exchange program or when teachers develop learning cultures built on a cluster-based learning process

Figure 21.5. The visual metaphor for the *Making meaning from lived experiences* chapters

Figure 21.6. The *Wordle* word cloud for the *Making meaning from lived experiences* chapters

aimed at school renewal, or when a researcher captures the lived experiences of Saudi Arabian nursing students studying at an Australian university campus (see Figs. 21.5 and 21.6).

• Fundamental to the meaning underlying the previous two metaphors is the need to develop a language of learning which is context specific. As Conway (2008) exposed, such a language is based on *values*, beliefs, *principles* of practice, *community*, and *network* shared understandings, and is distinctly *pedagogical* in nature and nurture (see Figs. 21.5 and 21.6). This language is one that builds shared understandings, and is built by shared understandings. It is a language that relies on the willingness of the participants in the cultural exchanges (culture in this context can be nationality-based or education-context based) to *listen* to the voices of others and to take them into account, regardless of the language used.

DEVELOPING VIRTUAL CONNECTIONS

Within this final grouping, the stand out message is one about learning. This is evident in Figs. 21.7 and 21.8. The metaphor is about crossing time and space, as well as contextual and cultural divides, through the creative use of digital learning, and teaching tools imaged as constructing virtual bridges to learning.

The ability of the online learning format to provide all the students with the tools to participate in learning, through giving them *presence* and enabling *engagement*, *understanding*, avenues of *discourse* and *knowledge creation* is fore-fronted as a means of facilitating *learning*. As the words in Figs. 21.7 and 21.8 demonstrate, learning is paramount.

Figure 21.7. The visual metaphor for the *Developing virtual connections* chapters

Figure 21.8. The *Wordle* word cloud for the *Developing virtual connections* chapters

REFLECTING ON THE METAPHORICAL APPROACH

The use of *Wordle* to make visual links and to show the relative emphases of concepts (see Figs. 21.2, 21.4, 21.6, and 21.8) worked well in conjunction with the visual metaphors (see Figs. 21.1, 21.3, 21.5, and 21.7), with each highlighting and reinforcing the other. The use of new technologies to create understandings is closely linked to the imaging of educators as neo-pedagogical experimenters. Both relate to the need to mobilize and share intellectual discoveries. As Hargreaves (2003) pointed out:

> In a dynamic knowledge economy, the capacity of organizations to mobilize intellectual capital in the process of knowledge creation is critical, for the production of new knowledge feeds successful innovation. Linked with this is the process of knowledge transfer or knowledge sharing. (p. 4)

For us, metaphors—both visual and verbal—became integral to the transference of knowledge within this book.

By weaving the varying metaphorical threads together—the opening of minds; being positive change agents; dynamic learning partnerships; nurturing learning; contemporary curriculum ecosystems; educational terrains; multiple pathways signposted by multiple narratives; cultural and intercultural reflections; a language of learning; and constructing virtual bridges to learning—we now possess a montage of images which in its entirety suggests the presence of the *new professional* at work.

THE "NEW PROFESSIONAL" FROM DIFFERENT PERSPECTIVES

To seize the "instant pudding" opportunity of a description of the *new professional* as being that of the teacher re-imaging the professional "look" would be unfair and irresponsible to the depth of meanings that have been presented in the chapters of this book. Further, to adopt the description of *new professional* would surely give rise to questions about the *old* and *new* professionals, and about *new* in relation to which particular period of time. However, as has been obvious throughout the chapters of this book, the contributing authors have presented a wide diversity of ideas about the teaching and learning field, and the concomitant challenges for educators.

The metaphors presented in earlier sections of this chapter have clarified connections in teaching and learning in a range of complex contexts. Many of the contributing authors have emphasized the key role of educators and how they are adapting, changing, and transforming pedagogies to meet the needs of learners. Thus, it is fair to say that there is the emergence of the new professional at work, even though some clarification of the intended meaning is necessary. As a result, we have devoted the latter part of this chapter to discussing a number of issues related to the new professional.

Meaning making has a barbed tail, when one considers the limitations of specific perspectives, so we are presented with the challenge of presenting a multi-perspective viewpoint. A study which adopted the multi-perspective analysis of teachers' work (Conway, 2008) observed that "participants were engaged in a unique experience of recognizing the complexity of making significant new meaning of their pedagogical work for the enhancement of student achievement" (p. 190). In so doing, teachers took responsibility for their professional development, resulting in the image of the professional as "one who collaboratively works confidently and creatively in recognition of responsibility for their part in the whole" (p. 190). In the vein of collaboration, several of the chapters within this volume are in line with the claims of Andrews and Crowther (2006) that:

> The power of teachers' collective engagement in processes of holistic school development, and the realization in their workplaces of their talents and gifts, as individual professionals [give rise to] a significant cadre within the teaching profession ... *teacher leaders* ... poised to transform the image and status of the teaching profession. (p. 18)

These are the new professionals who are leading with pedagogical responsibility. They are confronting, challenging, and helping change the workplace of teaching and learning with ethical autonomy and the courage to act upon it (Palmer, 2007).

From a hermeneutic phenomenological perspective, the work of Conway (2008) further pressed "the need for re-imaging the professional teacher as a character of proactive confidence, creativity, and responsive connection with others" (p. 228). By upholding a trusting and respectful culture, the professional educator can generate new ways of thinking and projecting new levels of working, juxtaposed with the risks and demands of complex systems. Such phenomena must surely herald "a future of new hope and confidence [and] the need for a new form of leadership and management" (Conway, 2008, p. 228). The varied contexts of the chapters of this book have challenged us to consider the importance of the new professional, as one who develops the capacity for thinking and acting with simultaneous individuality and collectivity in learning organizations. As Conway emphasized, it would appear, that organizations must recognize the interdependency of individual and collective, value the context, celebrate diversity, and acknowledge the collective as more important than the collection of its parts.

Of further significance in the collection of chapters in this book is the revelation that professional educators—from a range of different contexts, cultures, and aspirations, recognized for their value orientation and their personal skills and talents, and linked through a commitment to improving pedagogy—suggest an image of the teacher professional. The question of whether or not this is a *new professional* image is muddied, but the crystal view is that the new image of the teacher professional "highlights the multi-dimensional nature of value orientations and individual personality types within any single workplace" (Conway, 2008, p. 235). Hence, we recognize and reinforce the importance of the trusting and respectful culture of collaboration, and the valuing of the key role of educators.

In keeping with the multi-perspective viewpoint in defining the new professional, it would be remiss not to cast a critical perspective, perhaps most eloquently upheld through the work of Freire (2004) and his challenge for the educator "to unveil opportunities for hope" (p. 3). Recently, Giroux (2011) troubled the teaching profession to remember that:

> They also provide the knowledge, skills, social relations, and modes of peda-
> gogy that constitute a formative culture in which the historical lessons of
> democratization can be learned, the demands of social responsibility can be
> thoughtfully engaged, the imagination can be expanded, and critical thought
> can be affirmed. (para. 10)

Giroux's ideas are further explained through the connection of learning to fulfilling capacities for self and social determination. Giroux (2010) posed that educators have a role to play in "connecting truth to reason, learning to social justice, and knowledge to modes of self and social understanding" (para. 12) with a commitment on the part of the educators to acknowledge the marriage of education, with politics and matters of social responsibility. Overall, a sense of hope for a better future begins to emerge if new professional educators build capacity for a heightened consciousness of social responsibility. We are not let loose before considering the role we have to play as responsible educators. As Wrigley (2003) explained:

> Teaching is a profession of hope. We are driven by desires—for our students to discover a taste for learning, a feel for justice and care for each other. We aspire to turn children into thoughtful, creative, and concerned citizens. Inspirational teachers are motivated by their dreams of a better world. (p. 1)

In this sense, hope is interpreted beyond the confines of wishful thinking, dreams, or expectations of something desired. It manifests in passion and confidence, played out with conviction by the professionals demonstrating that they can create something better in their own lives, their students' lives, and their broader worlds (see Conway, 2008). So, we are left to mull over the role and responsibility of self, in any meaningful adoption of the term *new professional* and we might do well to be reminded that, in order to change, one must first take stock and consider the necessary transformations of self.

CONCLUSION

The initial call for chapters in this book was most certainly a leap of faith by us, the editors, as prospective authors were asked to consider some of the many ways of creating connections in teaching and learning. Did we really envisage that such a rich array of creative connections was available? We have learned much from our colleagues, and are confident that discerning readers might now be ready to critique their own educational settings, with the following set of questions:

- Which factors help to facilitate and/or restrict the possibilities for creating connections in an educational context?
- What implications or outcomes with regards to learning and/or teaching arise from the connections created?
- What realizations have emerged for educators and researchers, working to create current connections to guide future directions?
- What contributions do/can connections make to a broader society?

Finally, we are in debt to the authors of the chapters of *Creating Connections in Teaching and Learning*, as they have unveiled opportunities for enhancing new ways of thinking and acting for the new professional. The capacity for making links, crossing divides, forming relationships, building frameworks, and generating new knowledge in a range of diverse educational contexts is certainly a reality for sustainable pedagogy.

REFERENCES

Alvesson, M. (2002). *Understanding organizational culture*. London: Sage.
Andrews, D., & Associates. (2011). Capacity building for school improvement: An Australian research study. Saabrücken, Germany: VDM Verlag Dr Müller CmbH & Co.
Andrews, D., & Crowther, F. (2006). Teachers as leaders in a knowledge society: Encouraging signs of a new professionalism. *Journal of School Leadership, 16*(5), 534–549.
Barab, S. A., & Roth, W. M. (2006). Curriculum-based ecosystems: Supporting knowing from an ecological perspective. *Educational Researcher, 35*(5), 3–13.
Beare, H. (2001). *Creating the future school*. London: RoutledgeFalmer.
Conway, J. M. (2008). *Collective intelligence in schools: An exploration of teacher engagement in the making of significant new meaning*. Unpublished doctoral thesis, University of Southern Queensland, Toowoomba, Australia.
Denzin, N. K., & Lincoln, Y. S. (2005). *The SAGE handbook of qualitative research*. Thousand Oaks, CA: Sage.
Feinberg, J. (2009). Wordle [Website]. Retrieved from http://www.wordle.net/credits.
Freire, P. (2004). *Pedagogy of hope* (R. R. Barr, Trans.). New York: Continuum.
Gee. J. P. (1996). Literacy and social minds. In G. Bull & M. Anstey (Eds.), *The literacy lexicon* (pp. 5–14). Sydney: Prentice Hall.
Giroux, H. A. (2010). Lessons to be learned from Paulo Freire as education is being taken over by the mega rich. *truthout*. Retrieved from http://www.truth-out.org/lessons-be-learned-from-paulo-freire-education-is-being-taken-over-mega-rich65363
Giroux, H. A. (2011). Beyond the swindle of the corporate university: Higher education in the service of democracy. *truthout*. Retrieved from http://www.truth-out.org/beyond-swindle-corporate-university-higher-education-service-democracy66945.
Hargreaves, D. (January 5, 2003). *From improvement to transformation*. Keynote lecture presented at the National Congress for School Effectiveness and Improvement, Schooling the Knowledge Society, Sydney, Australia.
Jacobs, C., & Heracleous, L. (2004). *Constructing shared understanding: The role of embodied metaphors in organization development* [Working paper 57]. Switzerland: Imagination Lab.
Jakobson, R., & Halle, M. (1956). *Fundamentals of language*. The Hague: Mouton.
Kövecses, Z. (2005). *Metaphor in culture—Universality and variation*. Cambridge, UK: Cambridge University Press.

Lakoff, G., & Johnson, M. (1980). *Metaphors we live by*. Chicago: The University of Chicago Press.

McNaught, C., & Lam, P. (2010). Using Wordle as a supplementary research tool. *The Qualitative Report, 15*(3), *630–643*. Retrieved from http://www.nova.edu/ssss/QR15-3/mcnaught.pdf

Morgan, G. (1980). Paradigms, metaphors and puzzle solving in organizational theory. *Administrative Science Quarterly, 25*, 605–622.

Nonaka, I., & Takeuchi, H. (1995). The knowledge-creating company: How Japanese companies create the dynamics of innovation. New York: Oxford University Press.

Ortony, A. (1975). Why metaphors are necessary and not just nice. *Educational Theory, 25*, 45–53.

Palmer, P. J. (2007). A new professional: The aims of education revisited. *Change: The Magazine of Higher Learning, 39*, 6–12.

Steen, G. (2008). The paradox of metaphor: Why we need a three-dimensional model of metaphor. *Metaphor and Symbol, 23*(4), 213–241.

van Manen, M. (1991). *The tact of teaching: The meaning of pedagogical thoughtfulness*. Albany, NY: SUNY Press.

van Manen, M. (1997). *Researching lived experience: Human action for an action sensitive pedagogy*. Albany, New York: SUNY Press.

van Manen, M. (2000). Moral language and pedagogical experience. *The Journal of Curriculum Studies, 32*(2), 315–327. Retrieved from http://www.phenomenologyonline.com/max/articles/moral_language.html

Visser-Wijnveen, G. J., Van Driel, J. H., Van der Rijst, R. M., Verloop, N., & Visser, A. (2009). The relationship between academics' conceptions of knowledge, research and teaching—a metaphor study. *Teaching in Higher Education, 14*(6), 673–686.

Wrigley, T. (2003). *Schools of hope*. Stoke-on-Trent: Trentham Books.

ABOUT THE AUTHORS

Lindy Abawi is a lecturer in Curriculum and Pedagogy at the Toowoomba Campus of the University of Southern Queensland, Australia. She has taught secondary school art and English, primary school music, and English as a second language. She is a core team member of the Leadership Research group (LRI) at the University of Southern Queensland. She is a facilitator for the Innovative Designs for Enhancing Achievement in Schools (IDEAS) project, and has worked in this role at school, state, and interstate levels. Her doctoral research is linked to understanding how a context specific pedagogical language may help facilitate and sustain school improvement.

Margaret Baguley is a senior lecturer in Arts Education at the University of Southern Queensland, Australia. She has extensive teaching experience across a range of education sectors. Her research interests are in the areas of arts education, creative collaboration, leadership, and arts engagement. Her current research projects are investigating how to maximize learning pathways for low socioeconomic and non-traditional students (USQ Equity Incentives Fund), in addition to evaluating how the arts can engage children more effectively in their learning (Primary Arts Network Ipswich, Arts Queensland, and Australia Council for the Arts).

Lyn Brodie is an associate professor in the Faculty of Engineering and Surveying at the University of Southern Queensland, Australia, and a University Teaching Fellow. She has won several teaching awards, including the 2007 Carrick Award for Australian University Teaching (Team Leader). Her work involves the design and delivery of Problem Based Learning (PBL) courses, staff training, and the continuing development of the PBL strand in the faculty. She has a strong research interest in engineering education, problem-based learning, and transitions to university, and is director of the Faculty Centre for Engineering Education Research.

J. Anne Casley is currently involved in part-time diagnostic teaching in the areas of literacy and numeracy. She is also a part-time doctoral student at the University of Southern Queensland, Australia. Her dissertation involves a case study of one school and its approach to values education and citizenship education. In the past, she taught secondary school art for a considerable period of time. She also has experience teaching in the primary grades. In recent years she has enjoyed reviewing articles for a number of different publications.

Joan M. Conway is a lecturer at the University of Southern Queensland, Australia. She is a core team member of the Leadership Research group (LRI), a high-profile research and development group within the Faculty of Education. She has been involved over a number of years in the research, development, and delivery of the highly successful Innovative Designs for Enhancing Achievement in Schools (IDEAS) project. She has a strong interest in the concept of collective intelligence when learning communities develop enhanced levels of collaboration and build capacity for sustainable improvement, with a particular focus on teachers as leaders and new images of teacher professionalism.

P. A. Danaher is professor (Education Research) in the Faculty of Education at the Toowoomba Campus of the University of Southern Queensland, Australia. His research interests include educational mobilities; educational research ethics, methods, and politics; academics', educators', and researchers' work and identities; lifelong learning; rural education; social education; university learning and teaching; and vocational education. He is the co-author of *Mobile learning communities: Creating new educational futures* (New York: Routledge, 2009) and *Teaching Traveller children: Maximising learning outcomes* (Trent, UK: Trentham Books, 2007). He is also sole and co-editor of eight research books.

Marie Davis is from the U.S.A., but has spent her career teaching, counseling, and learning in international schools around the world. She is currently settled in the Alps of Switzerland, working with the many English speakers in the area as an educational psychologist. She enjoys giving workshops to teachers and parents about personality types and how they affect teaching and learning styles and relationships with others, be they colleagues, children, partners, or friends. When she is not otherwise occupied, she spends her time outdoors in the fresh mountain air.

Ian Fraser has been Head of English at Nanango State High School, a rural school in southeast Queensland, Australia, for the past 23 years. Prior to that, he taught in schools in the west and southeast of the state and in Cornwall (UK). He has a deep passion for developing student voice in schools and won a Queensland government scholarship to investigate student voice in schools across the UK in 2007. In 2010, he completed a Master of Education degree at the University of Southern Queensland (Toowoomba), focusing on student voice.

Helmut Geiblinger is a lecturer in the Faculty of Education at the University of Southern Queensland, Australia. His doctoral research examined the biomechanical perspectives of competition landings in gymnastics and was a result of his earlier interest and involvement as a competitor, coach, judge, and scientific investigator at five different world gymnastics championships. His research and teaching areas are primarily focused on education and sports science. His most recent research has used narrative inquiry to explore his own understandings as an educational researcher, examining both strategies and practical considerations for controlled gymnastics landings.

Peter Gibbings possesses a Bachelor of Surveying Degree, a Graduate Diploma in Technology Management, a Master of Geomatics, and a Doctor of Education from the Queensland University of Technology, Australia. He also has over 25 years experience in the surveying profession. He is now an associate dean at the University of Southern Queensland. In 2008, he won the individual Queensland Spatial Excellence Award for Education and Professional Development, and in the same year went on to win the individual Asia Pacific Spatial Excellence Award for Education and Professional Development.

C. E. Haggerty is the associate dean in the Faculty of Health at Whitireia Community Polytechnic, New Zealand. She led the delivery of postgraduate mental health nursing education prior to taking up her associate dean role. Her research interests include e-learning issues for academic staff, student access, and use in e-learning, new graduate nurses' first year of practice experiences, and preceptorship for practice. She was the lead author of *Growing our own: An evaluation of nurse entry to practice programmes in New Zealand 2006–2009* (Wellington, NZ: Ministry of Health, 2010).

R. E. (Bobby) Harreveld is associate professor in the School of Education and the Foundation Director of the Learning and Teaching Education Research Centre (LTERC) at CQUniversity, Australia. She also holds a position as an adjunct with the Centre of Education Research at the University of Western Sydney. She is currently investigating questions around the knowledge constructions of undergraduate and postgraduate teaching and teacher education in cross-cultural, open, and distance learning environments. This work is located among the education systems of universities, vocational colleges, schools, workplaces, and community learning settings.

Junichi Hatai has taught Japanese in Australia since 1989, after teaching English in Tokyo for 10 years. He has a Master of Education and a Master of Applied Linguistics (Honours), and advocates that teaching languages using students' well-known topics in the target language enhances language learning. In his role as educator, he has established Sister School Exchange Programs, Japanese Assistant Teacher programs, and Sister City English programs for Japanese primary school teachers. He has also worked as an interpreter and translator for government agencies and companies including law firms.

Karen Hawkins works part-time at Southern Cross University, Australia. Before retirement from full-time work in early 2011, she was the course coordinator for the Bachelor of Education (Early Childhood) program. As well as her first teaching degree, she holds a Graduate Diploma in Special Needs Education, a Masters of Education, and a Doctor of Philosophy. Her research interests gravitate toward early childhood education, social justice, literacy, wholeness, and well-being. She has a deep respect for and interest in collaborative research methods as socially just modes of inquiry that uphold and value participant knowledge, history, and expertise.

Robyn Henderson is an associate professor in Literacies Education in the Faculty of Education at the Toowoomba Campus of the University of Southern Queensland, Australia. She teaches literacy education courses for both undergraduate and postgraduate students. Her research interests include multiliteracies, digital and academic literacies, literacy pedagogy, and the implications of mobility for school-based literacy learning. She has co-edited three research books, and is currently sole-editing another which focuses on literacy learning. All of her work is underpinned by a concern for social justice issues.

Laurie Kocher is currently an instructor in the Early Childhood Education Programme at Douglas College near Vancouver, BC, Canada. She taught kindergarten in the public school system for many years. Her adult teaching experience includes working with graduate and undergraduate students at college and university levels, both in early years and school age contexts. Her doctoral research, undertaken at the University of Southern

Queensland, Australia, focused on the pedagogical documentation practices of the preschools of Reggio Emilia. She has also explored how this work has been transformative for teachers in other contexts.

Christine McDonald is a lecturer in statistics and mathematics in the Faculty of Sciences at the Toowoomba Campus of the University of Southern Queensland, Australia. Her research interests are in the fields of statistics education, distance education, and online learning. The title of her doctoral research is *Evaluating the use of online synchronous communication to enhance learning in statistics*. Before moving into the tertiary field of education, she taught secondary school mathematics, as well as science for a number of years.

Brad McLennan is a lecturer in literacy education at the University of Southern Queensland, Australia, and was a classroom teacher at the time of writing the chapter in this book. With 20 years teaching experience, he realizes that acknowledging student success breeds further success. Together with his teaching partner of 11 years, Karen Peel, he won a Queensland NEiTA award in 2009 for innovative practice. While a middle years teacher, he developed and implemented a teaching framework known as motivational pedagogy to motivate learners and lead them toward intrinsic self-directed competence. The approach fosters resilience, pride, belonging, unity, and self-esteem among students.

Warren Midgley is a lecturer in curriculum and pedagogy in the Faculty of Education at the University of Southern Queensland, Australia. His research interests include second language acquisition and use, cultural and linguistic adjustment in cross-cultural contexts, and the methodology and ethics of cross-cultural research. He is co-editor of and contributor to the research books *Beyond binaries in education research* (New York: Routledge, 2011) and *Sustaining synergies: Collaborative research and researching collaboration* (Teneriffe, Qld, Post Pressed, 2010). He also contributed to the book *Troubling terrains: Tactics for traversing and transforming contemporary educational research* (Teneriffe, Qld, Post Pressed, 2008).

Karen Noble is associate dean (Teaching and Learning) and Program Coordinator (Early Childhood) in the Faculty of Education at University of Southern Queensland, Australia. She has a strong leadership and management role, but maintains her teaching profile in the area of early childhood education, play and pedagogy, professional practice, and contemporary issues in early childhood. Her research interests include early childhood education, workforce capacity building, pedagogy and learning in higher education, learner agency, and parent participation in education. She has been invited to present a number of public addresses—locally, nationally, and internationally.

Lindsay Parry is professor of education and the Dean/Head of School of Education at James Cook University, Queensland, Australia. He has held senior academic management positions in New Zealand and Australia. His current research interests include educational policymaking, curriculum development and reform, and values-based curriculum leadership. He has published extensively on curriculum reform and development in the U.S.A. and the UK.

Cec Pedersen is a senior lecturer (Management and Organisational Behaviour) in the Faculty of Business at the University of Southern Queensland, Australia. Previously he had been the Queensland Administrator for the Royal Australian College of General Practitioners Training Program. Prior to his role as administrator, he had spent over 14 years in general management and consulting positions in small- and medium-sized organizations. His current research and educational interests are leadership in tertiary education, human resource development, and Eastern business education.

Karen Peel is a lecturer in Literacy Education at the University of Southern Queensland, Australia, and was a classroom teacher at the time of writing the chapter in this book. With 25 years teaching experience in middle years schooling, she remains at the forefront of modern teaching techniques and technologies. She is committed to sharing her practical knowledge with others. With her teaching partner Brad McLennan, she sought to inspire middle years students to be productive citizens and lifelong learners. With Brad, she received a Queensland NEiTA award for innovative practice in 2009. She aims to impart her knowledge and love of teaching to preservice teachers.

Petrea Redmond is a lecturer in the Faculty of Education at the Toowoomba Campus of the University of Southern Queensland, Australia. Prior to coming to USQ, she was a Head of Department in Business, ICT, and Technology. She also worked as an Education Advisor in learning technology, working with students, staff, and principals from preschool through to year 12. Her current teaching and research interests include teaching and learning in the middle and senior years, ICT integration, authentic learning, higher order thinking, and blended and online learning.

Richard Scagliarini began his career in education as a high school teacher in Victoria, Australia. He has been teaching in international schools for 15 years, where he developed an interest in the development and implementation of middle school curriculum reform. His doctoral studies with the University of Southern Queensland, Australia, focused on the process and dynamics of reforming the middle years curriculum in the international school context. His thesis has been published as *Reforming the middle years curriculum: A new paradigm for middle schooling*.

Tina van Eyk owns a learning design business and works with diverse clients across Australia. Her work combines her extensive knowledge and experience of human resource management, information technology, and education. Throughout her career, she has designed interactive learning resources for clients in both tertiary and vocational education and training sectors, as well as for clients working in the photographic, banking, superannuation, workers' compensation, agricultural, and veterinary industries. She loves the flexibility which online technologies offer and looks forward to the designing, developing, and researching of best practice learning environments in the future.

Henriette van Rensburg is a lecturer in Pedagogy and Curriculum (Blended Learning focus) and Postgraduate Program Coordinator in the Faculty of Education at the Toowoomba Campus of the University of Southern Queensland, Australia. Her research interests include linguistics, technology education, and postgraduate education. She has published research about Afrikaan speakers in Australia, and the postgraduate and higher degrees journey. Her PhD research was in the specific field of computer-aided education for milieu-deprived learners in mathematics in the senior primary phase.

Robert D. White is a doctoral candidate at the University of the Sunshine Coast, Australia, where he is writing a thesis about the determinants of propensity to lifelong learning. His background includes the banking and horticulture industries. He has also taught accounting and business studies to international students for the Open Access College at the University of Southern Queensland, Australia. He has written and reviewed extensively for international journals and conferences, receiving an award for outstanding reviewing from the editorial committee of the 5th International Conference on Lifelong Learning in 2008.

Joe Peng Zhou is a lecturer in the Faculty of Business at the University of Southern Queensland (USQ), Australia. Before coming to Australia in 1998, he was a business lecturer with a Chinese regional university. After completing his doctoral thesis in 2002, he was employed to coordinate a Mandarin MBA program which the USQ jointly operated with its Chinese partners. His current research interests are in cross-cultural issues in business education, the international marketing of higher education services, and Chinese consumer behavior.